THE *Simply Superb* COOKBOOK

TORMONT

Art direction and photography: Michel Paquet
Food Stylist: Laurent Saget
Food Assistant: Thérèse Meilleur-Maurice
Props: Mychèle Painchaud

Editor: Dominique Chauveau
Graphic Design: Zapp
English adaptation: Robyn Bryant

338 St. Antoine St. East
Montreal, Canada H2Y 1A3
Tel: (514) 954-1441
Fax: (514) 954-5086

ISBN 2-89429-639-8

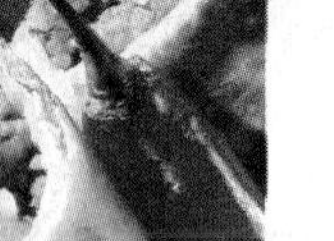

Appetizers

SAUCY SHRIMP WITH FETA

4 SERVINGS

1 tbsp	olive oil	15 mL
1 cup	chopped onion	250 mL
2	garlic cloves, minced	2
28 oz	can tomatoes, drained	796 mL
2 tbsp	dry white vermouth	30 mL
1	bay leaf	1
1 tsp	crumbled dried oregano	5 mL
1	pinch dried basil	1
1 lb	raw shrimp, shelled and deveined	450 g
¾ cup	pitted, sliced black olives	175 mL
6 oz	feta cheese, diced	180 g
	pepper	

GARNISH

½ cup	chopped fresh parsley	125 mL
2	garlic cloves, minced	2
1 tsp	grated lemon zest to taste	5 mL

- Heat oil in a skillet. Sauté onion and garlic over medium-high heat 5 minutes. Add tomatoes and vermouth. Break up tomatoes with back of wooden spoon.
- Add bay leaf, oregano and basil. Bring to a boil, lower heat and simmer 30 minutes to thicken sauce.
- Stir shrimp into sauce and cook over medium heat 4 to 5 minutes. Add olives, feta and pepper.
- Let heat several minutes, without stirring, then pour onto heated serving platter.
- In small bowl, combine parsley, garlic and lemon zest. Sprinkle over shrimp mixture and serve.

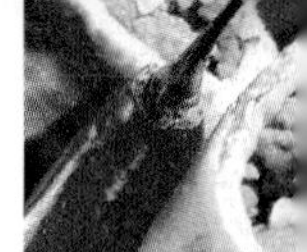

MARINATED MUSHROOMS AND MELON

2 SERVINGS

¼ tsp	dry mustard	1 mL
½ tsp	black pepper	2 mL
½ tsp	brown sugar	2 mL
1 tsp	onion, finely chopped	5 mL
2 tbsp	olive oil	30 mL
1 tbsp	water	15 mL
2 tbsp	dry white vermouth	30 mL
¼	melon	¼
12	mushroom caps	12
2 tsp	dried basil	10 mL
1 tsp	chopped fresh mint	5 mL

• In a bowl, combine mustard, pepper, brown sugar, onion and oil.

• Add water and vermouth.

• Cover with plastic wrap and refrigerate until serving time.

• Just before serving time, cut melon into balls with a melon baller.

• Put mushrooms caps and melon balls into marinade. Add basil and mint, and mix well.

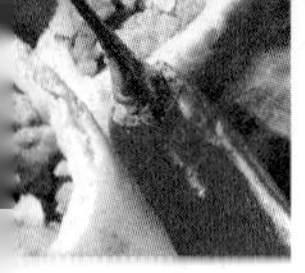

SPRING ROLLS

10 SERVINGS

2 oz	soy vermicelli	60 g
4	beaten eggs	4
1	onion, finely chopped	1
2 oz	fresh *or* canned mushrooms, chopped	60 g
2 oz	dried Chinese mushrooms, soaked 2 to 3 hours, chopped (optional)	60 g
3 oz	small shrimp, chopped	90 g
1 lb	ground lean pork *or* turkey	450 g
2 tbsp	vegetable oil	30 mL
1	carrot, grated	1
2 oz	crabmeat	60 g
3 oz	canned bean sprouts, drained	90 g
2	pinches pepper	2
1 tbsp	soy sauce	15 mL
3 tbsp	nuoc mam sauce	45 mL
1	garlic clove, chopped	1
20	rice paper wrappers	20
	oil for deep frying	
	SAUCE	
5 tbsp	nuoc mam sauce	75 mL
1 tbsp	lemon juice	15 mL
1	pinch sugar	1
1	garlic clove, finely chopped	1

Nuoc mam is a highly flavored, rather salty sauce made from fermented fish. If you cannot find it, substitute mashed anchovies.

• Soak vermicelli ½ hour in warm water. Drain and reserve. In a bowl, combine all spring roll ingredients except rice paper wrappers and frying oil.

• Using a damp tea towel, moisten rice wrappers one by one. Spoon 2 to 3 tbsp (30 to 45 mL) filling in center of each wrapper. Roll wrapper up around filling, tucking in ends. Let stand 30 minutes.

• Heat 2 inches (5 cm) oil in a large saucepan to 375°F (190°C). Fry spring rolls one or two at a time until golden. Drain on paper towels.

• Combine sauce ingredients in a small bowl. Serve with spring rolls.

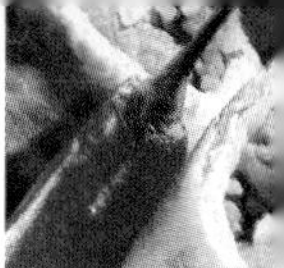

MELON STUFFED WITH CHICKEN AND FRUIT

2 SERVINGS

1	cantaloupe, halved and seeded	1
1½ cups	diced cooked chicken	375 mL
⅓ cup	sliced celery	75 mL
2 tbsp	finely chopped fresh chives	30 mL
⅓ cup	plain yogurt	75 mL
3 tbsp	fresh *or* frozen raspberries, puréed	45 mL
2 tsp	raspberry vinegar *or* aromatic vinegar	10 mL
	red *or* green peppercorns (to garnish)	
	raspberries (to garnish)	

• Scoop out melon flesh with a melon baller, or cut it into cubes with a knife, taking care not to puncture melon shell.

• Combine melon flesh, chicken, celery and chives in a bowl. Set aside. In second bowl, combine yogurt, puréed raspberries and vinegar. Gently stir half of yogurt mixture into chicken mixture.

• Fill melon halves with chicken mixture and pour on remaining yogurt mixture. Garnish with peppercorns and raspberries, if desired.

SUGGESTION

Add diced peaches or pears to the chicken salad mixture.

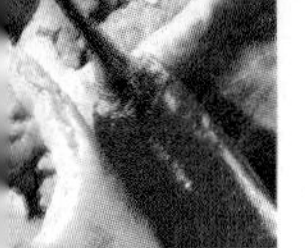

OYSTERS FLORENTINE

2 SERVINGS

8	fresh oysters	8
3 tbsp	dry white wine	45 mL
1 tbsp	butter *or* margarine	15 mL
1 tbsp	all-purpose flour	15 mL
1 cup	milk	250 mL
1	pinch nutmeg	1
1 cup	cooked drained spinach, chopped and seasoned	250 mL
3 tbsp	fine dry breadcrumbs	45 mL
2 tbsp	grated gruyère cheese	30 mL
	coarse salt	

(Continued on next page)

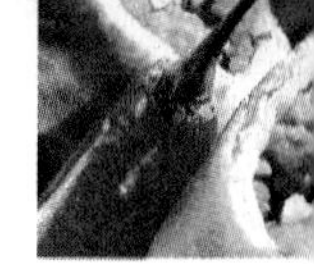

• Open oysters and remove from shells. Put oyster meats and their juice in a small saucepan.

• Spread a thick layer of coarse salt on a large baking pan or cookie sheet. Clean 8 deepest oyster shells, and pat dry. Arrange shells on salt and set aside.

• Pour white wine in saucepan with oysters and simmer 1 to 2 minutes over medium heat. Remove oysters from cooking liquid and reserve oysters and liquid separately.

• In a saucepan, melt butter, stirring in the flour. Cook 1 or 2 minutes, but do not let brown. Stir in milk, mussel cooking liquid and nutmeg. Cook until slightly thickened.

• Arrange cooked drained spinach in oyster shells. Top each with 1 oyster. Cover with sauce. Sprinkle with breadcrumbs and cheese.

• Brown under broiler. Serve hot.

AN EASY WAY TO OPEN OYSTERS

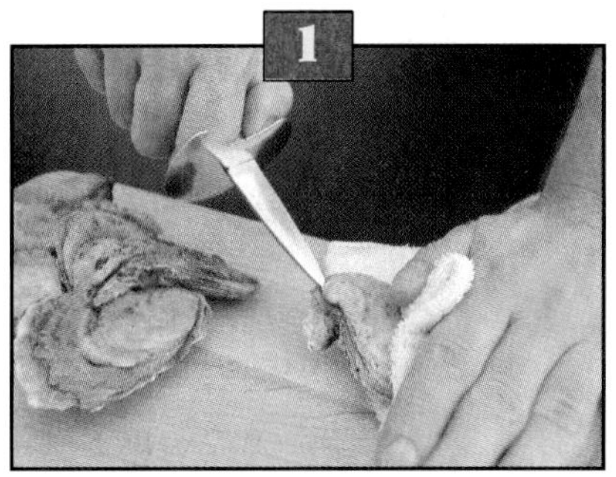

Hold oyster in a thick towel and place on work surface, with flatter shell facing upwards and hinge towards you. Holding oyster firmly with one hand, slide blade of an oyster knife into hinge of the shell.

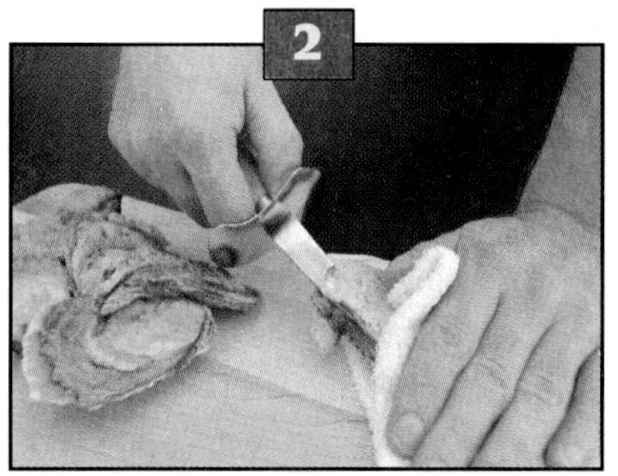

Turn knife at an angle to pry hinge open a bit.

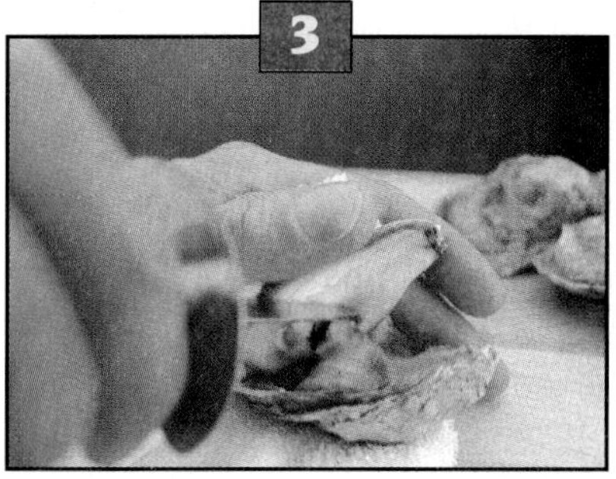

Holding oyster firmly, slide knife blade around upper shell to cut through the ligament and separate the shells. Remove any broken bits of shell.

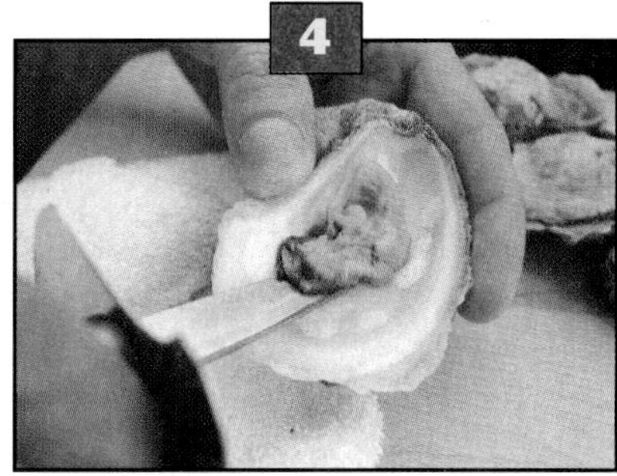

Detach oyster meat from deeper shell by cutting through ligament with knife blade.

Arrange oysters on their half shells in a circle on a tray *or* plate lined with coarse salt *or* crushed ice; serve with shallot-flavored vinegar, lemon and rye bread.

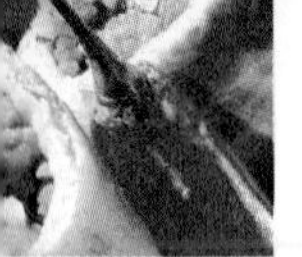

LAMB TARTLETS

16 TARTLETS

PASTRY CRUST

½ cup	butter *or* margarine	125 mL
½ cup	cream cheese	125 mL
1 cup	all-purpose flour	250 mL
1 cup	whole-wheat flour	250 mL
1 tsp	salt	5 mL

FILLING

2 tbsp	butter *or* margarine	30 mL
½ cup	finely chopped onion	125 mL
1 lb	ground lamb	450 mL
½ tsp	pepper	2 mL
1 tsp	ground cloves	5 mL
1 tsp	ground cinnamon	5 mL
½ tsp	ground nutmeg	2 mL
2 tbsp	chopped fresh parsley	30 mL
½ cup	pine nuts, toasted	125 mL
½ cup	plain yogurt	125 mL
½	cucumber, thinly sliced	½
	a few fresh mint leaves *or* parsley sprigs	

- Preheat oven to 350°F (180°C).
- To make dough: In food processor, combine ½ cup (125 mL) butter and cream cheese. Gradually blend in flours and salt, until dough forms a ball.
- Shape dough into ball, wrap in waxed paper and refrigerate 2 hours.
- Place dough between 2 sheets of waxed paper, then roll out with rolling pin to ⅛-inch (3 mm) thickness. Cut 16 circles to line 3-inch (7.5 cm) tartlet molds; set aside on a cookie sheet.
- For filling: Melt remaining butter in a non-stick pan. Cook onion in butter over medium-high heat until soft.

(Continued on next page)

• Add ground lamb and cook 3 to 4 minutes. Stir in pepper, cloves, cinnamon, nutmeg, chopped parsley and pine nuts.

• Let cool to room temperature. Stir in yogurt.

• Fill tartlet shells ¾ full and bake 30 minutes.

• Garnish with cucumber slices and mint or parsley sprigs. Serve warm.

SPANISH-STYLE SHRIMP

4 SERVINGS

20	**large raw shrimp**	20
3 tbsp	**olive oil**	45 mL
1	**garlic clove, minced**	1
2 tsp	**mixture of oregano, rosemary and thyme**	10 mL

• Shell, devein and rinse shrimp. Pat dry with paper towels.

• Heat oil in a non-stick skillet. Add garlic and herbs.

• Sauté shrimp in flavored oil until nice and pink, turning frequently.

• Drain well on paper towels and serve.

SUGGESTION

Serve these shrimp hot or cold, with a green salad dressed with olive oil and red wine vinegar.

CHICKEN FILO TRIANGLES

16 PASTRIES

1 tsp	**butter *or* margarine**	**5 mL**
2	**chicken tournedos**	**2**
3½ oz	**filo pastry**	**100 g**
2 tbsp	**Teriyaki sauce**	**30 mL**
¼ cup	**light soy sauce**	**50 mL**
2 tbsp	**honey**	**30 mL**
½ tsp	**slivered fresh ginger**	**2 mL**

• Preheat oven to 350°F (180°C).

• Melt butter in a non-stick skillet. Over medium heat, cook chicken tournedos about 5 minute until inside is no longer pink. Set aside and let cool.

• Cut each tournedos in half lengthwise, then each half in 4 crosswise. You will have 16 pieces in all.

• Unroll 3 sheets of filo pastry and stack them. Cut in 4 strips lengthwise. Arrange 1 chicken piece on top of filo strip and wrap. Press to seal. Cut off excess filo and use to wrap second chicken piece. (See step-by-step.) Repeat to make 8 triangles. Baste with butter.

• Repeat operation with another filo stack to make 8 more triangles. Place pastries on baking sheet. Bake until lightly golden, no more than 5 minutes.

• Meanwhile, combine Teriyaki sauce, soy sauce, honey and ginger in saucepan. Bring to a boil, remove pan from heat and remove ginger slivers.

• Serve hot filo triangles with sauce.

1

Sauté chicken tournedos.

2

Halve each tournedos lengthwise, then cut halves crosswise into 4 pieces, to make 16 pieces in all.

3

Arrange one chicken piece on top of 3-layer filo strip. Wrap, seal, and cut off excess filo. Repeat to make 8 triangles.

4

In saucepan, combine Teriyaki sauce, soy sauce, honey and ginger. Bring to boil.

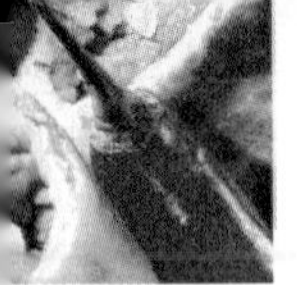

CHICKEN AND ASPARAGUS TERRINE

8 SERVINGS

1 lb	**boneless, skinless chicken breast, cut in strips**	**450 g**
1 tbsp	**finely chopped fresh tarragon**	**15 mL**
2	**egg yolks**	**2**
¾ cup	**plain yogurt**	**175 mL**
2	**egg whites**	**2**
½ lb	**cooked fresh *or* canned asparagus, cut in 1-inch (2.5 cm) pieces**	**225 g**
⅔ cup	**mayonnaise**	**150 mL**
	juice and zest of ½ lemon *or* lime	
	pepper	

• Preheat oven to 325°F (160°C). Grease a 9 x 5 inch (23 x 12.5 cm) loaf pan.

• In food processor, chop chicken with tarragon and lemon zest for 30 to 45 seconds.

• Add egg yolks and ¼ cup (50 mL) yogurt. Season and mix another few seconds. Set aside.

• In a bowl, beat egg whites to form stiff peaks. Fold into chicken mixture.

• Fold in asparagus pieces. Turn into loaf pan. Cover with waxed paper. Place loaf pan in larger pan with 1 inch (2.5 cm) water. Bake 1 hour. Let cool.

• In a small bowl, combine lemon juice, remaining yogurt and mayonnaise. Serve sauce with terrine.

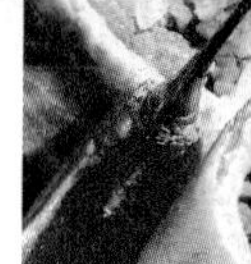

TOMATO BASIL BRUSCHETTA

4 TO 6 SERVINGS

1½ lbs	**fresh tomatoes *or* 28 oz (796 mL) can tomatoes, drained**	**675 g**
2	**garlic cloves, finely chopped**	**2**
1 tsp	**olive oil *or* vegetable oil**	**5 mL**
¼ tsp	**sugar**	**1 mL**
4 tbsp	**tomato paste**	**60 mL**
4	**fresh basil leaves, finely chopped**	**4**
4	**individual plain pizza shells**	**4**
1 cup	**grated mozzarella, gruyère *or* emmenthal**	**250 mL**
1 tsp	**chopped fresh parsley**	**5 mL**
	pepper	

- Coarsely chop the tomatoes.
- In a saucepan, combine garlic, oil, tomatoes, sugar, tomato paste and basil. Season with pepper.
- Partially cover and cook over medium-low heat 8 to 10 minutes.
- Spread resulting sauce on pizza shells. Sprinkle with cheese.
- Sprinkle with parsley and brown under broiler.

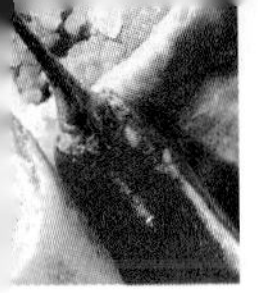

SUGGESTION

Use sesame oil sparingly; it has a pronounced flavor that goes particularly well with Oriental dishes.

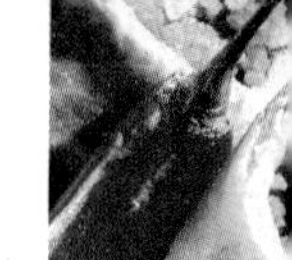

1

In food processor, coarsely chop scallops and half the smoked salmon.

2

Spoon into bowl. Stir in sesame oil and lemon juice.

3

Add red pepper and chives; mix.

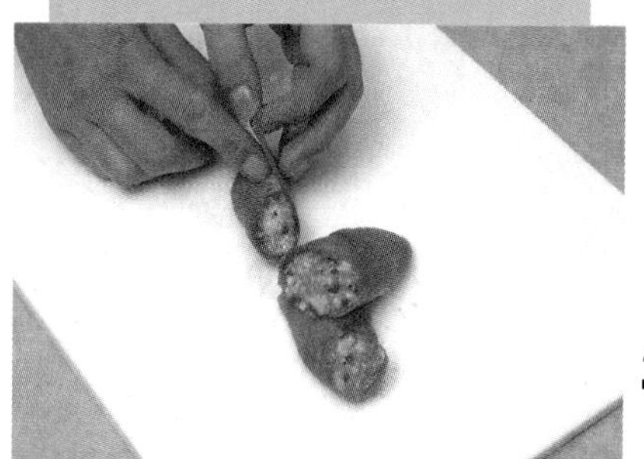

4

Spread scallop mixture on salmon slices and roll up. Cut each roll into 3.

SMOKED SALMON AND SCALLOP TARTARE WITH SESAME OIL

4 SERVINGS

10	fresh scallops	10
8	slices smoked salmon	8
2 tsp	sesame oil	10 mL
2 tbsp	fresh lemon juice	30 mL
1 tbsp	slivered red bell pepper	15 mL
1 tbsp	chopped chives	15 mL
	toasted bread, cut in triangles	

- In food processor, coarsely chop scallops with half the smoked salmon. Spoon into small bowl.
- Stir sesame oil into scallop mixture. Add lemon juice and mix again. Refrigerate 30 minutes.
- Blanch red pepper a few seconds in boiling water; drain and let cool. Stir red pepper and chives into scallop mixture.
- Lay out remaining salmon slices on work surface. Spread with scallop mixture and roll up. Cut each roll crosswise into 3. Keep refrigerated until serving time.
- Arrange 3 rolls on each plate. Serve with toast points.

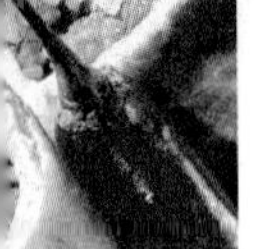

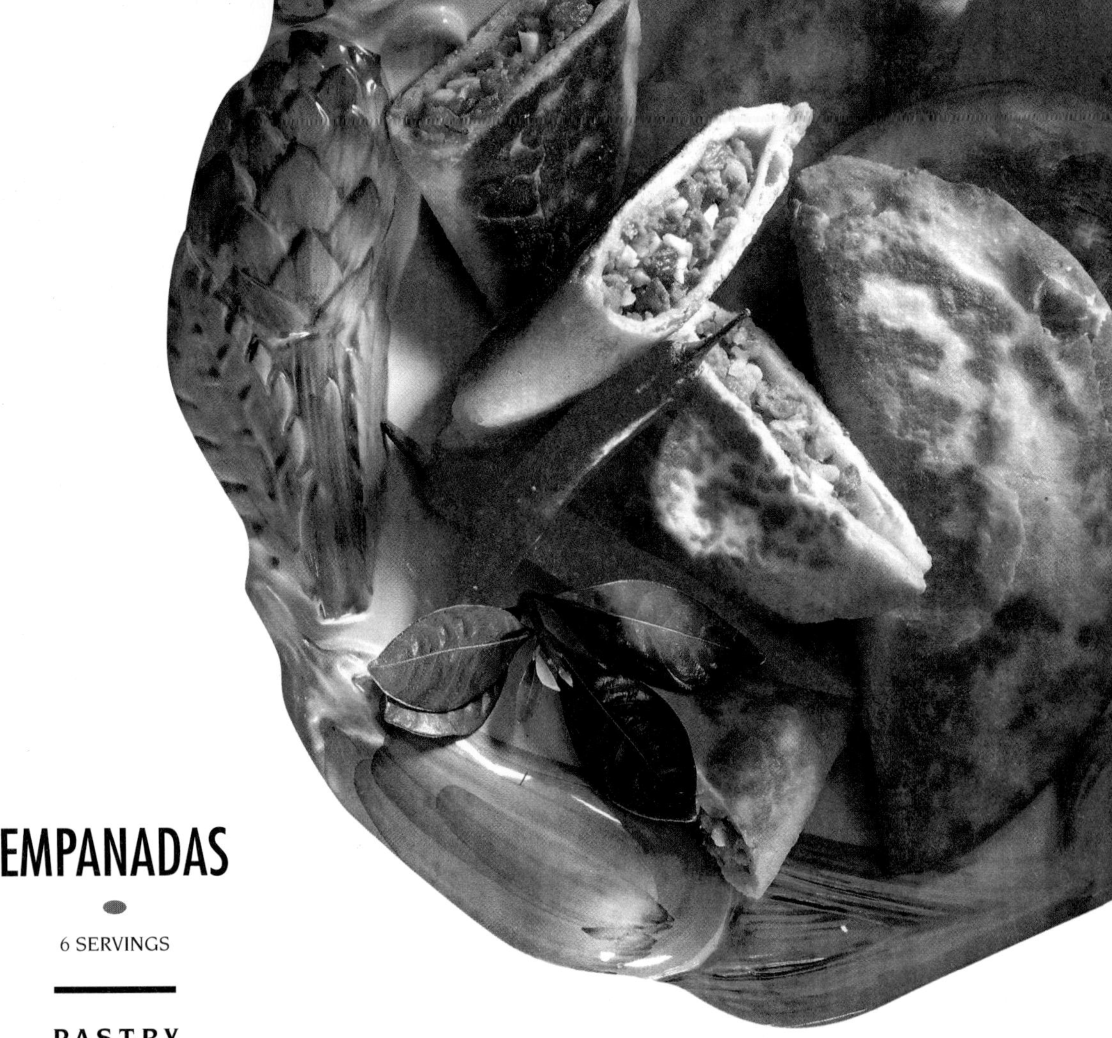

EMPANADAS

6 SERVINGS

	PASTRY	
4 cups	all-purpose flour	1 liter
1	pinch salt	1
½ tsp	dry yeast	2 mL
1 tbsp	warm milk	15 mL
2	eggs	2
¾ cup	soft butter *or* margarine	175 mL
	FILLING	
½ lb	ground lean beef, pork *or* veal	225 g
2	onions, finely chopped	2
1	garlic clove, minced	1
½	green pepper, finely chopped	½
3 tbsp	vegetable oil	45 mL
2	hard-boiled eggs, chopped	2
8	green olives, pitted	8
2 oz	raisins *or* currants	60 g
1	egg, beaten	1
	corn oil	
	paprika	
	marjoram (optional)	

- To make the pastry, combine flour, salt and yeast in a large bowl.
- Make a well in dry mixture and pour in milk and eggs. Stir to combine.
- Beat in soft butter and knead well. Cover and let rest about 2 hours.
- To make the filling, in a second bowl, combine meat, onions, garlic and green pepper.
- Heat oil in a non-stick skillet and cook meat mixture until meat is no longer pink. Let cool.
- Stir in chopped eggs, olives, raisins, paprika and marjoram.
- Divide pastry in 6 portions and roll out each into a circle.
- Spread ½ of each pastry circle with ⅙ filling mixture.
- Baste rim of each circle with beaten egg. Fold in half over filling and crimp to seal. Fry in hot corn oil on both sides until golden. Serve hot.

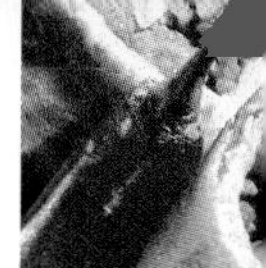

SMOKED SALMON-STUFFED CRÊPES

2 SERVINGS

4	**thin crêpes**	4
10 oz	**smoked salmon, cut in thin strips**	300 g
1 tsp	**grated Sbrinz *or* Parmesan cheese**	5 mL
2 tsp	**capers, drained**	10 mL
¾ cup	**plain yogurt**	175 mL
2 tsp	**black olives, sliced in rings**	10 mL
	sprigs of fresh dill *or* parsley	
	pepper	

• Preheat oven to 400°F (200°C).

• Lay out 2 crêpes side by side on a baking sheet. Arrange equal amounts of salmon on each. Pepper lightly.

• With a small knife, cut an X in center of 2 remaining crêpes.

• Arrange on top of first 2 crêpes, and fold back points of the X. Sprinkle with cheese.

• Bake in oven about 5 minutes.

• In a small bowl, mix capers, yogurt and olive slices.

• Remove crêpes from oven and garnish center with yogurt mixture and a strip of smoked salmon, rolled to make a rosette. Decorate with dill or parsley sprigs. Serve immediately.

GUACAMOLE

6 SERVINGS

2	**ripe avocados**	2
2	**tomatoes, peeled, seeded and finely chopped**	2
1	**hot pepper, seeded and finely chopped**	1
1	**onion, finely chopped**	1
1 tsp	**finely chopped fresh coriander**	5 mL
2 tsp	**lemon *or* lime juice**	10 mL
	raw vegetables *or* tortilla chips	
	salt and pepper	

• Cut avocados in half lengthwise and remove pits. Scrape out avocado flesh into food processor.

• Add tomatoes and hot pepper. Purée.

• Add onion and coriander, and mix at low speed. Add salt, pepper and lemon juice. Process to mix well.

• Serve guacamole with strips of various raw vegetables or tortilla chips.

CHEESE AND MUSHROOM MELTS

4 TO 6 SERVINGS

4	bacon strips, chopped	4
3 to 5 oz	mushrooms, chopped	90 to 150 g
1	onion, finely chopped	1
½ cup	dry white wine	125 mL
5 oz	gruyère cheese, grated	150 g
3 oz	emmenthal cheese, grated	90 g
2 oz	strong *or* medium cheddar, grated	60 g
3	egg yolks *or* 1 large egg	3
4 to 6	slices bread, lightly toasted	4 to 6
	paprika	

• In hot skillet, cook chopped bacon until soft but not crisp.

• Stir in mushrooms and onion. Cook 1 to 2 minutes.

• Pour in wine and cook, stirring and scraping, until liquid has evaporated. Remove from heat. Add grated cheeses. Mix well.

• Stir in egg yolks one by one to make a paste.

• Spread mixture thinly on toasted bread. Sprinkle with paprika. Brown under hot broiler.

• Cut into shapes with a cookie cutter or knife.

SUGGESTION

These cheese and mushroom melts freeze well before broiling.

To serve with cocktails, cut each bread slice into 8. Count on 4 pieces per person.

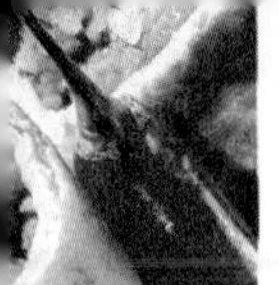

MUSHROOM RAVIOLI WITH CHICKEN WINGS

4 SERVINGS

3 tbsp	butter *or* margarine	45 mL
4	dry French shallots, chopped	4
1½ lbs	mushrooms, chopped	675 g
2 tbsp	chopped fresh parsley	30 mL
⅓ cup	grated gruyère cheese	75 mL
28	wonton wrappers	28
3 cups	chicken stock	750 mL
1½ cups	tomato sauce	375 mL
1 lb	chicken wings, seasoned with BBQ seasoning	450 g
2 tbsp	chopped fresh chives	30 mL

• In a non-stick skillet, melt 2 tsp (10 mL) butter over medium heat. Sauté shallots 4 minutes; stir in mushrooms. Cook about 10 minutes, until all liquid has evaporated. Stir in parsley. Place in a bowl and set aside.

• When mixture is completely cooled, stir in gruyère.

• Stuff wonton wrappers with mushroom mixture and fold into wonton shapes as shown. Seal edges with water.

• Bring chicken stock to a simmer in a large saucepan and cook mushroom ravioli, eight or ten at a time, 5 to 7 minutes. Remove ravioli from saucepan. Set aside in a little cold chicken stock.

• Reduce remaining stock over high heat until only a few ounces remain. Add tomato sauce and simmer 5 minutes over medium-low heat.

• In skillet, melt remaining butter and sauté seasoned chicken wings oven low heat until golden.

• Meanwhile, drain chicken stock from ravioli and heat to boiling. Heat ravioli in stock just until hot, about 1 minute.

• Pour tomato sauce on serving platter, arrange chicken wings and ravioli on top, sprinkle with chives and serve.

1 Cook mushrooms and shallots, then add parsley and cheese.

2 Stuff wonton wrappers with mushroom mixture and cook.

3 Add tomato sauce to reduced chicken stock; simmer to reduce.

4 Sauté chicken wings.

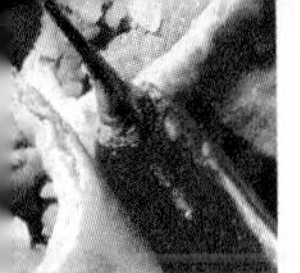

LOBSTER AND AVOCADO WITH GRAPEFRUIT

6 SERVINGS

PINK GINGER DRESSING

1 cup	plain yogurt	250 mL
2 tbsp	finely chopped parsley	30 mL
½ tsp	finely chopped fresh ginger	2 mL
1 tbsp	chili sauce	15 mL
½ tsp	tabasco sauce	2 mL
½ tsp	paprika	2 mL
1 tbsp	honey	15 mL
2 tsp	lemon juice	10 mL

SALAD

1 lb	cooked lobster meat	450 g
2 to 3	grapefruits, preferably pink	2 to 3
2	avocados	2
1	leaf lettuce, separated	1
1 cup	thinly sliced mushrooms	250 mL
	lemon juice	

• Stir together all dressing ingredients, cover and refrigerate 1 to 2 hours to allow flavors to meld.

• Put lobster meat in a covered bowl, and set aside.

• Peel skin and white pith from grapefruits, separate into segments and remove membranes. Set aside.

• Halve each avocado lengthwise, remove pit, and peel. Slice, and sprinkle avocado with lemon juice to prevent blackening.

• To serve, arrange lettuce leaves on plate with avocado slices, grapefruit segments and lobster meat on top. Pour dressing over. Decorate with mushroom slices.

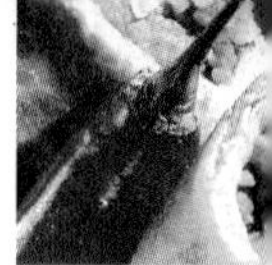

ESCARGOTS VOL-AU-VENT

4 SERVINGS

1	can of 12 large escargots (snails)	1
½ cup	butter *or* margarine, slightly softened	125 mL
2	garlic cloves, finely chopped	2
1	green onion, finely chopped	1
2 tbsp	chopped fresh parsley	30 mL
1	pinch ground nutmeg	1
2 tbsp	dry white wine	30 mL
12	miniature vol-au-vent shells, baked	12
12	mushroom caps	12
	pepper	

- Preheat oven to 400°F (200°C).
- Drain escargots, rinse in cold water and drain again.
- Combine well the butter, garlic, green onion, parsley, pepper, nutmeg and wine.
- Place about 1 tsp (5 mL) butter mixture in each vol-au-vent shell. Top each with 1 escargot, cover with butter mixture, and place mushroom cap on top.
- Arrange vol-au-vent shells on one large baking dish or 4 ovenproof plates. Bake 8 to 10 minutes.

If you wish, substitute rounds of toasted whole-wheat bread for vol-au-vent shells.

SUGGESTION

To serve, spoon fresh tomato purée on plates, top with vol-au-vent, and decorate with coarsely chopped parsley.

SOUFFLÉ MAKING

Grease and lightly flour a soufflé dish. Cut a double strip of aluminum foil slightly longer than circumference of dish and several inches (cm) wider than the depth of the soufflé dish.

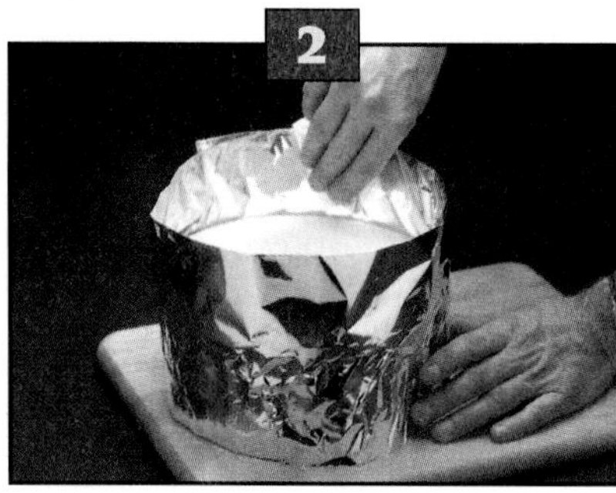

Tie foil band around soufflé dish, overlapping ends. Grease dish and inside surface of foil.

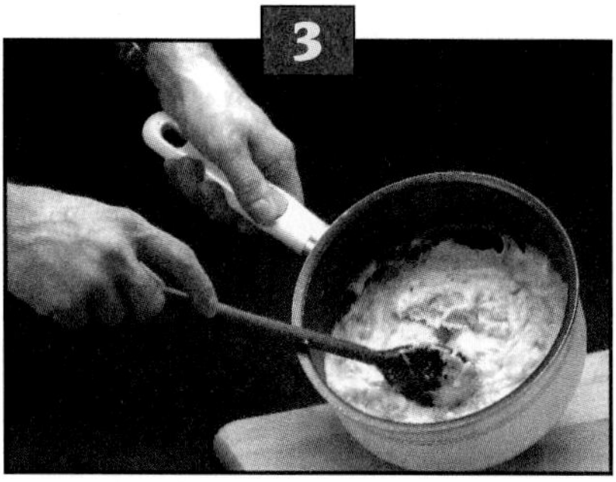

Prepare base mixture according to recipe instructions.

Beat egg whites until firm with clean whisk *or* egg beater. Using a spatula, gently fold beaten egg whites into base mixture.

Pour batter gently into soufflé dish. Bake 55 to 60 minutes or until knife inserted in center comes out clean.

Remove foil band from dish. Serve immediately.

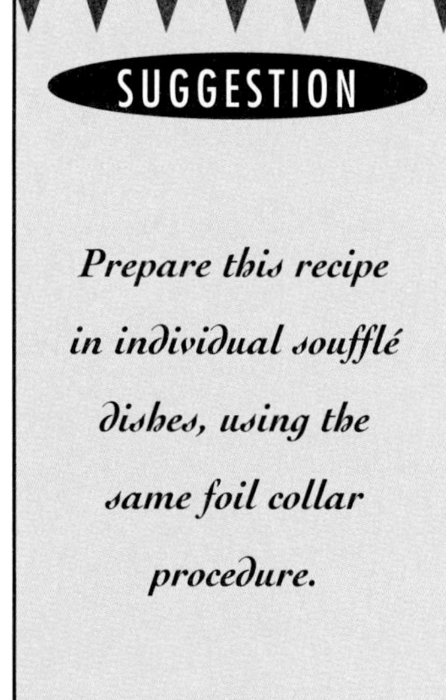

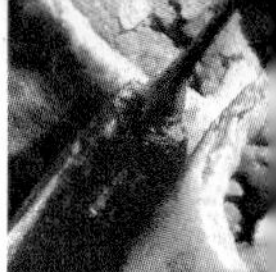

CHEESE AND HAM SOUFFLÉ

4 SERVINGS

6 tbsp	**butter *or* margarine**	**90 mL**
⅔ cup	**all-purpose flour**	**150 mL**
½ tsp	**dry mustard**	**2 mL**
1½ cups	**milk**	**375 mL**
1½ cups	**grated gruyère cheese**	**375 mL**
1 cup	**finely chopped cooked ham**	**250 mL**
1 tsp	**Worcestershire sauce**	**5 mL**
6	**eggs, separated**	**6**

- Preheat oven to 350°F (180°C).
- Prepare a soufflé dish according to technique on page 28.
- In a saucepan, melt butter over medium-low heat. Stir in flour and mustard. Bring to a boil, stirring occasionally.
- Lower heat, stir in milk bit by bit, and cook, stirring, until mixture is thick and smooth.
- Add cheese, chopped ham and Worcestershire sauce. Stir until cheese has melted. Remove from heat.
- Stir in egg yolks one at a time, beating well with wooden spoon after each addition. Reserve egg whites.
- Beat egg whites until stiff peaks form. Using spatula, fold egg whites into base mixture.
- Turn gently into soufflé dish. Bake 55 to 60 minutes or until knife inserted in center comes out clean. Remove foil collar. Serve immediately.

HUMMUS WITH PITA

6 SERVINGS

1	**can chickpeas, rinsed and drained**	1
½ cup	**chopped fresh parsley**	125 mL
½ cup	**plain yogurt**	125 mL
¼ cup	**chopped green onions**	50 mL
2 tbsp	**lemon juice**	30 mL
2	**garlic cloves, minced**	2
6	**whole-wheat pita breads**	6
	parsley sprigs to garnish	
	salt and pepper	

Chickpeas are a good source of nutrition. One serving of hummus provides as much calcium as ½ cup (125 mL) milk, as much fiber as 12 slices of whole-wheat bread, and as much iron as 3 ½ oz (100 g) chicken.

• In food processor, purée chickpeas to a paste with all remaining ingredients except pita bread and parsley sprigs.

• Place mixture in a serving dish, cover and refrigerate.

• At serving time, heat oven 350°F (180°C).

• Cut pita breads into 6 wedges each. Arrange on cookie sheet. Heat pita wedges in oven for a few minutes until crisp. Serve with hummus and parsley sprigs.

MANGO SALAD

2 SERVINGS

2 tbsp	unsweetened orange juice	30 mL
1 tbsp	red wine vinegar *or* aromatic vinegar	15 mL
1 tbsp	lemon juice	15 mL
2 tbsp	olive oil	30 mL
1	head Boston lettuce, torn into pieces	1
1	mango, peeled, pitted and diced (reserve several thin slices for garnish)	1
	pepper	

• In a bowl, combine orange juice, vinegar, and lemon juice. Pepper to taste.

• Gradually whisk in olive oil.

• Arrange lettuce on serving plate. Top with diced mango. Decorate with mango slices. Dress with orange vinaigrette.

1

Rinse and pat dry chicken livers.

2

Sauté onion and garlic. Add chicken livers.

3

Purée cooked livers with pan juices, cognac and cream. Add pistachios.

4

Turn mixture into a mold.

CHICKEN LIVER AND PISTACHIO PATÉ

4 TO 6 SERVINGS

½ lb	chicken livers, trimmed of membrane	225 g
2 cups	water	500 mL
¼ cup	butter *or* margarine	50 mL
1	onion, chopped	1
1	garlic clove, finely minced	1
2 tbsp	cognac *or* brandy	30 mL
2 tbsp	whipping cream	30 mL
½ cup	coarsely chopped pistachios	125 mL

- Rinse and pat dry chicken livers.
- Bring water to a boil in a saucepan and poach livers for 5 minutes. Drain and reserve.
- In a non-stick skillet, melt butter over medium heat; cook onion and garlic until transluscent.
- Add chicken livers and continue cooking about 4 minutes. Let cool 5 to 6 minutes.
- In food processor, purée cooked livers with pan juices, cognac or brandy, and cream.
- Add chopped pistachios and combine briefly at medium speed to a grainy consistency.
- Turn mixture into one or several molds. Cover and refrigerate. Serve with crackers.

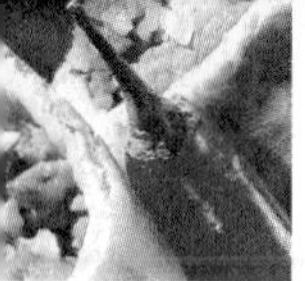

LAMB TURNOVERS WITH YOGURT SAUCE

24 TURNOVERS

2 tbsp	vegetable oil	30 mL
2	green onions, chopped	2
2	garlic cloves, minced	2
1 tbsp	chopped fresh ginger	15 mL
1 lb	lean ground lamb	450 g
2 tbsp	chopped blanched almonds	30 mL
¼ cup	lemon juice	50 mL
2 tsp	ground cumin	10 mL
¼ tsp	salt	1 mL
1	pinch hot red pepper flakes	1
1	egg, beaten	1
	puff pastry	

SAUCE

1 cup	plain yogurt	250 mL
3 tbsp	chopped fresh coriander	45 mL
1 tbsp	curry powder	15 mL
1	pinch salt	1

• In a non-stick skillet, heat oil over medium heat. Sauté onions, garlic and ginger 3 minutes. Add lamb and almonds, and continue cooking 5 to 7 minutes, stirring often.

• Stir in lemon juice, cumin, salt and hot pepper flakes. Simmer 5 minutes, stirring. Let cool to room temperature, then refrigerate.

• Preheat oven to 400°F (200°C). Divide puff pastry in half. Roll out each half to make 2 rectangles of 9 x 12 inches (23 x 30 cm). Cut each rectangle in 12 equal squares. Baste tops with beaten egg to edges. Divide lamb mixture equally between squares. Fold squares to make triangles. Pinch edges to seal.

• Arrange turnovers on baking sheet. Baste with remaining egg. Bake 15 to 20 minutes.

• Prepare yogurt sauce by combining all ingredients well. Serve with hot turnovers.

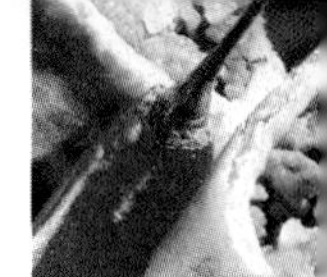

INDIVIDUAL SEAFOOD SOUFFLÉS

8 SERVINGS

½ lb	small raw shrimp, shelled and deveined	225 g
1 tbsp	lemon *or* lime juice	15 mL
2 tbsp	butter *or* margarine	30 mL
3 tbsp	all-purpose flour	45 mL
1⅓ cups	milk	325 mL
1 tbsp	tomato paste	15 mL
1	dash tabasco sauce	1
1	pinch cayenne pepper *or* paprika	1
6	eggs, separated	6
3	small bunches fresh parsley	3

• Preheat oven to 350°F (180°C). Grease 8 ramekins or small molds.

• Place shrimp in a bowl, sprinkle with lemon juice and set aside.

• In a saucepan, melt butter over medium-low heat. Add flour little by little, stirring constantly with wooden spoon, until smooth. Gradually add milk, stirring constantly. Bring to a boil and cook until thickened.

• Stir in tomato paste, tabasco and cayenne. Cook over very low heat 2 to 3 minutes.

• Place half the shrimp and 6 egg yolks in food processor. Mix 10 to 20 seconds. Add milk sauce and process to make grainy mixture. Add remaining shrimp and parsley and process briefly. Be careful not to reduce to purée. Set aside.

• Beat egg whites to stiff peaks. Using spatula, fold egg whites gently into shrimp mixture.

• Prepare ramekins using technique on page 28. Pour shrimp mixture into ramekins, filling no more than ¾ full. Bake in middle of oven 25 minutes.

SUGGESTION

To make a single large soufflé, fill 8-inch (20 cm) soufflé dish ¾ full and add 10 minutes to baking time.

SUGGESTION

To serve as a first course, accompany with fresh tomato sauce.

Reserve mushroom cooking liquid for use in soups.

STUFFED MUSHROOMS IN FILO

4 SERVINGS

8 tbsp	**butter *or* margarine**	**120 mL**
20	**mushroom caps**	**20**
½ cup	**water**	**125 mL**
1½ cups	**chopped mushrooms**	**375 mL**
1	**green onion, chopped**	**1**
1	**garlic clove, minced**	**1**
1 tbsp	**whipping cream**	**15 mL**
2 tsp	**chopped fresh parsley**	**10 mL**
20	**sheets filo pastry**	**20**

• In a saucepan, melt 1 tbsp (15 mL) butter. Add mushroom caps and cook to brown lightly. Add water and simmer 4 minutes over low heat. Drain and reserve mushroom caps.

• In saucepan, melt 1 tbsp (15 mL) butter. Add chopped mushrooms, onion and garlic. Cook several minutes, then stir in cream and parsley. Season. Fill mushroom caps with mixture. Let cool.

• Preheat oven to 375°F (190°C).

• In a skillet, melt 6 tbsp (90 mL) butter. Set aside.

• Cut each of 20 filo sheets into 4 equal rectangles. Using a brush, baste 4 filo rectangles with melted butter, then stack.

• Place a mushroom cap in center of filo stack and fold up sides of pastry over top. Repeat with remaining filo rectangles and mushrooms.

• Arrange on baking sheet. Bake in oven 15 to 20 minutes or until golden. Serve hot.

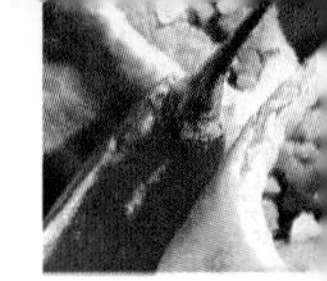

Note: You can use this same filo procedure to make various shapes with sweet or savory fillings of your choice.
Filo packages can be frozen prior to baking. Bake unthawed, increasing baking time.

USING FILO PASTRY

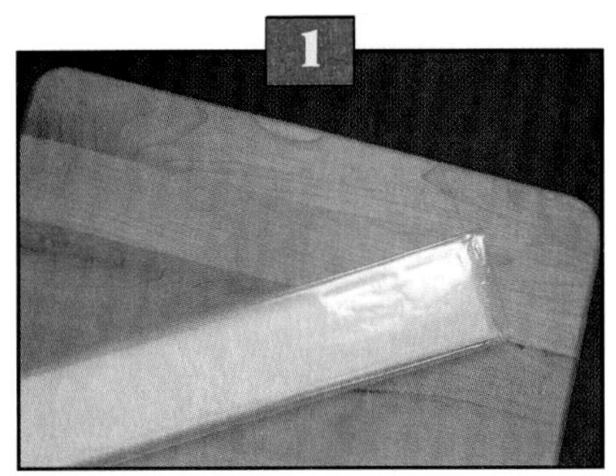

Defrost package of filo at room temperature about ½ hour before using.

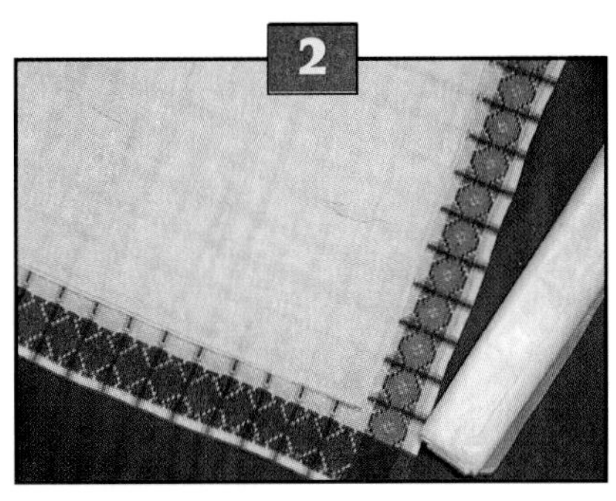

Unroll filo pastry, peel off required number of sheets and lay out on damp tea towel. (Seal and refreeze remaining filo.)

Stack 4 filo sheets, basting with melted butter.

Stuff filo sheets with filling of your choice.

Seal filo packets and baste again with melted butter. Arrange on baking sheet. Bake until golden in 350°F (180°C) oven. Serve immediately.

RUSSIAN BLINIS

15 BLINIS

3 cups	**whole-wheat flour**	**750 mL**
2½ cups	**milk**	**625 mL**
1	**envelope dry yeast**	**1**
3	**egg yolks**	**3**
½ cup	**butter *or* margarine, at room temperature**	**125 mL**
½ tsp	**salt**	**2 mL**
3	**egg whites**	**3**
	corn oil	
	caviar *or* lumpfish caviar, sour cream *or* yogurt, *or* smoked fish	

• Put 1 cup (250 mL) flour in a large bowl. Set aside.

• In a saucepan, warm ⅔ cup (150 mL) milk and add yeast. Remove from heat.

• Pour yeast mixture into bowl with flour. Cover and set aside in warm place for 1 hour.

• In another bowl, beat egg yolks together with butter or margarine. Gradually stir in yeast mixture, then remaining flour and milk. Add salt and mix until smooth. Let rise, covered, in warm place 30 minutes.

• Beat egg whites until peaks form, then stir into flour mixture.

• Oil a large skillet, then heat. Pour ladles of about ¼ cup (50 mL) batter, well-spaced, into pan. Brown on both sides.

• Serve with caviar or lumpfish caviar, sour cream or yogurt, or smoked fish.

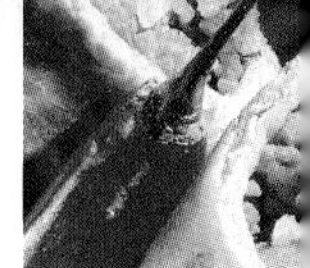

SMOKED SALMON DIP

4 SERVINGS

2½ oz	smoked salmon	75 g
⅓ cup	cottage cheese	75 mL
3 tbsp	plain yogurt	45 mL
2 tbsp	lemon juice	30 mL
1 tsp	hot mustard	5 mL
¼ lb	snow peas	110 g
1 cup	fresh fennel bulb cut into strips	250 mL
2	celery stalks, cut into strips	2
4	slices whole-wheat bread, toasted, cut in triangles	4
	freshly ground pepper	

• In food processor, purée until smooth the salmon, cottage cheese, yogurt, lemon juice, mustard and pepper. Refrigerate.

• Serve salmon mixture as dip for vegetable pieces, or to spread on toast points.

SUGGESTION

For added zing, stir some capers and lemon zest into salmon mixture.

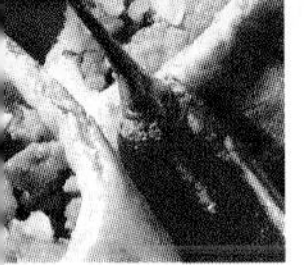

HAM AND CHEESE QUICHE

6 TO 8 SERVINGS

PASTRY CRUST

2 cups	**whole-wheat flour**	**500 mL**
2	**pinches salt**	**2**
½ cup	**butter *or* margarine**	**125 mL**
¼ cup	**ice water**	**50 mL**
1 tsp	**white vinegar**	**5 mL**

FILLING

4 oz	**grated emmenthal *or* gruyère cheese**	**120 g**
¾ cup	**diced cooked ham**	**175 mL**
3	**eggs**	**3**
1¼ cups	**milk**	**300 mL**
	salt and pepper	
	grated nutmeg	

• Combine flour and salt in a large bowl. Add butter and cut in with pastry cutter or two knives until butter is in pieces the size of peas. Add water and vinegar little by little, mixing gently with fork, to make a soft ball. Wrap pastry ball with plastic wrap and let rest 30 minutes in refrigerator.

• Preheat oven to 425°F (220°C).

• Grease a 9-inch (23 cm) quiche pan. Roll out pastry on lightly floured surface to fit quiche pan.

• Lay out and press pastry into pan, covering sides, and trimming off excess. Refrigerate.

• To make the filling, combine filling ingredients in a bowl. Pour into pastry crust.

• Place quiche in center of oven. Bake 40 to 50 minutes. Let stand a few minutes before serving.

QUICHE MAKING

1

Prepare pastry, roll it out and lay it into a greased quiche pan. Refrigerate.

2

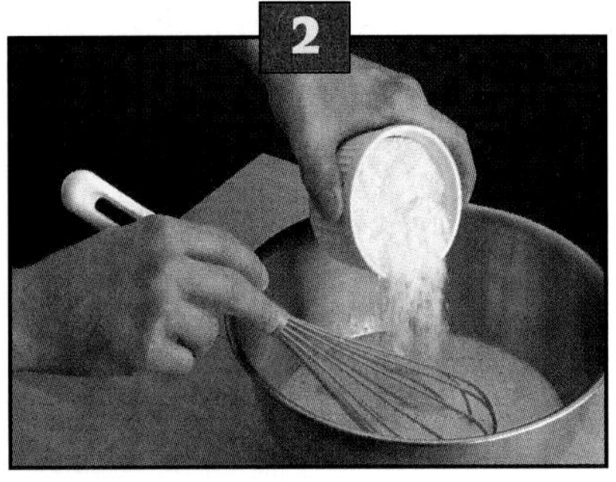

In a bowl, combine all filling ingredients.

3

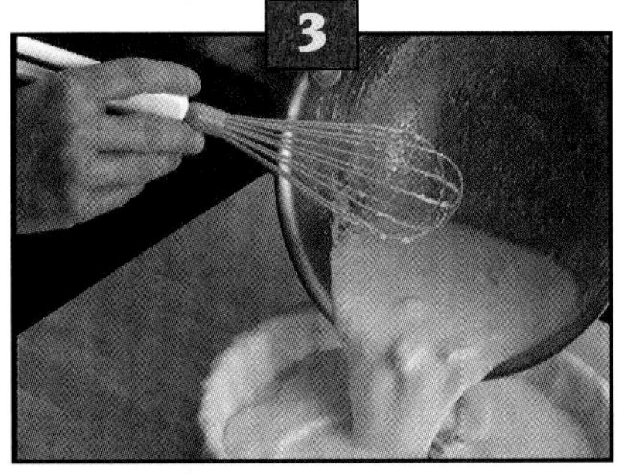

Turn filling mixture into pastry crust.

4

Place quiche in center of oven. Bake 40 to 50 minutes. Let stand several minutes before slicing and serving.

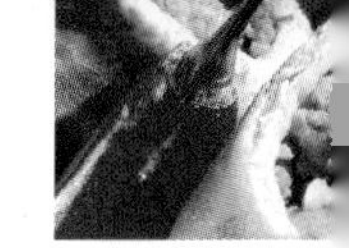

SUGGESTION

Prepare this recipe in small tart molds and serve as appetizers or with cocktails.

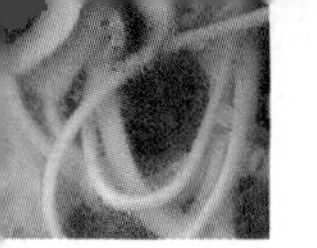

Soups

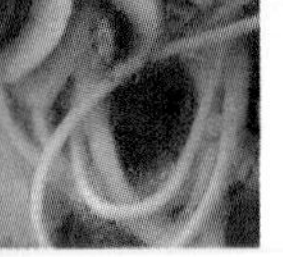

CREAM OF WATERCRESS

4 SERVINGS

2 tbsp	**butter *or* margarine**	**30 mL**
½ cup	**chopped onion**	**125 mL**
½ cup	**peeled, grated raw potato**	**125 mL**
1 tbsp	**chopped fresh parsley**	**15 mL**
2 cups	**chopped watercress**	**500 mL**
2 cups	**chicken stock**	**500 mL**
1 tsp	**dried oregano**	**5 mL**
1 cup	**10% cream**	**250 mL**
	pepper	

• Melt butter in a saucepan over low heat. Add onion, potato and parsley. Cover and cook 5 minutes.

• Add watercress, chicken stock and oregano. Bring to a boil. Let simmer 20 minutes over medium heat.

• Purée soup mixture in food processor. Return to saucepan and gently reheat. Add pepper to taste.

• Add the cream and stir well. Heat gently, without allowing soup to boil. Serve hot.

1

Melt, butter, and add onion, potato and parsley.

2

Add watercress, chicken stock and oregano. Bring to a boil.

3

Purée mixture in food processor. Return to saucepan. Add pepper.

4

Stir in the cream.

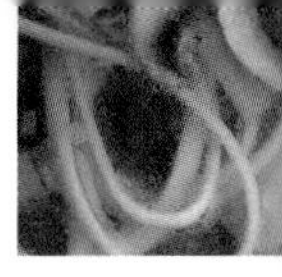

SUGGESTION

You can use this basic method to create a variety of cream soups. Replace the watercress with leeks, lettuce, or any leafy vegetable.

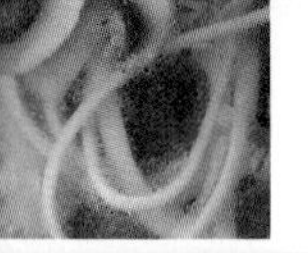

SUGGESTION

Add some imitation crabmeat or small shrimp along with the noodles.

CHINESE NOODLE SOUP

4 TO 6 SERVINGS

Noodles are a good source of energy, low in calories and fat, and easy to digest.

1 tbsp	butter *or* margarine	15 mL
2 cups	sliced mushrooms	500 mL
1 tsp	finely chopped garlic	5 mL
6 cups	chicken stock	1.5 liters
2 cups	fresh chow mein noodles *or* plain noodles	500 mL
1 tbsp	lemon juice *or* raspberry vinegar	15 mL
1	dash hot pepper sauce *or* chili oil (optional)	1
½ cup	chopped green onions	125 mL
1 tbsp	chopped fresh coriander	15 mL
1 tsp	chopped fresh ginger	5 mL

• Melt butter in a saucepan. Sauté mushrooms and garlic over high heat for 2 minutes.

• Add chicken stock and bring to a boil.

• Stir in noodles, lemon juice and pepper sauce.

• Lower heat, cover and let simmer 3 minutes. Stir in green onions, coriander and ginger. Serve at once.

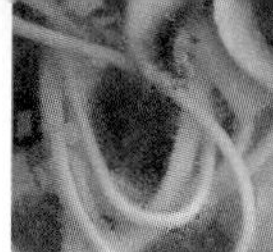

STRACCIATELLA

4 TO 6 SERVINGS

4 cups	chicken *or* beef stock	1 liter
2	eggs	2
2 tbsp	fine semolina *or* wheat germ	30 mL
½ cup	grated Sbrinz *or* Parmesan	125 mL
1 tbsp	chopped fresh parsley	15 mL
1	pinch nutmeg	1
	pepper	
	crackers *or* croutons (as accompaniment)	

• Reserve 1 cup (250 mL) cold stock.

• Bring remaining stock to a boil in a large saucepan.

• In a bowl, combine eggs, semolina, cheese, parsley and nutmeg. Stir in reserved cold stock.

• Using a whisk, stir this mixture quickly into the hot stock. Continue cooking over low heat until eggs set in long threads. Pepper to taste and serve with crackers or croutons.

SUGGESTION

Serve with a bowl of grated Sbrinz or Parmesan to sprinkle on top.

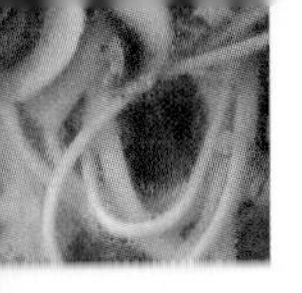

SUPER SIMPLE CLAM CHOWDER

4 SERVINGS

1 tbsp	butter *or* margarine	15 mL
1	onion, chopped	1
2	carrots, chopped	2
2	potatoes, peeled and diced	2
12 oz	can clams, with their juice	360 g
1 cup	water	250 mL
2 cups	milk	500 mL
	pepper	

Replace clams with any other shellfish such as mussels, oysters, or shrimp. If you use fresh or frozen shellfish instead of canned, add ½ cup (125 mL) chicken stock along with the shellfish.

- Melt butter in a large saucepan, and sauté vegetables 5 minutes, stirring.
- Add clams with their juice. Add enough of the water to cover ingredients. Let simmer over medium heat until vegetables are tender and liquid has reduced by half (about 15 minutes).
- Add milk and bring just to a boil, stirring constantly. Do not let boil. As soon as mixture starts to bubble, lower heat to keep soup barely simmering as long as possible (3 to 4 minutes).
- Pepper to taste and serve.

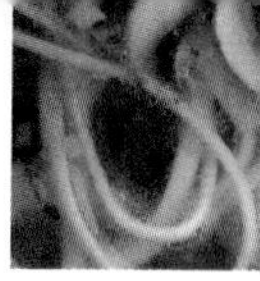

GAZPACHO

6 TO 8 SERVINGS

3	garlic cloves, crushed	3
1 lb	fresh tomatoes, peeled and seeded	450 g
1	cucumber, chopped	1
1	red pepper, chopped	1
6	green onions, chopped	6
1½ cups	tomato juice	375 mL
1 tbsp	red wine vinegar	15 mL
1 tsp	sugar	5 mL
½ tsp	pepper	2 mL
1 tbsp	olive oil	15 mL
	croutons	
	lemon slices	

- In food processor, combine all ingredients except croutons and lemon until fairly smooth.
- Pour into a large bowl and chill, covered.
- Serve in individual bowls garnished with croutons and lemon slices.

SUGGESTION

Consider serving gazpacho as a beverage with brunch, as an alternative to an alcoholic beverage.

Gazpacho is an easy and refreshing way to eat vegetables. Tomatoes are low in calories, as they are 95% water, but they are rich in vitamins A and C.

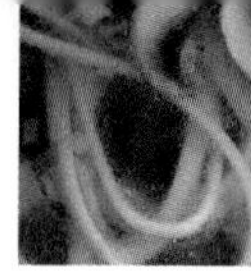

SEAFOOD AND ARTICHOKE SOUP

2 SERVINGS

2 tbsp	olive oil	30 mL
1	onion, finely chopped	1
1	can artichoke hearts, drained	1
1 cup	chicken stock	250 mL
¼ cup	dry white wine	50 mL
¾ cup	buttermilk	175 mL
2 tbsp	chopped fresh parsley	30 mL
½ tsp	ground nutmeg	2 mL
½ lb	seafood of your choice, chopped	225 g
	chopped fresh parsley	
	pepper	

• Heat olive oil in a large saucepan. Sauté onion about 5 minutes over low heat. Add artichoke hearts, chicken stock and white wine. Cover and let simmer 5 minutes.

• Purée mixture in food processor, then return to saucepan.

• Stir in buttermilk, parsley, nutmeg and pepper. Simmer over low heat about 8 minutes.

• Stir in seafood and cook another 5 minutes, without allowing to boil. Garnish with parsley to serve.

Be careful that seafood is not allowed to boil, or it will become rubbery.

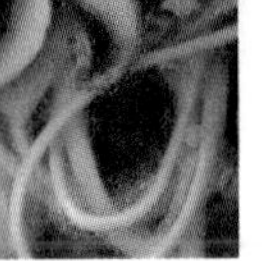

SPICY SOUP

4 SERVINGS

1 tbsp	**corn oil**	**15 mL**
1	**onion, finely chopped**	**1**
1	**garlic clove, sliced**	**1**
½ tsp	**ground cumin**	**2 mL**
1½ tsp	**curry powder**	**7 mL**
¼ tsp	**finely chopped fresh ginger**	**1 mL**
2½ cups	**chicken stock**	**625 mL**
1	**carrot, in julienne strips**	**1**
1 cup	**tomato *or* vegetable juice**	**250 mL**
1	**potato, peeled, in julienne strips**	**1**
¼ cup	**corn kernels, drained**	**50 mL**
	pepper	

- Heat corn oil in a large saucepan. Sauté onion, garlic, cumin, curry and ginger over medium heat until onion is tender.
- Add chicken stock, carrot and tomato juice. Mix well. Cook over medium heat 20 minutes, or until carrot is tender.
- Add potato. Cook 5 minutes.
- Stir in corn, cover, and continue cooking 2 to 3 minutes.
- Pepper to taste and serve.

1

Sauté onion, garlic, cumin, curry and ginger in hot oil.

2

Add chicken stock, carrot and tomato juice. Cook.

3

Add potato.

4

Stir in corn, cover and continue cooking. Pepper to taste.

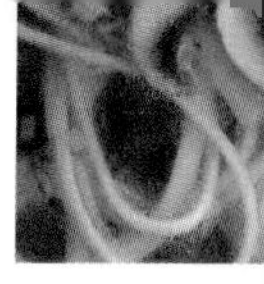

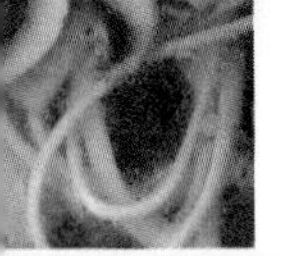

LENTIL AND SPINACH SOUP

4 SERVINGS

Dried lentils do not require soaking before cooking. They are an inexpensive source of protein, iron and fiber.

4 cups	chicken *or* vegetable stock	1 liter
19 oz	can tomatoes, diced	540 mL
19 oz	can lentils, drained *or* 2 cups (500 mL) cooked dried lentils	540 mL
2	celery stalks, chopped	2
1	carrot, grated	1
2	onions, chopped	2
2	garlic cloves, minced	2
1	bag spinach, chopped	1
1 tbsp	lemon juice	15 mL
	pepper	

GARNISH

¼ cup	grated cheddar cheese	50 mL
1 tsp	curry powder	5 mL
2	slices whole-wheat bread, toasted and cubed	2

- In a large saucepan, bring stock, tomatoes, lentils, celery, carrot, onions and garlic to a boil.
- Lower heat, cover and let simmer 5 minutes.
- Stir in spinach and let simmer 4 minutes.
- Add lemon juice and pepper to taste. Garnish with grated cheese, curry powder and croutons.

SUGGESTION

Purée this soup in the food processor to make a delicious cream-style soup.

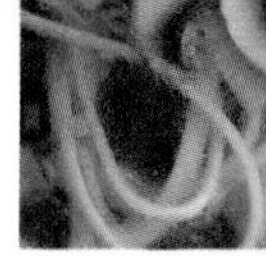

SUGGESTION

This recipe is a good way to use up wilted lettuce.

CREAM OF CHICKEN AND LETTUCE

4 SERVINGS

3 tbsp	butter *or* margarine	45 mL
½	leek, white part only, sliced	½
1	medium carrot, sliced	1
1	celery stalk, sliced	2
1	small onion, sliced	1
2 tbsp	all-purpose flour	30 mL
½ cup	milk	125 mL
3 cups	chicken stock	750 mL
1	pinch dried thyme	1
1	bay leaf	1
1	sage leaf *or* 1 pinch ground sage	1
½	head lettuce	½
1	pinch paprika	1
1 cup	diced cooked chicken *or* turkey	250 mL
	pepper	

• Melt butter over low heat in a large saucepan. Sauté all vegetables, except lettuce, 3 to 4 minutes. Sprinkle in flour and mix well.

• Gradually stir in milk and stock. Add thyme, bay leaf, sage and pepper. Let simmer over low heat about 15 minutes.

• Stir in lettuce leaves. Purée in food processor.

• Return soup to saucepan, add paprika and diced chicken. Reheat and serve very hot.

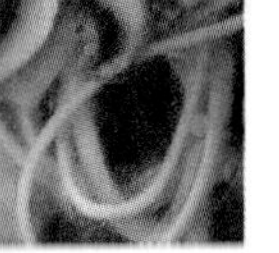

CRAB CHOWDER

6 SERVINGS

1 tbsp	**corn oil**	**15 mL**
1	**onion, finely chopped**	**1**
1 cup	**mushrooms, finely chopped**	**250 mL**
½ tsp	**dried thyme**	**2 mL**
2 cups	**finely chopped broccoli florets**	**500 mL**
1	**sweet red pepper, seeded and finely chopped**	**1**
2 cups	**chicken stock**	**500 mL**
2 cups	**milk**	**500 mL**
12 oz	**can cream-style corn**	**341 mL**
6 oz	**crabmeat *or* imitation crabmeat**	**180 g**
3 cups	**cooked rice**	**750 mL**
	pepper	

• In a non-stick skillet, heat corn oil over medium heat.

• Sauté onions and mushrooms in oil about 6 minutes until limp; season with thyme. Add broccoli and red pepper and continue cooking 4 minutes.

• Add chicken stock, milk and corn. Cook 5 to 7 minutes. Stir in crabmeat and rice. Cook another 2 minutes.

• Pepper to taste and serve immediately, garnished with canned baby corn, if desired.

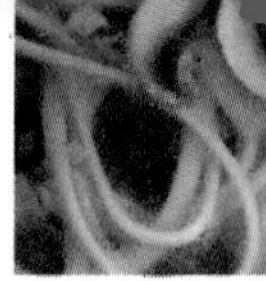

CHILLED AVOCADO AND SMOKED SALMON SOUP

6 SERVINGS

2	avocados, peeled and pitted	2
2 tbsp	lemon juice	30 mL
½ cup	sour cream *or* plain yogurt	125 mL
3 cups	chicken stock	750 mL
¼ tsp	tabasco sauce	1 mL
2 oz	smoked salmon, diced	60 g
4	slices whole-wheat bread, toasted and cubed	4
	pepper	

• In food processor, purée avocado, lemon juice, sour cream, stock and tabasco until smooth.

• Pour soup into large bowl. Pepper to taste, cover with plastic wrap and refrigerate at least 1 hour.

• Add ½ of the smoked salmon; stir in well.

• Garnish with remaining salmon and croutons to serve.

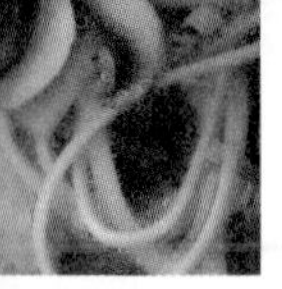

SPINACH SOUP

4 SERVINGS

1 tbsp	**corn oil**	**15 mL**
1 tsp	**cumin seeds**	**5 mL**
1	**garlic clove, finely chopped**	**1**
6 cups	**torn-up spinach**	**1.5 liters**
2½ cups	**chicken stock**	**625 mL**
½ cup	**sour cream**	**125 mL**
½ cup	**plain yogurt**	**125 mL**
	pepper	

• Heat corn oil in a large saucepan and lightly brown cumin seeds over medium heat.

• Stir in the garlic and spinach, reduce heat and let cook 5 minutes.

• Add chicken stock, bring to a boil, then let simmer over low heat 10 to 15 minutes. Remove from heat.

• Stir in sour cream and yogurt bit by bit. Pepper to taste. Serve hot or chilled.

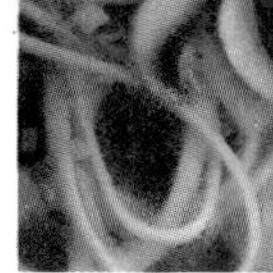

GARDEN HERB SOUP

4 SERVINGS

1 tbsp	butter *or* margarine	15 mL
1 cup	finely chopped celery	250 mL
¼ cup	finely chopped chives	50 mL
2 cups	chicken stock	500 mL
1 tbsp	chopped fresh parsley	15 mL
1 tsp	chopped fresh tarragon	5 mL
1 tsp	chopped fresh basil	5 mL
2 cups	milk	500 mL
2 tbsp	grated Parmesan	30 mL
	pepper	

• Melt butter in a large saucepan. Sauté celery and chives over low heat 3 to 4 minutes, stirring with a wooden spoon.

• Stir in chicken stock and herbs.

• Bring to a boil, add pepper and let simmer about 10 minutes.

• Add milk bit by bit, stirring constantly, and continue cooking a few more minutes over low heat.

• Sprinkle with Parmesan just before serving.

If you like a thicker soup, stir in a cooked mashed potato or a little cornstarch dissolved in cold water.

SUGGESTION

Replace the tarragon and basil with any other herbs of your choice.

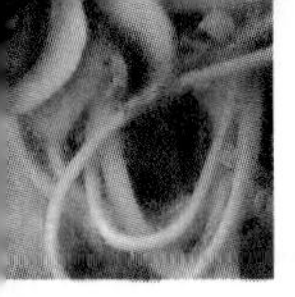

HEARTY CORN CHOWDER

4 SERVINGS

2	carrots, grated	2
1	large potato, peeled and diced	1
½	green pepper, diced	½
2 cups	chicken stock	500 mL
10 oz	can cream-style corn	284 mL
1 cup	processed cheese spread	250 mL
6	smoked sausages *or* wieners, cut into rounds	6
1 tsp	chopped fresh parsley	5 mL

• Put the carrots, potato, green pepper and chicken stock in a large saucepan. Bring to a boil.

• Cover and let simmer 8 to 10 minutes over medium heat, until vegetables are tender.

• Stir in the corn, cheese and sausage rounds. Cook until heated through, stirring from time to time. Sprinkle with chopped parsley to serve.

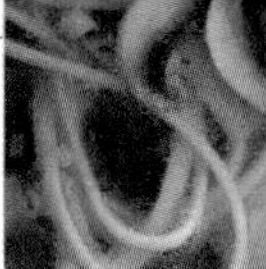

MINESTRONE ALLA CASALINGA

4 TO 6 SERVINGS

3 tbsp	olive oil	45 mL
2	onions, chopped	2
2	garlic cloves, crushed	2
2 to 3	bacon slices, chopped	2 to 3
4	tomatoes, peeled, seeded and finely chopped	4
½ cup	cooked *or* canned, drained red *or* white beans	125 mL
8 cups	chicken stock *or* water	2 liters
½ tsp	chopped fresh marjoram *or* basil	2 mL
1	pinch fresh thyme	1
2	carrots, peeled and diced	2
1 to 2	potatoes, peeled and diced	1 to 2
1	small turnip, peeled and diced	1
1 to 2	celery stalks, thinly sliced	1 to 2
1¼ cups	shredded cabbage	300 mL
½ cup	elbow macaroni *or* other pasta	125 mL
1 tbsp	coarsely chopped fresh parsley	15 mL
	salt and pepper	
	grated Parmesan	

• In a large saucepan, heat the olive oil and sauté the onions, garlic and bacon several minutes over medium heat until limp.

• Add the tomatoes, beans, stock, marjoram and thyme. Cover and let simmer about 1 hour.

• Add the carrots, and cook 10 minutes. Add potatoes, turnip, celery, cabbage and pasta; continue to cook until vegetables are tender and pasta is done.

• Season to taste, garnish with parsley and grated Parmesan, and serve.

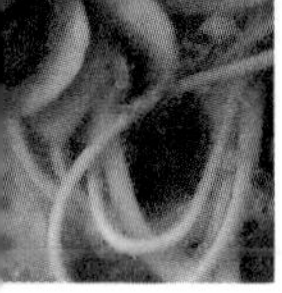

HOW TO SHELL A COOKED LOBSTER

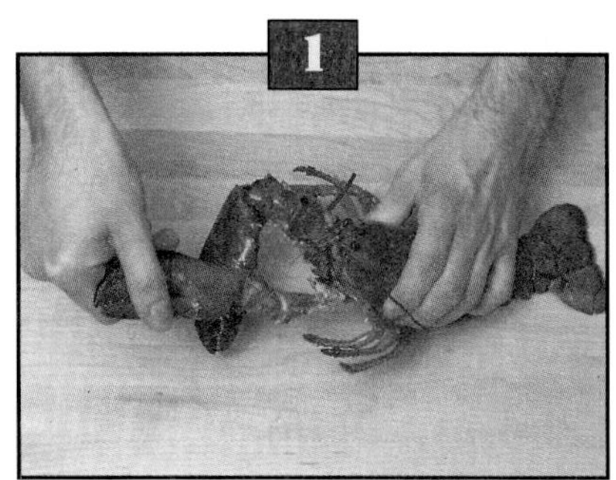

Twist off the claws.

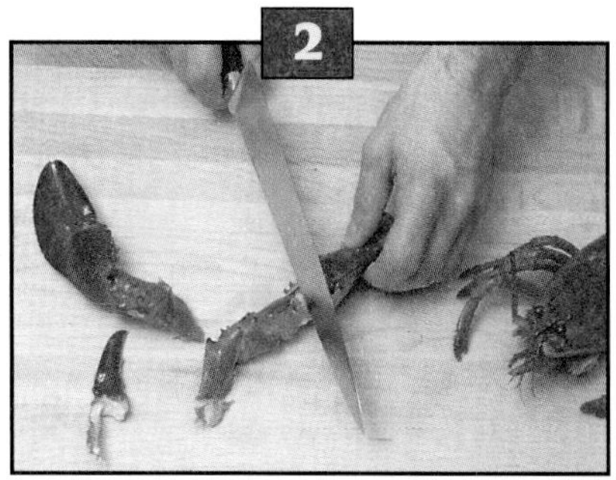

Crack them with a large knife or a nutcracker.

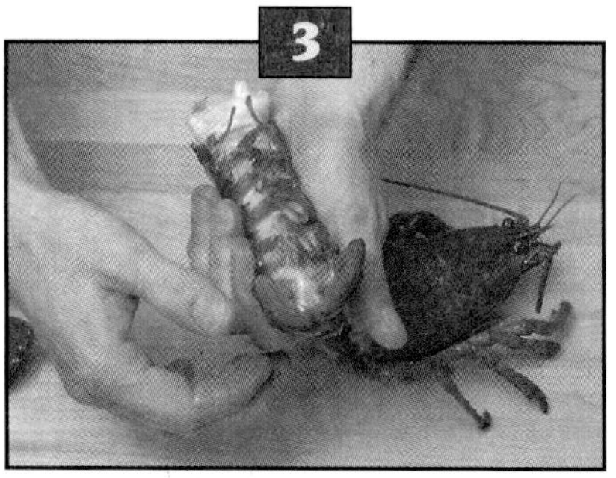

Arch the tail until it cracks off the body. Squeeze the shell to crack it open.

Pull out the flesh.

LOBSTER AND FISH CHOWDER

6 SERVINGS

1 tbsp	butter *or* margarine	15 mL
1	onion, chopped	1
2	celery stalks, diced	2
2 cups	peeled, diced potato	500 mL
2 cups	water	500 mL
1 lb	fresh *or* frozen fish fillets, in 1-inch (2.5 cm) cubes	450 g
3 cups	milk	750 mL
11 oz	cooked or canned lobster meat, drained and cubed	325 g
12 oz	can corn kernels, drained	341 mL
1	pinch paprika	1
1	pinch cayenne pepper (optional)	1
3 tbsp	grated Sbrinz *or* Parmesan	45 mL
3	slices whole-wheat bread, toasted and cubed	3
	chopped fresh parsley	
	pepper	

• Met butter in a large saucepan and sauté onion and celery 2 to 3 minutes over medium-high heat.

• Add potatoes, water and pepper. Cover and let simmer 10 minutes or until potatoes are nearly tender.

• Add fish cubes, cover and let simmer 5 minutes.

• Add milk and gently stir in lobster meat, corn, paprika and cayenne pepper. Heat over low heat without allowing to boil.

• Garnish with parsley and grated cheese. Serve with whole-wheat croutons.

1

Drain and cube lobster meat.

2

Cube fish fillets.

3

Sauté onion and celery in butter. Add potatoes, water and pepper.

4

Stir milk, lobster meat, corn, paprika and cayenne into fish mixture.

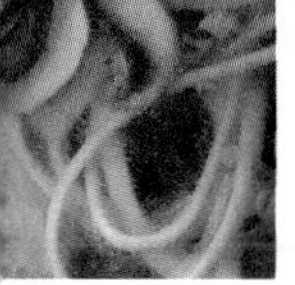

CHICKEN AND RICE SOUP

2 SERVINGS

2 cups	**chicken stock**	**500 mL**
¼ cup	**raw long grain rice**	**50 mL**
¼ cup	**chopped green onion**	**50 mL**
3 tbsp	**butter *or* margarine**	**45 mL**
⅓ cup	**all-purpose flour**	**75 mL**
¼ tsp	**dried sage**	**1 mL**
1	**pinch pepper**	**1**
1 cup	**15% cream *or* buttermilk**	**250 mL**
¾ cup	**diced, cooked chicken *or* turkey**	**175 mL**
2	**slices bacon, cooked crisp, drained and crumbled**	**2**
2 tbsp	**chopped green onion**	**30 mL**
2 tbsp	**sherry (optional)**	**30 mL**
	croutons	

• Pour chicken stock in a saucepan. Add rice and onions. Bring to a boil. Lower heat, cover and simmer 20 to 30 minutes or until rice is tender.

• In a medium-size saucepan, melt butter over moderate heat. Stir in flour, sage and pepper. Cook 1 minute, stirring. Gradually add cream and cook, stirring, until mixture is slightly thickened and smooth.

• Gently stir thickened mixture into rice mixture. Add remaining ingredients except croutons. Heat gently, stirring often, without allowing to boil.

• Garnish with croutons and serve immediately.

1

Combine chicken stock with rice and onions.

2

Melt butter and stir in flour, sage and pepper. Gradually stir in cream.

3

Stir thickened mixture gradually into rice mixture, along with remaining ingredients.

4

Garnish with croutons.

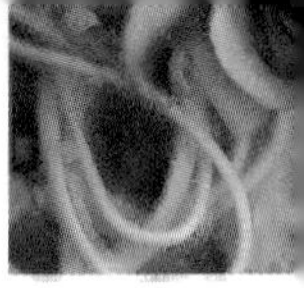

CREAM OF BARLEY

4 SERVINGS

1 cup	pearl barley	250 mL
4 cups	chicken stock	1 liter
2	celery stalks, sliced	2
½ cup	milk	125 mL
½ cup	15% cream	125 mL
1	pinch celery salt	1
	white pepper	

• In a bowl, cover barley with warm water; let soak 1 hour.

• Pour chicken stock into a saucepan. Drain barley and add to stock. Add celery. Bring to a boil, lower heat and let simmer about 1 hour.

• Strain soup, and return liquid to saucepan. (Discard solids.)

• Add milk, cream and seasonings. Reheat gently and serve.

SUGGESTION

To make a lighter soup, replace cream with an equal quantity of milk and add 1 tbsp (15 mL) commercial gravy thickener.

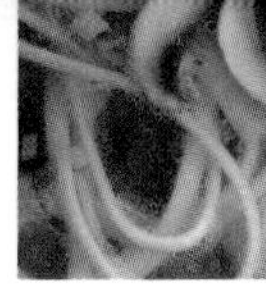

CURRIED CELERY SOUP

4 SERVINGS

1	onion, quartered	1
1	garlic clove	1
2 tbsp	butter *or* margarine	30 mL
2 tsp	curry powder	10 mL
2 tbsp	all-purpose flour	30 mL
3 cups	chicken stock	750 mL
½	head celery with leaves, coarsely chopped	½
1	potato, peeled and diced	1
3 tbsp	15% cream *or* buttermilk (optional)	45 mL
4 tbsp	grated cheese	60 mL
4	slices white bread, toasted	4
	pepper	

• Finely chop onion and garlic in food processor; set aside.

• Melt butter in a large saucepan. Over medium-high heat, sauté onion and garlic 2 minutes. Sprinkle in curry and flour and stir well.

• Add chicken stock and cook, stirring, until mixture is slightly thickened.

• Stir in celery and potato; cook 20 minutes over low heat, or until vegetables are tender.

• Purée mixture in food processor until creamy. Return to saucepan, reheat and season to taste.

• Add cream just before serving, stirring constantly.

• Sprinkle cheese on toast slices and brown in oven; serve with soup.

SUGGESTION

Replace chicken stock with vegetable stock and add a little tomato juice.

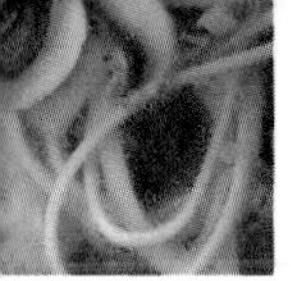

GOULASH SOUP

2 SERVINGS

1 tbsp	vegetable oil	15 mL
½ lb	lean stewing beef, in small cubes	225 g
1	onion, chopped	1
1	garlic clove, chopped	1
1 tbsp	paprika	15 mL
2½ cups	chicken stock	625 mL
½	envelope stew seasoning mix	½
½ cup	canned tomatoes, crushed	125 mL
½	green pepper, seeded and sliced	½
½	celery stalk, finely chopped	½
1	potato, peeled and diced small	2
	chopped fresh parsley	

• Heat oil in a large saucepan. Brown beef and onion over medium-high meat.

• Add garlic, paprika, chicken stock, and stew seasoning. Bring to a boil. Lower heat, cover and let simmer 45 to 50 minutes.

• Stir in tomatoes, green pepper, celery and potato. Cover and let simmer 15 minutes.

• Garnish with chopped parsley just before serving.

SUGGESTION

Add ½ tsp (2 mL) caraway seeds along with the chicken stock.

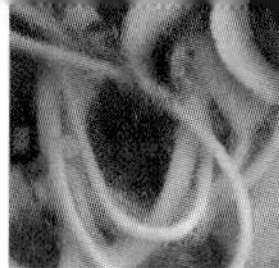

CREAM OF CUCUMBER

4 SERVINGS

2 tbsp	butter *or* margarine	30 mL
1	onion, chopped	1
1	garlic clove, chopped	1
3	medium cucumbers, peeled, seeded and coarsely chopped	3
3 tbsp	all-purpose flour	45 mL
4 cups	rich chicken stock	1 liter
4	mint leaves, finely chopped	4
½ cup	10% cream	125 mL
1 tbsp	chopped fresh parsley	15 mL
2 tbsp	diced red and green peppers	30 mL
	pepper	

• Melt butter in a large saucepan. Sauté onion over medium heat 2 to 3 minutes.

• Add garlic, cucumbers and pepper. Continue cooking 4 to 5 minutes.

• Sprinkle in flour and stir well.

• Stir in chicken stock bit by bit, and continue cooking until cucumber is tender. Add mint.

• Purée mixture in food processor until smooth, then reheat.

• Add cream just before serving, stirring constantly. Garnish with parsley and diced peppers.

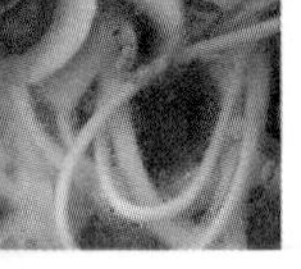

CARROT SOUP

2 SERVINGS

1 tbsp	butter or margarine	15 mL
1	garlic clove, crushed	1
1	onion, finely chopped	1
1 lb	carrots, peeled and coarsely grated	450 g
4 cups	chicken stock	1 liter
2 tbsp	unsweetened orange juice	30 mL
2 tbsp	commercial gravy thickener	30 mL
1 cup	milk	250 mL
½ cup	croutons	125 mL
	chopped fresh parsley	
	grated zest of 1 orange	
	pepper	

- Melt butter in a saucepan. Add garlic, onion, and carrots, cover and cook 5 minutes over low heat.
- Stir in chicken stock, orange juice and grated zest. Pepper to taste, cover and let simmer 25 minutes over low heat.
- Stir in gravy thickener and continue cooking about 5 minutes.
- Purée soup in food processor, stir in milk and reheat.
- Garnish with croutons and parsley just before serving.

A single carrot fulfils the minimum daily requirement for vitamin A. Vitamin A content is especially high in orange-colored or dark green vegetables, as well as liver, milk and egg yolks.

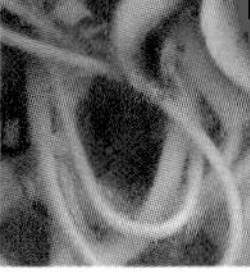

VEGETABLE AND SAUSAGE SOUP

6 TO 8 SERVINGS

3 cups	chicken stock	750 mL
1	medium onion, chopped	1
2 cups	chopped *or* julienned leeks	500 mL
1½ cups	peeled, diced potato	375 mL
2 cups	chopped green cabbage	500 mL
1 cup	drained and chopped canned tomatoes	250 mL
4	smoked *or* dry sausages, cut in 1-inch (2.5 cm) pieces	4
1 cup	milk	250 mL
	pepper	
	sliced green onions	

• Pour chicken stock into a saucepan and bring to a boil. Add onion, leeks and potato. Lower heat, cover and let simmer about 20 minutes, or until vegetables are tender.

• Stir in cabbage, tomatoes and sausages. Cook 5 to 8 minutes, or until cabbage is tender. Stir in milk and pepper to taste.

• Garnish with green onions just before serving.

SUGGESTION

Double the recipe and freeze in single-serving sizes for easy meals in a hurry.

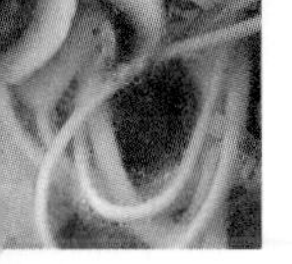

HERB AND APPLE SOUP

4 TO 6 SERVINGS

2 tbsp	butter *or* margarine	30 mL
2 cups	chopped onion	500 mL
2 cups	cored, peeled and diced apple	500 mL
2	garlic cloves, chopped	2
½ tsp	dried thyme	2 mL
1	bay leaf	1
1 tsp	chopped fresh coriander	5 mL
4 cups	chicken stock	1 liter
¼ cup	buttermilk	50 mL
1 tsp	fresh mint (to garnish)	5 mL
	pepper	

• Melt butter in a large saucepan and sauté onion until translucent.

• Add apple, garlic, thyme, bay leaf and coriander.

• Cook about 10 minutes, until onions are lightly browned.

• Add chicken stock and bring to a boil. Lower heat, cover and let simmer 15 to 20 minutes.

• Stir in buttermilk and simmer 1 minute. Remove bay leaf and add pepper to taste.

• Purée in food processor. Garnish with mint. Serve hot or chilled.

POTAGE PARMENTIER WITH GREEN ONIONS

4 SERVINGS

¼ cup	butter *or* margarine	50 mL
2	bunches green onions, sliced	2
4 cups	chicken stock	1 liter
2 cups	peeled, diced potato	500 mL
¼ tsp	pepper	1 mL
¼ cup	dry white wine (optional)	50 mL
1 cup	10% cream	250 mL
	chopped fresh chives	

• Melt butter in a large saucepan. Sauté green onions about 15 minutes, or until tender, without allowing them to brown. Add chicken stock and potato; cook 20 to 30 minutes. Add pepper.

• Purée mixture until smooth in food processor, then blend in wine. Return to saucepan and bring to a boil.

• Add cream, stirring constantly, and reheat without allowing to boil. Adjust seasoning, if necessary. Garnish with chives just before serving.

SUGGESTION

Add diced cooked ham, chicken or beef to the puréed soup to turn it into a meal-in-a-bowl.

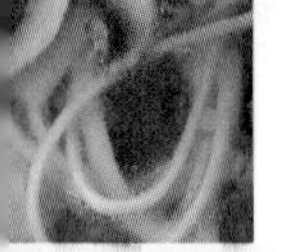

SUGGESTION

If you wish, you can flavor and color the soup with a sprinkling of paprika. Top with croutons for a meal-in-a-bowl.

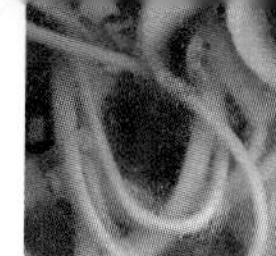

CREAM OF LEEK AND MUSSELS

4 SERVINGS

2 lbs	mussels, cleaned and debearded	900 g
¾ cup	dry white wine	175 mL
2	leeks, white parts only, sliced	2
4	potatoes, peeled, in 1-inch (2.5 cm) cubes	4
1 tbsp	chopped fresh thyme *or*	15 mL
1 tsp	dried thyme	5 mL
1½ cups	milk	375 mL
1 tbsp	cornstarch, dissolved in a little water	15 mL
1	sweet red pepper, cut in ¼-inch (.5 cm) dice	1
2 tbsp	chopped fresh parsley	30 mL
	pepper	

- Put the mussels and wine in a large saucepan and bring to a boil, covered. As soon as mussels have opened, remove them from the pan, let cool slightly, and remove from their shells. Set aside. Discard shells and any unopened mussels.

- Strain the cooking liquid through a fine strainer or cheesecloth and return to the saucepan.

- Add leeks and potatoes, and cook 20 to 25 minutes over medium heat. Season with thyme and pepper.

- Add milk, let simmer 5 minutes, then stir in dissolved cornstarch to thicken.

- Stir in mussels, red pepper and parsley. Serve very hot.

OLD-FASHIONED MUSHROOM BARLEY SOUP

4 TO 6 SERVINGS

4 cups	chicken stock	1 liter
¼ cup	pot barley *or* Scotch barley	50 mL
1	bay leaf	1
2	large carrots, peeled and chopped	2
1	celery stalk with leaves, chopped	1
1	medium onion, chopped	1
1	potato, unpeeled, diced	1
2	garlic cloves, sliced	2
¼ tsp	dried thyme	1 mL
1½ cups	sliced mushrooms	375 mL
	chopped fresh parsley	
	pepper	

• Put the chicken stock, barley and bay leaf in a large saucepan. Bring to a boil, partially cover and let simmer ½ hour.

• Add carrots, celery, onion, potato, garlic and thyme. Cover and continue cooking about 25 minutes. Add mushrooms and simmer another 5 minutes, or until vegetables are tender.

• Stir in parsley and pepper to taste. Remove bay leaf and serve.

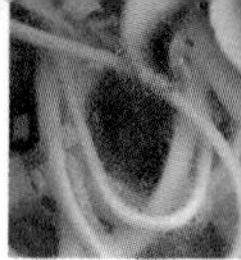

CREAM OF BEET SOUP

2 SERVINGS

1 tbsp	butter *or* margarine	15 mL
½	onion, finely chopped	½
2 cups	chicken stock	500 mL
2 tbsp	raw rice	30 mL
1	large beet, parboiled, peeled and cut up	1
1 tbsp	red wine vinegar *or* raspberry vinegar	15 mL
½ tsp	hot mustard	2 mL
1	egg yolk	1
3 tbsp	10% cream	45 mL
2 tbsp	chopped fresh parsley (optional)	30 mL
	pepper	
	croutons (optional)	

• Melt butter in a large saucepan over low heat. Sauté onion 3 minutes. Add chicken stock and rice, and bring to a boil. Add beet, vinegar, and pepper to taste. Let simmer about 20 minutes.

• Purée mixture until smooth in food processor. Strain and return to saucepan. Correct seasoning if necessary. Stir in mustard with a wire whisk. Return to heat and bring to a boil.

• In a small bowl, combine egg yolk with cream, using a wire whisk or fork. Stir gradually into beet mixture. Serve immediately, garnished with a swirl of cream, or parsley and croutons.

Turn leftover beet soup into a delicious sauce for pasta or chicken; simply sauté a few sliced mushrooms and ½ onion, sliced, and stir into soup.

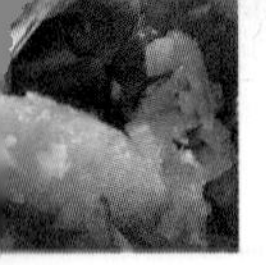

Salads

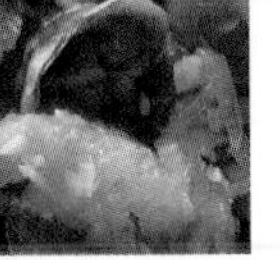

GINGERED CHICKEN SALAD

6 SERVINGS

3	skinless, boneless chicken breasts, ½ lb (225 g) each	3
1¼ cups	dry white wine	300 mL
1¼ cups	water	300 mL
1 tsp	peppercorns	5 mL
¼ cup	finely chopped fresh parsley	50 mL
2	celery stalks, finely chopped	2
¼	honeydew melon, peeled, seeded and cubed	¼
⅓ cup	mayonnaise	75 mL
⅔ cup	plain yogurt	150 mL
5 tbsp	lemon juice	75 mL
2 tsp	honey	10 mL
1 tsp	grated fresh ginger	5 mL
	celery leaves	
	grated zest of 1 lemon	
	pepper	

- Put chicken, wine and water in a saucepan. Add peppercorns and celery leaves. Bring to a boil, then simmer over low heat until chicken is tender.
- Remove chicken from stock and cut into bite-size pieces.
- Combine chicken, parsley and celery in a salad bowl. Top with the cubed melon. Set aside.
- In a small bowl, combine mayonnaise, yogurt, lemon zest, lemon juice and honey. Season with ginger and pepper.
- Pour dressing over salad and serve.

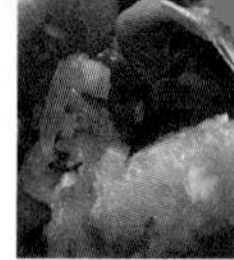

SPINACH AND RED CABBAGE SALAD

4 SERVINGS

⅓ cup	coarsely chopped pecans	75 mL
1	package fresh spinach, torn up	1
2 cups	shredded red cabbage	500 mL
½	red onion, sliced	½
4 tsp	red wine vinegar *or* raspberry vinegar	20 mL
½ tsp	hot mustard *or* grainy mustard	2 mL
3 tbsp	olive oil	45 mL
3 tbsp	buttermilk	45 mL
	freshly ground pepper	

- Preheat oven to 400°F (200°C).
- Spread pecans on a cookie sheet and toast in oven 8 minutes, stirring occasionally. Let cool and set aside.
- In a large bowl, combine spinach, cabbage and onion. Refrigerate until serving time.
- In a small bowl, combine vinegar with mustard. Whisk in olive oil and buttermilk. Pepper to taste.
- When ready to serve, toss dressing through salad. Garnish with toasted pecans.

Red cabbage is high in Vitamin C, which helps the body utilize the iron found in spinach.

SUGGESTION

At the last minute, peel and dice a fresh orange or two to scatter over the salad.

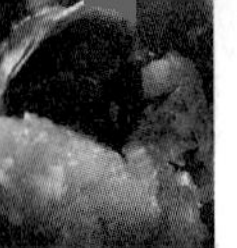

BOSTON LETTUCE WITH APPLE

4 SERVINGS

2	small heads Boston lettuce	2
1	apple, peeled	1
2 tbsp	lemon juice	30 mL
2	hard-boiled eggs, sliced	2
¼ lb	gruyère cheese, diced	110 g
1 tsp	hot mustard	5 mL
1 tbsp	corn oil	15 mL
1 tbsp	vinegar	15 mL
1 tbsp	water	15 mL
	pepper	
	chopped fresh chives	

• Wash and tear up lettuce. Cut apple in small dice and sprinkle with 1 tbsp (15 mL) lemon juice.

• Place lettuce, apple, eggs and cheese in a salad bowl.

• In a small bowl, combine mustard, remaining lemon juice, oil, vinegar and water. Pepper to taste.

• Pour dressing over salad, toss lightly, and garnish with chives to serve.

1

Wash and tear up lettuce. Cut apple into small dice and sprinkle with lemon juice.

2

Place lettuce, apple, eggs and cheese in a salad bowl.

3

Prepare dressing.

4

Pour over salad, toss lightly and garnish with chives.

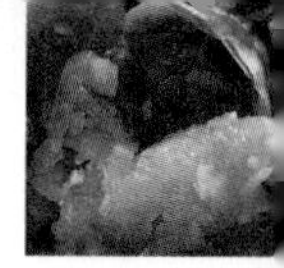

LUNCHEON RICE SALAD

4 SERVINGS

1 cup	cold diced meat of your choice	250 mL
½ cup	diced celery	125 mL
2	green onions, chopped	2
1½ cups	cooked rice	375 mL
	DRESSING	
¾ cup	plain yogurt	175 mL
2 tbsp	tomato juice	30 mL
½ tsp	chopped fresh coriander	2 mL
1	garlic clove, minced	1
	GARNISH	
	lettuce leaves	
	radish slices	

• In a bowl, combine meat, celery, green onions and rice. Set aside.

• To make the dressing, stir together yogurt, tomato juice, coriander and garlic.

• Pour dressing over rice mixture, stir well, cover and refrigerate 2 hours.

• Line 4 plates with lettuce leaves, top with rice salad and decorate with radish slices.

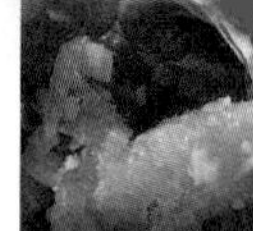

ZUCCHINI AND YOGURT SALAD

4 SERVINGS

1 cup	thinly sliced zucchini	250 mL
1 tbsp	chopped fresh tarragon	15 mL
1 tbsp	chopped fresh parsley	15 mL
4	curly lettuce leaves, torn up	4
4	radicchio leaves, torn up	4
¼ cup	chopped fresh chives	50 mL
	DRESSING	
⅓ cup	plain yogurt	75 mL
2 tbsp	lemon juice	30 mL
2 tsp	red wine vinegar *or* raspberry vinegar	10 mL
1 tsp	hot mustard	5 mL
1	garlic clove, minced	1
2 tbsp	olive oil	30 mL
1½ tsp	chicken stock	7 mL
	freshly ground pepper	

• In a bowl, combine zucchini with 1 tsp (5 mL) tarragon and 1 tsp (5 mL) parsley. Set aside.

• In another bowl, combine lettuce and radicchio with remaining tarragon, parsley and chives. Set aside.

• To make the dressing, whisk together yogurt, lemon juice, vinegar, mustard and garlic. Stir in oil and chicken stock. Pepper to taste.

• To serve, stir half the dressing into the zucchini. Toss remaining dressing with lettuce. Arrange lettuce on plates with zucchini mixture on top.

Use your imagination when it comes to garnishing: try chopped green or black olives, chopped fresh parsley, plain or garlic-flavored croutons, grated cheese, strips of cooked ham, etc.

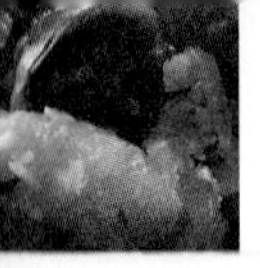

BEEF AND ORANGE SALAD

4 SERVINGS

1 tbsp	light soy sauce *or* tamari	15 mL
1	garlic clove, minced	1
1 tbsp	corn oil	15 mL
½ lb	beef sirloin *or* top round, sliced	225 g
1	Romaine lettuce, washed and torn up	1
2	large oranges, peel and pith removed, sliced	2
1 tbsp	chopped fresh parsley	15 mL
	DRESSING	
¼ cup	corn oil	50 mL
¼ cup	unsweetened orange juice	50 mL
2 tbsp	mayonnaise	30 mL
	salt and pepper	

• In a large bowl, combine soy sauce, garlic and corn oil. Add beef strips, stir, cover, and marinate 1 hour refrigerated.

• Remove beef from marinade and cook, without added oil, in a non-stick skillet over high heat 2 to 3 minutes, stirring from time to time.

• Arrange lettuce on salad plates. Top with beef and orange slices. Sprinkle with parsley.

• Stir together dressing ingredients until well mixed. Serve separately.

SUGGESTION

The beef can be served hot, chilled or at room temperature. Instead of orange slices, use canned mandarin wedges; use the mandarin juice in the dressing.

FENNEL AND CARROT SALAD

4 TO 6 SERVINGS

12	radishes	12
3	fennel stalks, thinly sliced	3
1	apple, cored and diced	1
2	carrots, peeled and cut in julienne strips	2
1 tbsp	lemon juice	15 mL
6 tbsp	plain yogurt	90 mL

• Put trimmed radishes in very cold water. Refrigerate 2 to 3 hours. Drain and reserve.

• In a large bowl, combine fennel, apple and carrot.

• Add lemon juice and yogurt and stir well.

• Arrange in salad dishes and garnish with radishes.

Whether raw or cooked, fennel can be used exactly like celery. However, fennel contains much more Vitamin C and A. Its mild licorice flavor goes well with fish and is delicious in salads.

SUGGESTION

Prepare the dressing several hours in advance to allow flavors to meld.

TURKEY AND FETA SALAD

4 SERVINGS

6 cups	Romaine lettuce, torn up	1.5 liters
2 cups	diced, skinless cooked turkey	500 mL
4 oz	feta cheese, crumbled	120 g
⅓	English cucumber, quartered then sliced	⅓
8	sliced radishes	8
8	pitted black olives	8
½	tomato, diced	½
	coarsely chopped fresh parsley	
	DRESSING	
1	garlic clove, minced	1
1 tsp	dried basil	5 mL
1 tsp	hot mustard *or* grainy-style mustard	5 mL
2 tbsp	lemon juice	30 mL
2 tbsp	red wine vinegar *or* raspberry vinegar	30 mL
¼ cup	olive oil *or* vegetable oil	50 mL
	pepper	

• Arrange lettuce on 4 plates.

• In a bowl, gently combine turkey, feta, cucumber, radishes, olives and tomato. Spoon on top of lettuce.

• Stir together dressing ingredients in small bowl.

• Sprinkle a little over each salad. Garnish with parsley to serve.

RAVIOLI SALAD NIÇOISE

4 SERVINGS

8 oz	cooked mini ravioli, stuffed with cheese *or* meat	225 g
3	tomatoes, thinly sliced *or* 12 cherry tomatoes, halved	3
1	English cucumber, thinly sliced	1
2	hard-boiled eggs, quartered	2
1	green pepper, cut in strips	1
1	red pepper, cut in strips	1
1	can anchovy fillets, chopped (optional)	1
⅓ cup	black olives, halved *or* quartered	75 mL
1	medium onion, sliced	1

DRESSING

2 tbsp	red wine vinegar *or* raspberry vinegar	30 mL
1 tsp	hot mustard	5 mL
1	garlic clove, minced	1
2 tbsp	chopped fresh parsley	30 mL
6 tbsp	olive oil	90 mL
	pepper	

- Combine all dressing ingredients in a large bowl.
- Add ravioli, tomatoes, cucumber, eggs, peppers, anchovies, olives and onion.
- Stir gently to mix. Serve chilled or at room temperature.

If anchovies are very salty, rinse them under cold water and drain on paper towels.

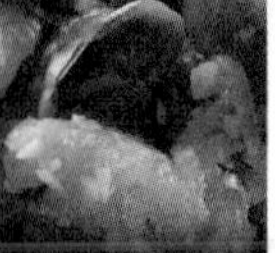

ITALIAN SALAD

4 SERVINGS

⅓ lb	rigatoni	175 g
1 tbsp	olive oil	15 mL
2	green peppers	2
2	red peppers	2
½ lb	sliced salami	225 g
½ cup	pitted black olives	125 mL
4	green onions, sliced	4
	DRESSING	
¼ cup	shallot-flavored vinegar	50 mL
2 tbsp	finely chopped fresh parsley	30 mL
¼ tsp	dried oregano	1 mL
¼ tsp	dried basil	1 mL
1	pinch crushed hot red pepper	1
3 tbsp	water	45 mL
3 tbsp	olive oil	45 mL
	salt and pepper	

• Cook rigatoni in boiling salted water. Drain, rinse, drain again, place in salad bowl, then sprinkle with olive oil.

• Put red and green peppers on baking pan and broil about 4 inches (10 cm) from the element, turning every 5 minutes, until skin is charred. Close peppers in a paper bag or sealable container and let sweat about 20 minutes.

• Pull off charred skin, seed, and cut peppers into strips about 1 inch (2.5 cm) wide. Stir pepper strips into pasta along with salami, olives, and green onions.

• In a small bowl, combine vinegar, parsley, oregano, basil, hot pepper, water, salt and pepper. Whisk in oil gradually. Pour dressing over salad and toss gently. Let sit 1 hour at room temperature or longer in refrigerator for flavors to meld.

1

Cook rigatoni, drain, rinse, and drain again. Toss with olive oil.

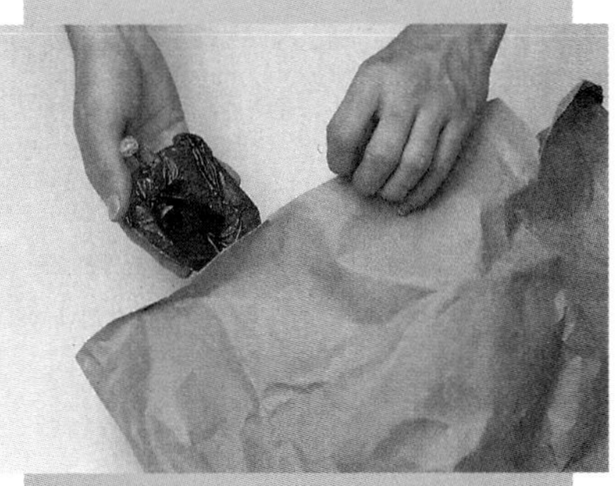

2

Broil peppers, then seal them in paper bag.

3

Combine rigatoni, peppers, salami, olives and onions.

4

Toss salad with dressing. Let sit 1 hour at room temperature.

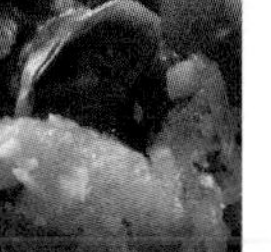

WARM SPINACH AND ORANGE SALAD

4 SERVINGS

2	oranges, segmented and membranes removed (reserve juice)	2
2	packages spinach, washed and drained	2
1 tbsp	corn oil	15 mL
1	onion, finely chopped	1
¼ cup	balsamic, red wine *or* raspberry vinegar	50 mL
1 tsp	dried tarragon	5 mL
1 tsp	julienned orange zest	5 mL
2 tbsp	grated Sbrinz *or* Parmesan	30 mL
2	slices bread, toasted and diced	2

• Combine orange pieces and their juice in a bowl. Set aside.

• Place spinach in salad bowl. Set aside.

• Heat oil in a skillet and cook onion, vinegar, tarragon and orange zest, covered, until onion is tender.

• Slowly stir in oranges and their juice, and mix well.

• Pour orange mixture over spinach. Toss gently. Sprinkle with cheese and croutons to serve.

CHICKEN AND ORANGE SALAD

3 SERVINGS

2	oranges, segmented and membranes removed	2
6 oz	cooked boneless, skinless chicken, cubed	180 g
6	slices chicken pepperoni, cut in strips	6
½ cup	alfalfa sprouts	125 mL
6 oz	bean sprouts	180 g
3 tbsp	unsweetened orange juice	45 mL
1 tbsp	lemon juice	15 mL
½ tsp	soy sauce *or* tamari	2 mL
2 tbsp	mayonnaise	30 mL
½ tsp	grated fresh ginger	2 mL
	chopped fresh parsley	
	chopped, unsalted cashews (optional)	
	pepper	

• In a salad bowl, combine orange pieces, chicken, pepperoni, alfalfa sprouts and bean sprouts. Set aside.

• In another bowl, stir together orange and lemon juice, soy sauce, mayonnaise, ginger and pepper.

• Pour over chicken mixture. Sprinkle with parsley and chopped nuts to serve.

FATTOUCHE

2 SERVINGS

½	green pepper, chopped	½
1 to 2	tomatoes, chopped	1 to 2
6	Romaine lettuce leaves, torn up	6
½	cucumber, diced *or* sliced	½
6 to 8	radishes, quartered *or* sliced	6 to 8
2	green onions, sliced	2
1	garlic clove, minced	1
	DRESSING	
½	onion, minced	½
½ tsp	salt	2 mL
1 tbsp	dried sumac*	15 mL
4 tbsp	olive oil	60 mL
	lemon juice	

- Combine all dressing ingredients in a small bowl; set aside.
- Combine salad ingredients in a large bowl.
- Pour dressing over salad and toss gently. Serve immediately.

* See glossary

MUSTARD VINAIGRETTE

MAKES 1 CUP (250 ML)

1 tbsp	grainy-style mustard	15 mL
1 tbsp	hot mustard	15 mL
1 tbsp	red wine vinegar	15 mL
¾ cup	canola oil	175 mL
	pepper	

- Whisk together the mustards, vinegar and pepper to taste.
- Pour in oil in a thin stream, whisking constantly.
- Beat with whisk until creamy.

WARM BEEF SALAD WITH LEMON

4 SERVINGS

2	slices lean beef, about 7 oz (200 g) each	2
8	Boston *or* Romaine lettuce leaves	8
4	radicchio leaves	4
1	Belgian endive	1
1 cup	watercress	250 mL
1	green apple, diced	1
1	red pepper, cut in strips	1
1 tbsp	lemon juice	15 mL
¼ cup	olive oil	50 mL
	pepper	

• Season the meat with pepper to taste, then barbecue or grill to desired degree of doneness. Set aside for 5 minutes.

• Tear up lettuce and radicchio and chop the endive. Cut beef into thin strips and toss with lettuce, radicchio, endive, watercress, apple and red pepper.

• Add lemon juice and olive oil. Toss well and serve.

SHRIMP AND RICE SALAD

6 SERVINGS

2 cups	unsweetened orange juice	500 mL
1¼ cups	long grain rice	300 mL
1 tsp	butter *or* margarine	5 mL
1	red *or* green pepper, diced	1
1	onion, minced	1
¼ lb	snow peas, cut diagonally and steamed	110 g
5 oz	small cooked, shelled and deveined shrimp, coarsely chopped	150 g
2	oranges, segmented and membranes removed	2
	DRESSING	
2 tbsp	corn oil	30 mL
2 tbsp	water	30 mL
2 tbsp	raspberry vinegar	30 mL
1	pinch sugar	1
1	pinch dry mustard	1
	pepper	

- In a saucepan, combine orange juice, rice and butter. Bring to a boil and stir once.
- Lower heat, cover and let simmer 15 to 20 minutes, or until rice is tender and orange juice absorbed.
- Put rice in a bowl and stir gently with a fork. Let cool.
- Add diced pepper, onion, snow peas and shrimp. Set aside.
- Combine dressing ingredients in a bowl.
- Pour over salad and toss gently.
- Garnish with orange segments to serve.

PASTA SHELL SURPRISE

4 SERVINGS

½	head broccoli, cooked *or* raw, in florets	½
1 cup	canned *or* frozen, thawed peas	250 mL
3	tomatoes, diced	3
1	green *or* red pepper, diced	1
3	green onions, chopped	3
10 to 12	black olives, coarsely chopped	10 to 12
4	smoked chicken sausages *or* weiners, cooked and cut up	4
14 oz	pasta shells, cooked	420 g
3	hard-boiled eggs, sliced	3
2 tbsp	chopped fresh parsley	30 mL

DRESSING

¼ cup	honey	50 mL
¼ cup	lemon juice	50 mL
2 tsp	raspberry *or* other vinegar	10 mL
1 tsp	dry mustard	5 mL
¼ cup	corn oil	50 mL

- In a bowl, combine vegetables, sausage and pasta shells. Set aside.
- In another bowl, combine dressing ingredients.
- Pour dressing over pasta mixture and toss gently.
- Arrange on chilled plates.
- Garnish with slices of hard-boiled eggs, sprinkle with parsley and serve.

TOMATO, FENNEL AND GOAT'S CHEESE SALAD

4 SERVINGS

3	tomatoes, peeled, seeded and diced (reserve juice and seeds)	3
1	fennel bulb, halved, then cut in strips	1
¼ cup	finely chopped red onion	50 mL
¼ cup	torn up fresh basil leaves	50 mL
⅓ cup	crumbled goat's cheese	75 mL
3 tbsp	red wine vinegar	45 mL
⅓ cup	canola oil	75 mL
¼ tsp	salt (optional)	1 mL
¼ tsp	pepper	1 mL
4	slices whole-wheat bread	4
1	garlic clove, halved	1

- Preheat broiler.
- In a bowl, combine tomatoes with their juice and seeds, fennel, onion, basil and cheese.
- Add vinegar and 2 tbsp (30 mL) oil. Season and mix well. Set aside.
- Baste both sides of bread slices with remaining oil, then brown under broiler.
- Rub toasted bread with garlic, let cool, then dice.
- Add toast croutons to salad and toss just before serving.

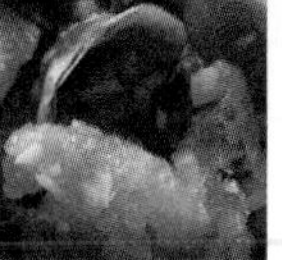

ORIENTAL TURKEY SALAD

4 SERVINGS

¼ cup	soy sauce	50 mL
1 tsp	grated fresh ginger	5 mL
1	garlic clove, minced	1
1 lb	boneless, skinless turkey breast, cut in strips	450 g
¼ cup	chopped fresh coriander (optional)	50 mL
3 cups	shredded Chinese lettuce	750 mL
1 cup	bean sprouts	250 mL
4	green onions, sliced	4
¼ lb	snow peas, steamed	110 g
	DRESSING	
¼ cup	sesame seeds	50 mL
¼ cup	peanut oil *or* vegetable oil	50 mL
2 tbsp	sesame oil	30 mL
2 tbsp	rice vinegar *or* cider vinegar	30 mL
2 tsp	cornstarch	10 mL

• Combine soy sauce, ginger and garlic in a small bowl. Set aside.

• Place turkey strips in a bowl and pour soy mixture over; cover and marinate 3 hours, refrigerated.

• In a salad bowl, combine coriander, lettuce, bean sprouts and onions.

• Toast sesame seeds in a skillet over medium heat 3 to 4 minutes. Remove from skillet and reserve.

• Drain turkey, reserving ¼ cup (50 mL) of the marinade. Heat 1 tbsp (15 mL) peanut oil in the same skillet over medium-high heat and cook turkey on all sides about 4 minutes or until it loses its pinkish hue. Toss into salad.

• In a saucepan, combine reserved marinade, remaining peanut oil, sesame oil, vinegar and cornstarch. Bring to a boil, then boil 3 minutes, stirring constantly. Pour over salad, and toss gently. Sprinkle with sesame seeds and garnish with snow peas. Serve immediately.

SPINACH SALAD WITH WALNUT DRESSING

4 SERVINGS

¼ cup	chopped walnuts	50 mL
2	garlic cloves	2
¼ cup	balsamic vinegar *or* raspberry vinegar	50 mL
1 tbsp	hot mustard	15 mL
1 tsp	pepper	5 mL
⅓ cup	olive oil *or* vegetable oil	75 mL
2	packages spinach, washed and well-drained	2
2 tbsp	crumbled crisp-cooked bacon	30 mL
½ cup	diced goat's cheese *or* other cheese	125 mL
¼ cup	grated carrot	50 mL

- Crush walnuts and garlic in food processor.
- Add vinegar, mustard and pepper. Mix well.
- Gradually pour in oil, with processor on, until dressing thickens. Set aside.
- Tear spinach leaves into a large bowl. Sprinkle with dressing.
- Garnish with bacon, cheese and carrots to serve.

SUGGESTION

Add segments of fresh peeled orange with pith and membrane removed.

CABBAGE AND FRUIT SALAD

4 SERVINGS

1 cup	drained pineapple pieces	250 mL
2 cups	grated cabbage	500 mL
⅔ cup	cored, diced apple	150 mL
½ cup	grated carrot	125 mL
¼ cup	diced green pepper	50 mL
1 tbsp	pineapple juice	15 mL
1 tbsp	corn oil	15 mL
1 tbsp	honey	15 mL
1 tbsp	lemon juice	15 mL
1	pinch ground ginger	1
4 tbsp	plain yogurt	60 mL

• In a large bowl, combine pineapple, cabbage, apple, carrot and green pepper. Set aside.

• Place pineapple juice, corn oil, honey, lemon juice, ginger and yogurt in a jar with a tight-fitting lid. Shake well to blend.

• Pour dressing over salad and toss gently. Cover and refrigerate 4 to 24 hours. Stir before serving.

CANTONESE CHICKEN SALAD

4 SERVINGS

⅓ cup	mayonnaise	75 mL
⅓ cup	plain yogurt	75 mL
1 tbsp	light soy sauce	15 mL
1½ tsp	dried dill	7 mL
¼ tsp	pepper	1 mL
2 cups	diced, cooked, boneless chicken	500 mL
10 oz	can water chestnuts, quartered (optional)	284 mL
½ cup	chopped green onions	125 mL
2	kiwis, peeled, halved and sliced *or* ½ cup (125 mL) diced melon *or* halved green grapes	2
1 tbsp	sesame seeds	15 mL
	lettuce leaves	

• In a bowl, stir together mayonnaise, yogurt, soy sauce, dill and pepper.

• Add diced chicken, water chestnuts, onions and kiwis.

• Stir gently to mix.

• Arrange on lettuce leaves. Sprinkle with sesame seeds to serve.

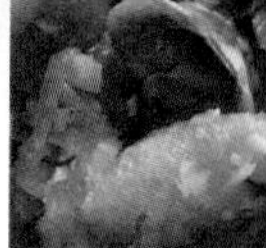

FRUITY CHICKPEA SALAD

4 SERVINGS

2½ cups	canned chickpeas, rinsed and drained	625 mL
3	red *or* green apples with peel, cored and diced	3
2	green onions, chopped	2
1 cup	chopped celery	250 mL
	lettuce leaves to garnish	

DRESSING

3 tbsp	cider vinegar *or* raspberry vinegar	45 mL
⅓ cup	canola oil	75 mL
1	garlic clove, minced	1
2 tbsp	chopped fresh parsley	30 mL
	a few fresh basil, coriander *or* mint leaves, chopped	

- In a bowl, combine chickpeas, apples, onions and celery. Set aside.
- Stir together dressing ingredients in a small bowl.
- Pour dressing over chickpea mixture. Stir, cover and refrigerate 30 minutes.
- Arrange on lettuce leaves to serve.

SUGGESTION

Chickpeas are an excellent source of dietary fiber, and are so rich in protein that they make a good meat substitute.

SALMON SALAD WITH PEACHES

4 SERVINGS

If you must use canned fruit for this recipe, be sure to select fruit that is canned in its own juice, not in syrup.

1	head Boston *or* Romaine lettuce, washed and dried	1
4	salmon fillets, about 3 oz (90 g) each, cooked	4
3	fresh peaches, peeled and sliced *or* 14 oz (398 mL) can sliced peaches in natural juice, drained	3
4 tbsp	halved pecans	60 mL
½ cup	mayonnaise	125 mL
1 tbsp	raspberry vinegar	15 mL
½ tsp	finely chopped fresh ginger	2 mL

- Arrange lettuce leaves on 4 plates.
- Place cooked fillet on each.
- Arrange peaches and nuts on top. Set aside.
- In a bowl, stir together mayonnaise, vinegar and ginger.
- Spoon dressing over each salad.

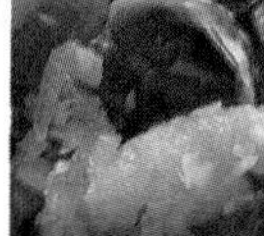

WARM SPINACH AND SMOKED SAUSAGE SALAD

4 SERVINGS

2	packages fresh spinach, washed and drained	2
4	smoked sausages, cut in pieces	4
1	medium onion, finely chopped	1
3 tbsp	sunflower oil *or* other oil	45 mL
1 tbsp	raspberry vinegar	15 mL
2 tsp	hot mustard	10 mL
2 oz	slivered almonds	60 g
1	pinch paprika	1
	pepper	

- Tear spinach into a large bowl. Set aside.
- Grill or broil sausages. Keep warm.
- Soften onion in the oil over medium heat, without allowing to brown.
- In food processor, combine onion, vinegar, mustard and pepper until smooth.
- Toss spinach with onion mixture and sausage pieces. Add almonds and paprika.
- Toss well and serve.

SUGGESTION

Just before serving, top the salad with garlic-flavored croutons and grated cheese of your choice.

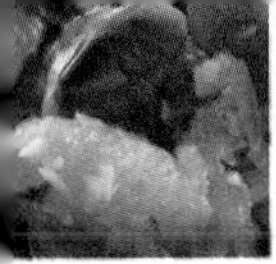

SUGGESTION

If you wish, use diced canned beets instead of fresh. Beets are a rich source of potassium, calcium and folic acid.

BEET AND WALNUT SALAD

2 SERVINGS

2 tsp	**white wine vinegar**	**10 mL**
2 tsp	**canola oil**	**10 mL**
2 tsp	**mayonnaise**	**10 mL**
2	**raw beets, peeled and grated**	**2**
6 tbsp	**chopped walnuts**	**90 mL**
1 tbsp	**chopped fresh parsley**	**15 mL**
	pepper	

- Whisk together vinegar and oil in a bowl.
- Add mayonnaise and pepper. Whisk to blend.
- Combine beets and walnuts in salad bowl.
- Toss with dressing. Sprinkle with parsley and refrigerate. Serve well chilled.

1

Combine vinegar and oil in bowl.

2

Whisk in mayonnaise and pepper.

3

Combine beets and walnuts in salad bowl.

4

Toss with dressing and sprinkle with parsley.

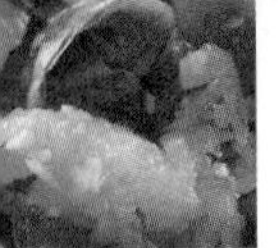

ARTICHOKE HEART SALAD

2 SERVINGS

3 tbsp	**olive oil**	**45 mL**
1 tbsp	**lemon juice**	**15 mL**
1 tsp	**finely chopped onion**	**5 mL**
1	**pinch dried thyme**	**1**
16	**canned artichoke hearts, whole *or* quartered**	**16**
1 tbsp	**finely chopped fresh parsley**	**15 mL**
2 tbsp	**grated Sbrinz *or* gruyère cheese**	**30 mL**
	pepper	

Artichokes are a good source of Vitamin A and potassium.

• In a large bowl, combine oil, lemon juice, onion and thyme. Pepper to taste.

• Add artichoke hearts and stir gently.

• Refrigerate 1 to 2 hours, stirring occasionally.

• Arrange artichoke hearts on a serving dish. Garnish with parsley and cheese.

POTATO SALAD WITH THYME

4 SERVINGS

4	potatoes, cooked, peeled and halved *or* quartered	4
2 tbsp	dry white wine	30 mL
1 tsp	chopped fresh thyme	5 mL
4 tsp	red wine vinegar	20 mL
1 tsp	hot mustard	5 mL
1	pinch pepper	1
2 tbsp	corn oil	30 mL
1 tbsp	chopped fresh chives	15 mL

• Combine potatoes, wine and thyme in a bowl.

• In a second bowl, whisk together vinegar, mustard and pepper. Gradually whisk in oil.

• Pour dressing over potatoes. Toss gently. Sprinkle with chives and serve.

Poultry

STUFFED CHICKEN THIGHS WITH THYME

4 SERVINGS

¾ cup	cooked white rice	175 mL
¼ cup	cooked wild rice	50 mL
1	pinch dried thyme	1
4	boneless chicken thighs	4
1 cup	chicken stock	250 mL
	freshly ground pepper	
	SAUCE	
3 tbsp	butter *or* margarine	45 mL
1	green onion, finely chopped	1
½ cup	chopped lettuce	125 mL
¼ cup	chopped spinach	50 mL
1 cup	chicken stock	250 mL
½ cup	dry white wine	125 mL
½ cup	whipping cream	125 mL
	freshly ground pepper	

• In a bowl, combine white rice, wild rice, thyme and pepper. Stuff chicken thighs with rice mixture and close to form a neat package, fastening with toothpicks.

• Preheat oven to 400°F (200°C).

• Arrange stuffed chicken thighs in baking pan, pour chicken stock over, and bake 10 to 15 minutes or until chicken is cooked.

• To make the sauce, melt 1 tbsp (15 mL) butter in a saucepan with chopped green onion. Add lettuce, spinach, chicken stock and wine. Simmer 5 minutes.

• Stir in cream and bring to a boil. Purée until smooth in blender. Add remaining butter and pepper to taste. Keep hot.

• To serve, pour sauce on 4 plates and arrange chicken on top. Garnish with vegetables of your choice.

SUGGESTION

Replace fresh ginger with 1 tsp (5 mL) ground ginger. A few sprigs of fresh coriander add greatly to the aroma and visual appeal.

TURKEY TOURNEDOS WITH GINGER

4 SERVINGS

1 tbsp	corn oil	15 mL
2 tbsp	grated fresh ginger	30 mL
1	garlic clove, sliced	1
4	turkey tournedos*	4
2	onions, chopped	2
1	red pepper, cut in strips	1
10	chopped mushrooms	10
2	green onions, chopped	2
1 tbsp	light soy sauce	15 mL

- Heat oil in a non-stick skillet. Add ginger and garlic, and cook just until garlic turns slightly golden.
- Add tournedos and cook over medium-high heat about 10 minutes, until meat is browned. Turn halfway through.
- Add vegetables, and continue cooking 10 minutes over medium heat.
- Stir in soy sauce. Serve with rice.

* See glossary

Like chicken, the white meat of turkey contains half the fat and cholesterol of the dark meat.

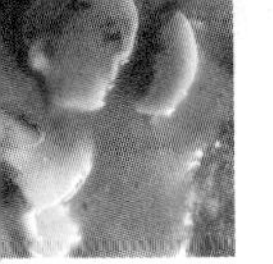

BARBECUED TURKEY WITH CRANBERRY

4 SERVINGS

4	small turkey thighs	4
1 tbsp	vegetable oil	15 mL
1 tbsp	butter *or* margarine	15 mL
2 tbsp	finely chopped green onion	30 mL
1	garlic clove, sliced	1
¼ cup	cranberry jelly	50 mL
½ cup	dry red wine	125 mL
¼ cup	chicken stock *or* orange juice	50 mL
1 tsp	grated orange zest	5 mL
½ tsp	dry mustard	2 mL
½ tsp	ground ginger	2 mL

- Place turkey thighs in a glass dish, cover with plastic wrap and set aside.

- In a small saucepan, heat oil and butter. Add green onion and garlic and cook over medium heat 5 minutes. Stir in remaining ingredients.

- Heat until jelly melts. Remove from heat and let cool. Pour mixture over turkey. Let marinate 3 hours in refrigerator, covered.

- Remove turkey and pour marinade into a saucepan. Bring to a boil, then simmer 4 minutes over medium-high heat. Set aside.

- Arrange turkey on preheated barbecue grill at high, or in very hot skillet. Cook 20 minutes, basting with marinade from time to time. Turn over and cook another 10 minutes.

- Serve with grilled vegetables.

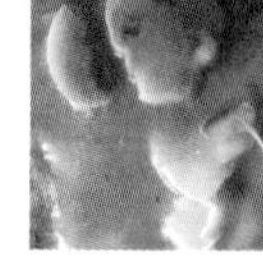

TURKEY BURGERS WITH BASIL

4 SERVINGS

1	egg, beaten	1
¼ cup	fine breadcrumbs	50 mL
3 tbsp	chicken stock *or* water	45 mL
2 tbsp	chopped fresh basil	30 mL
2 tbsp	chopped green onion	30 mL
2 tbsp	grated Parmesan	30 mL
1 tbsp	pine nuts *or* slivered almonds	15 mL
1 lb	ground turkey, cooked *or* raw	450 g
4	Kaiser rolls *or* hamburger buns	4
	salt and pepper	

• In a large bowl, combine egg, breadcrumbs, chicken stock, basil, onion, Parmesan, nuts, salt and pepper. Add ground turkey and mix well. Shape into 4 patties.

• Grill burgers 5 minutes on oiled, preheated barbecue grill or in a skillet. Turn over and cook another 7 minutes.

• Serve on lightly toasted rolls, with garnishes of your choice.

MANGO-STUFFED CHICKEN BREASTS

6 SERVINGS

¼ cup	finely chopped mango	50 mL
1 tbsp	fruit catsup	15 mL
3 tbsp	butter *or* margarine	45 mL
1 tbsp	lemon juice	15 mL
1	pinch ground ginger	1
1	pinch cayenne pepper	1
1	pinch ground cloves	1
1	garlic clove, crushed	1
2	mangoes, peeled, pitted and cut in long strips	2
6	boneless, skinless chicken breasts	6
	juice of ½ lime	

• In a bowl, combine chopped mango, catsup, butter, lemon juice, ginger, cayenne, cloves, and garlic. Set aside.

• Sprinkle mango strips with lime juice. Set aside.

• Slit chicken breasts deeply along one side to make a pocket. Fill slit with chopped mango mixture.

• Heat remaining chopped mango mixture in skillet.

• Grill chicken breasts on oiled, preheated barbecue 7 to 8 minutes on each side, basting with hot mango mixture.

• Serve garnished with fresh mango strips.

ROAST STUFFED TURKEY BREAST

4 SERVINGS

1½ lbs	**turkey breast, skin removed**	**675 g**
½ cup	**quick-cooking rice, uncooked**	**125 mL**
1 cup	**sliced mushrooms**	**250 mL**
⅓ cup	**sliced green onions**	**75 mL**
½ cup	**drained canned tomatoes, crushed**	**125 mL**
⅓ cup	**grated mozzarella**	**75 mL**
¼ cup	**chicken stock**	**50 mL**
	freshly ground pepper	

• Slit turkey breast deeply along one side to make a pocket. Sprinkle with pepper and set aside.

• In a bowl, combine remaining ingredients except chicken stock.

• Preheat oven to 350°F (180°C).

• Stuff breast with rice mixture. Close and hold shut with toothpicks. Place on baking pan, pour chicken stock over and cover.

• Bake 35 to 40 minutes. Let rest several minutes before carving.

• Serve turkey slices with sauce or gravy of your choice.

NEW ORLEANS BARBECUED CHICKEN

4 SERVINGS

1 cup	all-purpose flour	250 mL
½ tsp	mixed salt, pepper, powdered garlic and cayenne	2 mL
4	grain-fed chicken legs	4
2 cups	oil for frying	500 mL
	MARINADE	
1 cup	catsup	250 mL
½ cup	brown sugar	125 mL
1 tsp	Worcestershire sauce	5 mL
1 tsp	white vinegar	5 mL
½ tsp	mixed salt, pepper, powdered garlic and cayenne	2 mL
2	dashes tabasco sauce	2
1 tsp	prepared horseradish	5 mL
1½ cups	chopped onion	375 mL

- Preheat oven to 300°F (150°C).
- Stir ½ tsp (2 mL) mixed spice mixture into flour. Coat chicken legs with mixture.
- Heat oil in deep fryer and cook chicken legs one by one until lightly browned.
- Dry legs with paper towels.
- Arrange chicken in baking pan and set aside.
- Combine marinade ingredients in a bowl. Pour marinade over chicken.
- Bake, covered, about 2 hours.

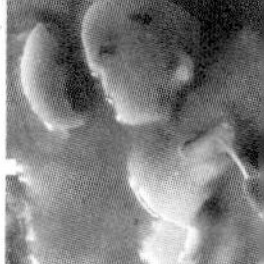

ROLLED STUFFED TURKEY SCALLOPINI

4 SERVINGS

7 oz	cooked ham, fat trimmed, diced	200 g
1	green *or* red pepper, diced	1
2 tbsp	finely chopped fresh parsley	30 mL
2 tbsp	port, sherry *or* unsweetened apple juice	30 mL
1	egg white	1
2	pinches dried tarragon *or* dried thyme	2
4	very thin turkey scallopini*	4
8	leaves Romaine lettuce *or* cabbage, blanched	8
½ cup	chicken stock	125 mL
2 cups	tomato sauce, heated	500 mL
	pepper	

- Preheat oven to 350°F (180°C).
- In a bowl, combine ham, green pepper, parsley, port, egg white, tarragon and pepper.
- Divide mixture between scallopini, roll them up, and season with pepper.
- Wrap each in 2 blanched lettuce leaves.
- Arrange in baking pan, pour chicken stock over, cover, and bake 20 to 25 minutes.
- Cut each roll crosswise into thick slices. Arrange on plates on top of tomato sauce. Garnish with parsleyed boiled potatoes.

* See glossary

CHICKEN WITH MUSHROOMS AND YOGURT SAUCE

6 SERVINGS

6	chicken pieces, about 4 oz (120 g) each	6
1 tbsp	all-purpose flour	15 mL
3 tbsp	butter *or* margarine	45 mL
2	onions, sliced	2
1½ cups	sliced mushrooms	375 mL
½ cup	water	125 mL
½ cup	plain yogurt	125 mL
1 tsp	cornstarch, dissolved in a little water	5 mL
	pepper	

• Lightly flour the chicken pieces.

• Melt butter in a heavy-bottomed skillet. Cook chicken on both sides over medium heat until golden. If the chicken contains bones, lower heat and cook another 8 to 10 minutes on each side. Remove chicken from skillet and keep warm.

• In same skillet, cook onions and mushrooms over medium heat until tender.

• Add water and bring to a boil. Cook 1 minute. Remove from heat, and stir in yogurt, dissolved cornstarch and pepper.

• Return chicken to skillet and stir until hot before serving.

1

Flour chicken pieces and brown in skillet. Keep warm.

2

Cook onions and mushrooms.

3

Add water and cook to reduce. Stir in yogurt, cornstarch and pepper.

4

Return chicken to skillet.

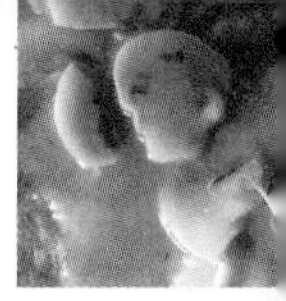

TURKEY BREAST STUFFED WITH NUTS AND RAISINS

6 TO 8 SERVINGS

1	turkey breast	1
½ cup	cooked white rice	125 mL
¼ cup	cooked wild rice	50 mL
⅓ cup	chopped walnuts	75 mL
2 tbsp	chopped fresh parsley	30 mL
2 tsp	chopped fresh mint	10 mL
¼ cup	raisins	50 mL
1	egg	1
2 cups	chicken stock	500 mL
	pepper	

- Preheat oven to 350°F (180°C).
- Slit open turkey breast along one side to make a deep pocket. Pepper and set aside.
- In a bowl, combine white and wild rice, walnuts, parsley, mint, raisins and egg. Stuff turkey breast with this mixture, and fasten shut with toothpicks.
- Put turkey breast in baking pan, pour chicken stock over, cover, and bake 20 to 30 minutes.
- Pour off cooking juices and boil in saucepan until reduced by half.
- To serve, slice so that each piece contains stuffing, and pour cooking juices over.

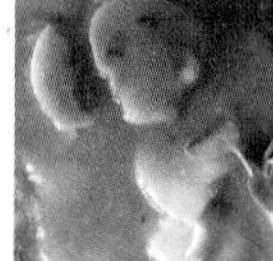

TERIYAKI CHICKEN KEBABS

8 SERVINGS

1½ lbs	boneless, skinless chicken breasts, cut in large cubes	675 g
3	cans water chestnuts, drained	3
¼ cup	dry sherry	50 mL
¼ cup	dry white wine	50 mL
¼ cup	light soy sauce	50 mL
2	garlic cloves, crushed	2
3 tbsp	corn oil	45 mL

GARNISH

lettuce, torn up

onion rings

lemon wedges

paprika

• Put chicken and water chestnuts in a bowl.

• In a second bowl, combine sherry, wine, soy sauce and garlic. Pour over chicken and water chestnuts. Cover and refrigerate 1 hour, stirring from time to time.

• Remove chicken and water chestnuts from marinade and thread on 8 skewers. Reserve marinade.

• Baste kebabs with oil and cook on preheated grill 10 minutes, turning often and basting with marinade.

• Arrange kebabs on a bed of lettuce. Garnish with onion rings, lemon wedges and paprika to serve.

CHICKEN AND CELERY REMOULADE

2 SERVINGS

⅔ cup	**mayonnaise**	**150 mL**
2 tbsp	**chopped fresh parsley**	**30 mL**
2 tsp	**hot mustard**	**10 mL**
1	**celery root (celeriac) peeled and grated *or* 1 jar prepared celery root, rinsed and drained**	**1**
4	**small chicken fillets**	**4**
2	**lemon slices, halved**	**2**
	white pepper	
	lettuce leaves to garnish	

Celery root is a good source of phosphorous.

• In a bowl, combine mayonnaise, parsley, mustard and pepper.

• Add celery root, mix well and refrigerate 3 to 6 hours before serving.

• Preheat oven to 350°F (180°C).

• Arrange chicken fillets on oiled baking pan. Bake 15 to 20 minutes. Remove and keep warm.

• Line serving dish with lettuce leaves and top with celery remoulade. Arrange chicken on top and serve with lemon.

CHICKEN WITH PEACHES

4 SERVINGS

4	chicken legs, skin removed	4
1 tbsp	canola oil	15 mL
2	onions, chopped	2
2	garlic cloves, sliced	2
1 tsp	ground cinnamon	5 mL
1 tsp	turmeric	5 mL
1 tsp	ground nutmeg	5 mL
½ tsp	paprika	2 mL
1¼ cups	chicken stock	300 mL
2	drops tabasco sauce	2
2	fresh peaches, sliced	2
1 tbsp	cornstarch	15 mL
	juice of 1 lemon	

• In a non-stick skillet, brown chicken in hot oil on all sides.

• Remove chicken from skillet and keep warm. Drain off any excess oil from pan, then brown onions and garlic over medium heat. Stir in spices, lower heat and cook another 3 minutes.

• Stir in 1 cup (250 mL) chicken stock, tabasco and lemon juice. Return chicken to skillet.

• Add peaches to skillet and cover. Cook over low heat 20 minutes. With slotted spoon, lift out chicken and other solids and arrange on serving plate.

• Dissolve cornstarch in ¼ cup (50 mL) cold chicken stock. Stir into cooking juices and cook 2 minutes.

• Pour sauce over chicken just before serving.

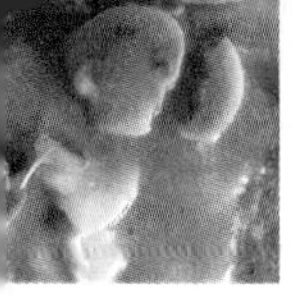

ORIENTAL MARINADE*

MAKES 1¼ CUPS (300 ML)

½ tsp	**chopped fresh ginger**	**2 mL**
¼ cup	**corn oil**	**50 mL**
	juice and grated zest of 4 limes	
	juice and grated zest of 1 lemon	
	ground pepper	

- Combine all ingredients in a bowl.
- Cover and refrigerate 12 to 24 hours.
- Use as is, or strain out citrus zest.

* This marinade can be used for chicken, pork or fish.

SWEET AND SOUR MARINADE*

MAKES 1¼ CUPS (300 ML)

⅓ cup	**honey *or* maple syrup**	**75 mL**
4	**fresh mint leaves, finely chopped**	**4**
⅓ cup	**raspberry vinegar *or* wine vinegar**	**75 mL**
2 tbsp	**soy sauce**	**30 mL**
2 tbsp	**walnut oil, sesame oil, vegetable oil *or* olive oil**	**30 mL**
	juice and grated zest of 1 orange	

- Combine all ingredients in a saucepan.
- Bring to a boil and let simmer, uncovered, until reduced by ⅓.

* This marinade can be used for lamb, chicken or beef.

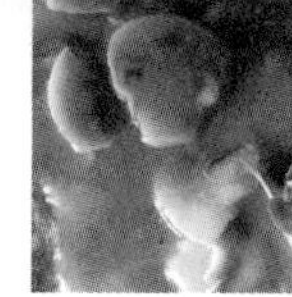

SPICY GRILLED CHICKEN TOURNEDOS

6 TO 8 SERVINGS

⅓ cup	tomato paste	75 mL
3 tbsp	dry white vermouth *or* dry white wine	45 mL
2 tbsp	Worcestershire sauce	30 mL
2 tbsp	molasses	30 mL
½ tsp	pepper	2 mL
1 tsp	hot mustard	5 mL
1 tsp	hot pepper sauce	5 mL
1 tsp	paprika	5 mL
2 tbsp	corn oil	30 mL
6 to 8	chicken tournedos*	6 to 8
	juice of ½ lemon	

- In a large bowl, combine all ingredients except tournedos.
- Add tournedos to marinade. Cover and refrigerate 1 hour, turning the meat from time to time.
- Remove tournedos from marinade and wrap separately in foil. Cook on preheated barbecue grill a maximum of 10 to 12 minutes, turning from time to time.
- Serve with vegetables of your choice.

* See glossary

QUAILS WITH GLAZED GRAPES

4 SERVINGS

8	quails, gutted and plucked	8
3 tbsp	olive oil	45 mL
2 tbsp	raspberry vinegar	30 mL
3	sprigs thyme	3
4 to 5	juniper berries	4 to 5
½	carrot, cut in rings	½
½	onion, cut in rings	½
	SAUCE	
2 tbsp	butter *or* margarine	30 mL
1 to 2	dry French shallots, finely chopped	1 to 2
6	oyster mushrooms, finely chopped	6
¼ cup	dry white vermouth	50 mL
1 cup	prepared brown sauce *or* chicken *or* beef stock	250 mL
20	seedless green grapes	20
1 tbsp	liquid honey	15 mL
	salt and pepper	

• Place your hands on both sides of each quail breast, and break leg joints by pressing so as to partially flatten the breast and legs. Slit the skin on the drumsticks and ease out drumstick bones. Sprinkle with pepper and savory. Set aside.

• In a shallow dish, combine oil, vinegar, thyme, juniper berries, carrot and onion.

• Arrange quails in mixture and marinate 2 to 3 hours, covered, turning from time to time.

• Preheat oven to 425°F (220°C).

• Drain quails thoroughly and arrange in roasting pan. Reserve thyme and juniper berries from marinade. Place quails in center of oven, lower heat immediately to 350°F (180°C) and bake 12 to 15 minutes.

• To prepare the sauce: Melt butter in a skillet and sauté shallots and mushrooms over high heat.

• Add vermouth and cook until liquid has evaporated. Stir in brown sauce, reserved thyme and juniper berries, and salt and pepper. Simmer 2 to 3 minutes.

• In another skillet, heat honey, add grapes and stir to glaze.

• Arrange quails on serving plate, pour sauce over and garnish with glazed grapes.

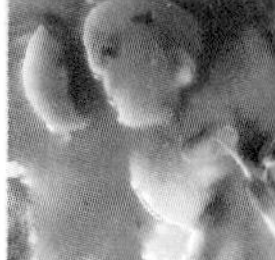

CHICKEN SCALLOPINI IN HUNTER SAUCE

4 SERVINGS

½ cup	fine breadcrumbs	125 mL
¼ cup	grated Sbrinz *or* Parmesan cheese	50 mL
4	chicken *or* turkey scallopini*, well-flattened	4
2 tbsp	butter *or* margarine	30 mL
1½ cups	sliced mushrooms	375 mL
2	dry French shallots, finely chopped	2
2 tbsp	all-purpose flour	30 mL
¼ cup	dry white wine (optional)	50 mL
1½ cups	chicken stock	375 mL
¼ tsp	dried thyme	1 mL
1 tsp	finely chopped fresh parsley	5 mL
1 tbsp	tomato paste	15 mL
1 tbsp	corn oil	15 mL
	pepper	

• Combine breadcrumbs and cheese. Coat scallopini well with mixture. Cover and set aside.

• In a non-stick skillet, melt 1 tbsp (15 mL) butter. Cook mushrooms and shallots 3 to 4 minutes over high heat.

• Sprinkle flour over. Stir well with wooden spoon. Add wine and chicken stock.

• Add thyme, parsley and tomato paste. Simmer over medium heat, stirring, until sauce is creamy. Keep hot.

• Heat remaining butter and oil in a second skillet. Cook scallopini on both sides over high heat until interior is no longer pink.

• Arrange scallopini on plates with sauce on top.

* See glossary

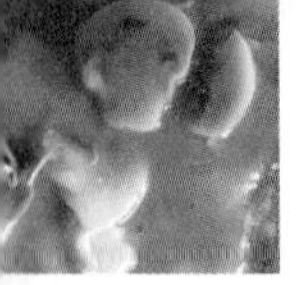

CHICKEN SATAY

4 SERVINGS

1 lb	boneless, skinless chicken breasts, cut in strips	450 g
12	cubes cantaloupe	12
	MARINADE	
¼ cup	soy sauce *or* tamari	50 mL
¼ cup	dry sherry	50 mL
	juice and grated zest of 1 lemon	
	PEANUT SAUCE	
½ cup	crunchy-style peanut butter	125 mL
¼ cup	milk	50 mL
2 tbsp	soy sauce *or* tamari	30 mL
2 tbsp	lemon juice	30 mL
2 tbsp	brown sugar	30 mL
½ tsp	curry powder	2 mL
5	drops tabasco sauce	5
1	garlic clove, crushed	1

• Combine marinade ingredients in a dish.

• Add chicken, cover, and let marinate in refrigerator 2 to 3 hours.

• Thread chicken strips on presoaked wooden skewers. Cook on preheated barbecue grill 4 minutes, turning once during cooking.

• Thread 1 piece of cantaloupe on each skewer and cook 1 more minute.

• To make peanut sauce, combine all ingredients in a saucepan and bring to a boil.

• Serve 3 brochettes per serving, accompanied with peanut sauce.

SUGGESTION

Soak wooden skewers in water 30 minutes before using so that they do not burn during cooking.

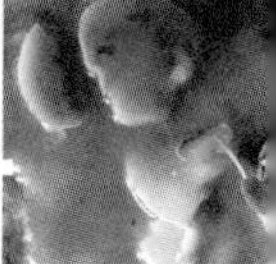

THAI CURRIED CHICKEN WITH COCONUT MILK

3 TO 4 SERVINGS

1 tbsp	vegetable oil	15 mL
1 tbsp	Thai hot pepper and curry paste	15 mL
1	chicken, deboned and cut up *or* 2 boneless, skinless chicken breasts	1
¾ cup	canned coconut milk	175 mL
½ tsp	sugar	2 mL
1 cup	cooked green beans, in pieces	250 mL
½	red pepper, in strips	½
½	green pepper, in strips	½
	canned bamboo shoots, in strips	
	basil leaves to garnish	
	salt	

• Heat oil with pepper paste in a saucepan. Add chicken pieces. Cook several minutes over high heat.

• Add coconut milk, reduce heat and continue cooking 10 minutes, or until chicken is cooked. Add salt and sugar at end of cooking.

• Meanwhile, steam the vegetables until tender-crisp.

• To serve, arrange chicken on serving plate, pour sauce over, and garnish with vegetables and fresh basil leaves, if desired.

SUGGESTION

Replace hot pepper and curry paste with tomato paste seasoned highly with hot pepper, curry and ground ginger.

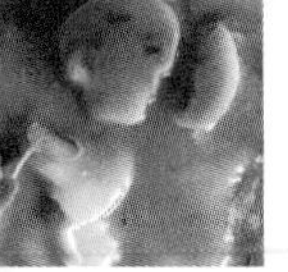

DUCK WITH RED CABBAGE

4 SERVINGS

½ cup	raisins	125 mL
3 cups	diced day-old bread	750 mL
2 cups	diced cooking apples	500 mL
¼ cup	melted butter	50 mL
1	egg, lightly beaten	1
1 tsp	salt	5 mL
¼ tsp	pepper	1 mL
½ tsp	dried marjoram	2 mL
1	duck, about 4½ lbs (2 kg)	1
1	large onion, coarsely chopped	1
2	large carrots, coarsely chopped	2
½ cup	boiling water	125 mL
1 tbsp	liquid honey	15 mL
1 cup	dry red wine	250 mL
1	red cabbage, about 2 lbs (900 g), chopped	1
¾ cup	boiling water	175 mL
2	large cooking apples, peeled and thinly sliced	2
3 tbsp	brown sugar	45 mL
1½ tsp	all-purpose flour	7 mL
1½ tsp	salt	7 mL
1	pinch pepper	1
¼ cup	white vinegar	50 mL
3 tbsp	melted butter	45 mL

- Preheat oven to 325°F (160°C).
- In a large bowl, combine raisins, bread, diced apples, ¼ cup (50 mL) melted butter, egg, salt, pepper and marjoram.
- Stuff duck with raisin mixture, close opening with skewers, and tie wings close to body.
- Place onion and carrots in roasting pan with duck on top. Pour in ½ cup (125 mL) boiling water.
- Bake in oven about 2 hours, or until duck is very tender; baste duck with liquid honey 15 minutes before end of cooking time. Remove duck from pan and keep warm.
- Deglaze roasting pan with wine and heat quickly to a boil, stirring to loosen any browned bits. Strain the sauce, pour into a gravy boat, skim off fat, and keep warm.
- Meanwhile, put cabbage with ¾ cup (175 mL) water in a large saucepan, cover and boil 10 minutes.
- Add apple slices and boil another 10 minutes or until cabbage and apples are tender. Do not drain. Set aside.
- In a bowl, combine brown sugar, flour, salt and pepper. Stir in vinegar, then 3 tbsp (45 mL) melted butter. Stir this mixture into cabbage and return to a boil.
- Arrange duck on a serving plate. Surround with cabbage and pass the gravy boat.

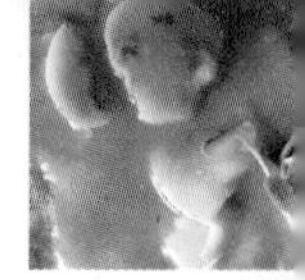

TURKEY TERIYAKI

4 SERVINGS

¼ cup	**sugar**	50 mL
¼ cup	**soy sauce**	50 mL
¼ cup	**Japanese cooking wine *or* sherry**	50 mL
1	**garlic clove, finely chopped**	1
1 tbsp	**chopped fresh ginger**	15 mL
4	**thick turkey scallopini***	4
2 tbsp	**sesame seeds**	30 mL
	vegetable oil	

• In a saucepan, combine sugar, soy sauce, wine, garlic and ginger. Cook over medium heat 5 to 10 minutes, or until the sauce is slightly syrupy.

• Oil and heat the barbecue grill or a skillet. Arrange turkey on grill and baste with sauce. Grill 3 minutes. Baste again and cook another 3 minutes. Turn turkey pieces over, baste again, and continue cooking until interior is no longer pink.

• Sprinkle with sesame seeds and serve with plain rice.

* See glossary

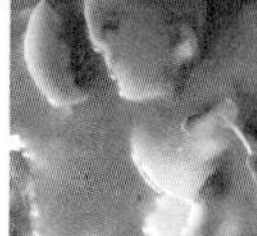

CHICKEN AND VEGETABLE STEW

4 SERVINGS

1 cup	dried navy beans	250 mL
3 tbsp	butter *or* margarine	45 mL
1½ lbs	boneless chicken, cubed	675 g
½ cup	raw brown rice	125 mL
2	celery stalks, cubed	2
2	carrots, cut in rings	2
1	onion, chopped	1
2 tsp	chopped fresh parsley	10 mL
3 cups	chicken stock	750 mL

• Put beans in a saucepan, cover with cold water, bring to a boil and let boil 2 minutes. Turn off heat and let stand, covered, 1 hour in cooking liquid.

• Drain beans, put them in a casserole dish, and set aside.

• Preheat oven to 300°F (150°C).

• In a non-stick skillet, melt butter and brown the chicken lightly.

• Add chicken to beans along with all remaining ingredients. Bake, covered, about 4 hours.

SUGGESTION

This stew is even tastier if you bake it for 8 hours at 200°F (100°C).

SUGGESTION

Bread the chicken rolls before cooking by dipping first in flour, then a beaten egg, and finally in breadcrumbs.

STUFFED CHICKEN ROLLS

4 SERVINGS

4	skinless chicken breasts	4
4	thin slices cooked ham	4
4	thin slices Emmenthal cheese	4
4	spears cooked fresh *or* canned asparagus	4
2 tbsp	all-purpose flour	30 mL
1 tbsp	butter *or* margarine	15 mL
1 tbsp	corn oil	15 mL
1 cup	fresh tomato sauce, heated	250 mL
	lemon wedges	
	pepper	

• Put chicken breasts between 2 sheets of waxed paper and flatten slightly with a rolling pin.

• Pepper each chicken breast, then top with a piece each of ham, cheese and asparagus. Roll carefully and fasten with toothpicks. Sprinkle with flour.

• In a non-stick skillet, heat butter with oil. Brown chicken over low heat 12 to 15 minutes, turning often. Remove to a serving plate and keep warm.

• Serve hot with tomato sauce and lemon.

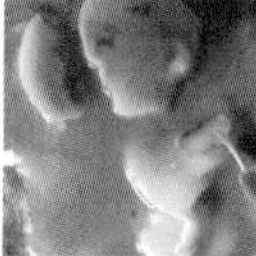

TURKEY CABBAGE ROLLS WITH YOGURT

4 SERVINGS

1 lb	ground turkey, cooked *or* raw	450 g
1	large onion, finely chopped	1
2	slices Italian-style bread, diced, soaked in milk	2
2	eggs, beaten	2
4	large cabbage leaves, blanched	4
1 tbsp	butter *or* margarine	15 mL
2 tbsp	lemon juice	30 mL
½ cup	chicken stock *or* water	125 mL
	plain yogurt	
	pepper	

• In a bowl, combine ground turkey, onion, bread, eggs and pepper.

• Divide mixture in 4 and shape into balls. Wrap each ball with a blanched cabbage leaf, fastening shut with toothpicks. Set aside.

• Melt butter in a saucepan. Arrange cabbage rolls carefully on top. Add lemon juice and stock, cover and cook over very low heat 20 minutes, or until turkey is no longer pink.

• Remove cabbage rolls from liquid and keep warm.

• Cook liquid over high heat a few minutes until slightly thickened. Pour over bottom of 4 plates.

• Arrange cabbage rolls on top and serve with yogurt.

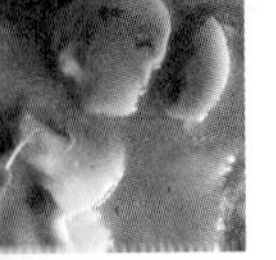

CHICKEN WITH CURRY AND HERBS

4 SERVINGS

½ cup	coarsely chopped parsley	125 mL
4	celery stalks	4
2 tbsp	chopped fresh chives	30 mL
2	onions, quartered	2
1 tbsp	fresh peeled ginger	15 mL
1 lb	boneless chicken fillet	450 g
2 tsp	curry powder	10 mL
2 tbsp	all-purpose flour	30 mL
2 tbsp	sunflower oil *or* peanut oil	30 mL
2	garlic cloves, crushed	2
1 cup	chicken stock	250 mL
3 tbsp	dry white vermouth (optional)	45 mL
	pepper	

• In food processor, finely chop parsley, celery and chives. Set aside.

• Again using food processor, coarsely chop onion and ginger. Set aside.

• Dry chicken fillet with paper towels and cut in strips ½ inch (1 cm) wide.

• Combine curry, flour and pepper in a plastic bag. Add chicken strips and shake to coat well with flour mixture.

• Heat oil in a non-stick skillet and lightly brown the garlic.

• Remove garlic, add onions and ginger, and cook 1 minute over medium-high heat.

• Add chicken and cook to brown, turning frequently. Add stock and vermouth, and stir in reserved celery mixture. Mix well, let simmer 2 to 3 minutes, and serve.

SUGGESTION

Drain chicken wings well on paper towels after baking to remove as much fat as possible.

CHICKEN WINGS WITH VEGETABLE SAUCE

4 SERVINGS

12	chicken wings, coated with barbecue spice	12
1 tbsp	butter *or* margarine	15 mL
½ cup	sliced mushrooms	125 mL
½ cup	chopped fresh spinach	125 mL
2 cups	tomato juice	500 mL
1 tbsp	commercial white sauce thickener	15 mL
1	garlic clove, finely chopped	1
3 cups	cooked rice	750 mL
	pepper	

- Preheat oven to 400°F (200°C).
- Arrange wings on baking pan and bake about 12 minutes, or until crispy.
- Melt butter in a non-stick skillet. Add mushrooms and cook 2 minutes over medium-high heat. Add spinach and stir well.
- Stir in tomato juice and cook until slightly thickened.
- Add sauce thickener, stirring constantly.
- Add garlic and pepper.
- Arrange chicken wings on a bed of rice, with sauce poured over.

TURKEY TOURNEDOS WITH RED CABBAGE

4 SERVINGS

1 tbsp	butter *or* margarine	15 mL
4	turkey tournedos*, about 4 oz (120 g) each	4
½	onion, sliced	½
2 cups	shredded red cabbage	500 mL
2	juniper berries (optional)	2
¾ cup	dry white wine *or* chicken stock	175 mL
1	apple, with peel, cored and diced *or* in wedges	1
1	garlic clove, halved	1
2 tbsp	corn syrup	30 mL
	pepper	

• Heat butter in a non-stick skillet. Add tournedos and cook over high heat about 2 minutes to lightly brown both sides. Remove from skillet and keep warm.

• Add onion, cabbage, juniper berries and wine to skillet. Cover and cook over medium heat until cabbage is barely tender, about 4 minutes.

• Arrange tournedos on top of red cabbage mixture, and add apple pieces, garlic, and pepper. Continue cooking until tournedos are cooked through.

• Arrange on an oven-proof serving dish, baste tournedos with corn syrup, and brown a few seconds under the broiler before serving.

* See glossary

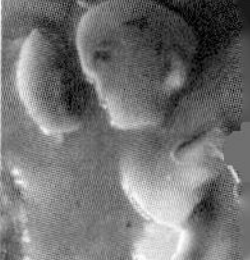

CRISPY CHICKEN

4 SERVINGS

¼ cup	all-purpose flour	50 mL
½ cup	plain *or* Italian breadcrumbs	125 mL
8	chicken pieces, skin removed	8
3 tbsp	olive oil	45 mL
	pepper	

- Preheat oven to 400°F (200°C).
- Combine flour, breadcrumbs and pepper in a plastic bag. Add chicken pieces and shake to coat chicken well with mixture.
- Heat olive oil in a very hot non-stick skillet. Add chicken and brown over hight heat 3 to 4 minutes.
- Arrange chicken on a baking pan and bake about 15 to 20 minutes, or until meat easily falls from bone.
- Remove from oven and serve at once.

SUGGESTION

Serve crispy chicken with sweet and sour sauce or tartar sauce.

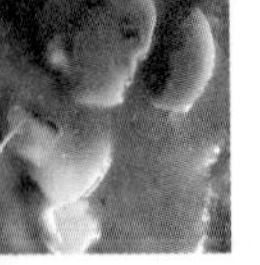

CHICKEN LIVER SAUTÉ

6 SERVINGS

1½ lbs	chicken livers, trimmed	675 g
¼ cup	all-purpose flour	50 mL
1 tbsp	butter *or* margarine	15 mL
1 tbsp	canola oil	15 mL
1	garlic clove, finely chopped	1
1 cup	peeled baby white onions	250 mL
3 tbsp	water	45 mL
1	pinch sugar	1
2 tbsp	vinegar	30 mL
2 tbsp	dry red wine	30 mL
	salt and pepper	

Organ meats, especially liver, are a rich source of iron and Vitamin A.

- Wipe chicken livers, and cut in half if large.
- Combine flour, salt and pepper in a plastic bag. Add livers and shake to coat well.
- Preheat oven to 200°F (100°C).
- Heat butter and oil in a large skillet. Add garlic and cook over high heat 10 seconds. Add chicken livers and cook 4 minutes, stirring occasionally to brown all sides. Remove livers from skillet and keep warm in oven.
- Put onions in saucepan with water and sugar, cover and cook over high heat until onions are tender. Remove onions.
- Over high heat, add vinegar and wine to skillet, and scrape bottom to deglaze. Let sauce reduce 20 seconds. Stir in chicken livers and onions and serve immediately.

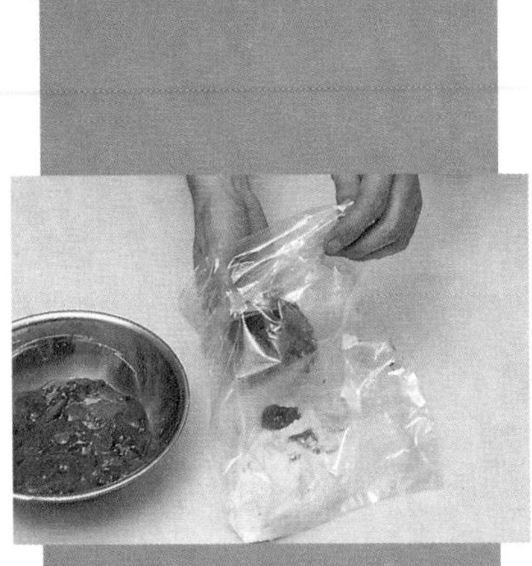

1

Flour the chicken livers.

2

Cook garlic over high heat in butter and oil. Add chicken livers, cook 4 minutes, then keep warm.

3

Cook onions in covered pan. Remove onions.

4

Deglaze skillet with vinegar and wine. Simmer sauce to reduce, then add livers and onions.

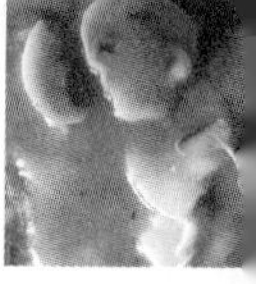

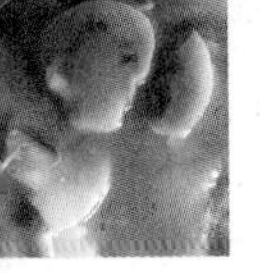

TURKEY PARMIGIANA

4 SERVINGS

¼ cup	breadcrumbs	50 mL
2 tbsp	grated Parmesan	30 mL
4	turkey scallopini*, about 3½ oz (100 g) each	4
2 tbsp	milk	30 mL
28 oz	can stewed tomatoes	796 mL
2 tsp	cornstarch, dissolved in a little cold water	10 mL
½ tsp	crushed Italian seasoning	2 mL

- Preheat oven to 350°F (180°C).
- Combine breadcrumbs and Parmesan in a shallow dish.
- Dip scallopini in milk, then into breadcrumb mixture on both sides.
- Oil a cookie sheet, arrange scallopini on it, and bake in oven 8 to 10 minutes.
- Combine tomatoes and cornstarch in a saucepan with Italian seasonings. Cook, stirring constantly, until sauce is thickened.
- Pour sauce on plates, arrange scallopini on top and serve.

* See glossary

HONEY-LEMON CHICKEN

4 SERVINGS

4	**skinless, boneless chicken breasts**	4
3 tbsp	**all-purpose flour**	45 mL
1 tbsp	**corn oil**	15 mL
1 tbsp	**butter *or* margarine**	15 mL
2 tbsp	**honey**	30 mL
2 tsp	**julienned lemon zest**	10 mL
1	**pinch dried marjoram**	1

- Preheat oven to 350°F (180°C).
- Coat chicken lightly with flour.
- Heat oil and butter in a non-stick skillet over medium heat. Add chicken and cook 5 minutes.
- Arrange chicken on a baking pan and bake in oven 10 minutes, or until chicken is cooked through.
- Pour off grease in skillet and add honey. Stir in lemon zest and marjoram. Cook over very low heat until honey bubbles.
- Add chicken pieces and toss to coat with honey.

To prepare boneless chicken breasts at home, cut a whole chicken breast in half lengthwise along the bone. Pull off skin, then remove fillets from bone by following along the bone with a sharp knife. One whole breast will make 2 boneless breasts.

CHICKEN BURGERS WITH CAESAR SAUCE

8 SERVINGS

8	chicken burgers, unbreaded type	8
8	hamburger buns	8
8	Romaine leaves, coarsely chopped	8
8	slices tomato	8
	crisp-cooked bacon, crumbled (optional)	

SAUCE

1	garlic clove, sliced	1
2 tbsp	red wine vinegar	30 mL
1 tbsp	capers	15 mL
1 tbsp	lemon juice	15 mL
1 tbsp	hot mustard	15 mL
2 tbsp	canola oil	30 mL
1 tbsp	water	15 mL
¼ cup	mayonnaise	50 mL
3 tbsp	grated Sbrinz *or* Parmesan cheese	45 mL
1 tsp	Worcestershire sauce	5 mL
2 tbsp	crumbled, crisp-cooked bacon (optional)	30 mL
	pepper	

• In a bowl, combine all sauce ingredients. Cover and refrigerate.

• Cook burgers on oiled, preheated barbecue and toast the buns.

• Baste each bun with sauce, then layer on a burger, some lettuce and a tomato slice. Sprinkle with bacon if desired.

SUGGESTION

Instead of bacon, use chopped anchovies as a garnish.

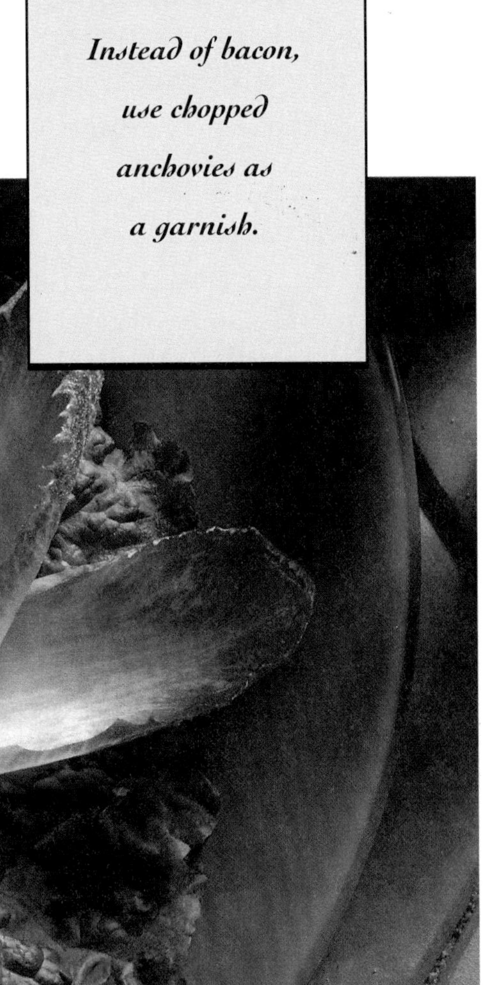

SUGGESTION

The calcium content of this chicken pie will be higher if you use yogurt instead of sour cream.

COUNTRY-STYLE CHICKEN PIE

6 TO 8 SERVINGS

FILLING

¾ cup	diced carrot	175 mL
¾ cup	chopped onion	175 mL
½ cup	diced celery	125 mL
¼ cup	chicken stock	50 mL
10 oz	can cream of chicken soup	284 mL
½ cup	sour cream *or* plain yogurt, drained	125 mL
3 cups	diced cooked chicken	750 mL
½ cup	sliced mushrooms	125 mL
1 tsp	Worcestershire sauce	5 mL
1	pinch pepper	1

TOPPING

1 cup	all-purpose flour	250 mL
2 tsp	baking powder	10 mL
2	eggs, beaten	2
½ cup	milk	125 mL
1 tbsp	chopped green pepper	15 mL
1 tbsp	chopped red pepper	15 mL
1¼ cups	grated Emmenthal cheese	300 mL

- Preheat oven to 350°F (180°C).
- Cook carrot, onion and celery in chicken stock 20 minutes.
- Add remaining filling ingredients and mix well. Pour into a baking dish. Set aside.
- In a large bowl, combine all topping ingredients except ¼ cup (50 mL) grated cheese. Spread over chicken vegetable mixture. Bake 40 to 45 minutes.
- Sprinkle with reserved cheese just before end of baking.

SUGGESTION

Hot pear or peach halves filled with berry jelly make an attractive garnish.

BREAST OF DUCK WITH GREEN PEPPERCORNS

4 SERVINGS

2 to 3 tbsp	green peppercorns	30 to 45 mL
2	large boneless duck breasts, with skin, excess fat removed	2
1 tbsp	butter *or* margarine	15 mL
1 tbsp	vegetable oil	15 mL
	salt	

SAUCE

1 tbsp	butter *or* margarine	15 mL
1	small dry French shallot, finely chopped	1
1 tbsp	green peppercorns	15 mL
½ tsp	hot mustard	2 mL
2 tbsp	calvados, brandy *or* unsweetened apple juice	30 mL
1 cup	prepared brown sauce	250 mL
¼ cup	15% cream *or* plain yogurt	50 mL
	chopped fresh parsley	

• Preheat oven to 400°F (200°C).

• Crush peppercorns with flat edge of knife, and spread over duck breasts.

• Heat butter and oil in an ovenproof skillet. Add duck breasts skin side down and cook over high heat about 5 minutes, or until skin is lightly browned. Add salt.

• Put skillet with duck in oven and cook another 10 to 15 minutes. The interior should still be slightly pink when done. Remove duck and keep warm on serving plate.

• To make the sauce, melt butter in a skillet. Cook shallot and peppercorns over high heat 1 minute. Stir in mustard. Deglaze pan with calvados. Stir in brown sauce and cook until slightly reduced. Add cream and parsley, stirring well.

• Slice the duck breasts into thin slices lengthwise. Arrange on hot plates. Garnish with sauce and accompaniments of your choice.

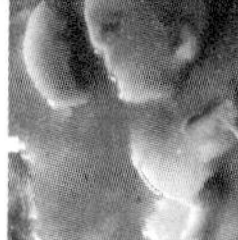

JAMAICAN CHICKEN TOURNEDOS

2 SERVINGS

2	chicken tournedos*	2
½	onion, chopped	½
1	garlic clove, chopped	1
½	hot pepper, chopped (optional)	½
¼ cup	orange juice	50 mL
1 tbsp	soy sauce	15 mL
1 tsp	corn oil	5 mL
1 tsp	wine vinegar	5 mL
1 tsp	allspice	5 mL
1 tsp	dried thyme	5 mL
1 tsp	sugar	5 mL
1 tsp	black pepper	5 mL
¼ tsp	ground cinnamon	1 mL
¼ tsp	ground nutmeg	1 mL
	few drops tabasco sauce	

- Arrange tournedos in a glass dish.
- In food processor, chop all other ingredients well. Pour over tournedos, making sure they are well covered in marinade.
- Cover and refrigerate overnight.
- Preheat oven to 450°F (230°C).
- Remove tournedos from marinade and drain. Place on baking pan and cook 20 to 25 minutes in oven, basting lightly with marinade from time to time.

* See glossary

SUGGESTION

This easy, spicy chicken dish is delicious served with a cabbage salad and rice.

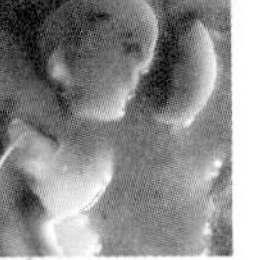

CARIBBEAN CHICKEN

8 SERVINGS

3 lbs	chicken, in serving pieces	1.3 kg
3	garlic cloves, chopped	3
2 tbsp	curry powder	30 mL
2	onions, cut in strips	2
2 cups	water	500 mL
½ tsp	chopped fresh parsley	2 mL
1	pinch dried thyme	1
1	pinch dried sage	1
2	medium potatoes, diced *or* sliced	2
1	zucchini, chopped	1
4	small green onions, chopped	4
1 tbsp	tomato paste	15 mL
1	small eggplant, diced	1
	freshly ground pepper	
	hot chili pepper	
	juice of 3 lemons	
	corn oil	
	salt and pepper	

• Wipe chicken, and season with pepper, hot chili pepper, 2 chopped garlic cloves and juice of 2 lemons.

• Heat a little corn oil in a large non-stick skillet. Add chicken, sprinkle with curry, add onions and cook uncovered until lightly browned, stirring often.

• Add water, parsley, thyme and sage. Let simmer 10 minutes.

• Add potato, zucchini and salt and pepper to taste. Cook another 10 minutes.

• Stir in green onions, tomato paste and eggplant. Cook another 15 minutes.

• Just before serving, season with juice of 1 lemon and 1 chopped garlic clove.

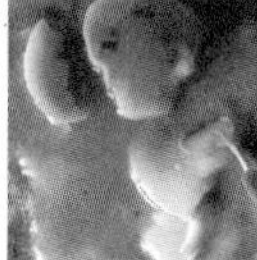

TURKEY SCALLOPINI STUFFED WITH SPINACH

4 SERVINGS

8	turkey scallopini*, about 2 oz (60 g) each	8
1 tbsp	butter *or* margarine	15 mL
2 tbsp	finely chopped green onion	30 mL
½ tsp	garlic powder	2 mL
½ tsp	dried thyme	2 mL
1½ cups	chopped cooked spinach	375 mL
½ cup	grated gruyère cheese	125 mL
	BREADING	
½ cup	crushed corn flakes	125 mL
1 tbsp	chopped fresh parsley	15 mL
1 tsp	paprika	5 mL
2 tbsp	melted butter *or* margarine	30 mL

• Place each scallopini between 2 sheets of plastic wrap and flatten with rolling pin to ⅛ inch (3 mm) thick. Set aside.

• Melt butter in a saucepan. Add green onion, garlic and thyme; cook 2 minutes. Stir in spinach and cook 5 more minutes. Let cool, then stir in cheese.

• Spread spinach mixture over scallopini. Roll up and set aside.

• Preheat oven to 350°F (180°C).

• Combine breading ingredients. Coat each turkey roll well with breading. Place rolls in baking dish and bake 10 minutes or until tender. Serve hot.

* See glossary

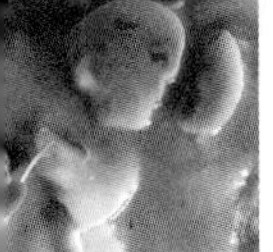

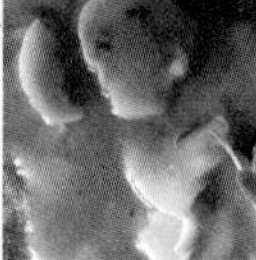

BANGKOK STIR-FRY

4 SERVINGS

½ lb	beef fillet mignon	225 g
½ lb	boneless, skinless chicken breast	225 g
1	garlic clove, chopped	1
½ cup	dry white wine	125 mL
½ cup	white sugar	125 mL
1¼ cups	rich chicken stock	300 mL
1 tsp	hot pepper paste	5 mL
2 tsp	cornstarch	10 mL
½ lb	raw peeled shrimp	225 g
4 oz	bean sprouts	120 g
4 oz	dried black mushrooms, soaked in cold water	120 g
¼ cup	cashews	50 mL
¼ cup	pine nuts	50 mL
	vegetable oil	

• Slice the beef and chicken in thin strips. Refrigerate.

• In a saucepan, cook garlic in a little oil, but do not let brown. Add wine, sugar, chicken stock and hot pepper paste. Simmer 5 minutes.

• Dissolve cornstarch in a little water, and stir into mixture. Simmer 5 more minutes.

• Sauté beef and chicken over high heat in a large non-stick skillet until no longer pink. Add shrimp, bean sprouts and mushrooms, and cook to heat through. Stir in sauce and nuts. Serve immediately.

CHICKEN TOURNEDOS WITH MUSHROOMS AND ASPARAGUS

4 SERVINGS

4	chicken tournedos*, about 4 oz (120 g) each	4
2 tsp	vegetable oil	10 mL
4	thin slices emmenthal cheese, 1 oz (30 g) each	4
12	asparagus spears, cooked	12
	pepper	
	SAUCE	
½ cup	sliced oyster *or* ordinary mushrooms	125 mL
2 tsp	chopped dry French shallot	10 mL
1	garlic clove, chopped	1
½ cup	dry white wine (optional)	125 mL
¾ cup	tomato sauce	175 mL
1 tbsp	chopped fresh parsley	15 mL
1	pinch dried thyme	1

• Preheat oven to 375°F (190°C).

• Pepper tournedos lightly.

• Heat oil in a non-stick skillet and add chicken. Cook over high heat 2 minutes each side to sear. Arrange on baking dish and cook in oven 10 to 15 minutes, or until chicken interior is no longer pink.

• After ¾ of the cooking time, cover tournedos with cheese slices and asparagus spears. Continue cooking with broiler on.

• To make the sauce, brown mushrooms lightly in lightly oiled skillet. Add shallot, garlic, white wine, tomato sauce, parsley and thyme. Cook until reduced slightly.

• To serve, pour a little sauce on the bottom of each plate and arrange tournedos on top.

* See glossary

GARDEN-STYLE TURKEY ROLLS

4 SERVINGS

4	turkey scallopini*, very thin	4
½ cup	carrots cut in julienne shreds	125 mL
½ cup	red pepper cut in julienne shreds	125 mL
½ cup	zucchini cut in julienne shreds	125 mL
½ cup	celery cut in julienne shreds	125 mL
3 tbsp	grated Sbrinz *or* Parmesan cheese	45 mL
¼ cup	all-purpose flour	50 mL
¼ tsp	paprika	1 mL
2 tbsp	vegetable oil	30 mL
⅔ cup	water	150 mL
¼ cup	lemon juice	50 mL
1	envelope commercial turkey gravy mix	1
½ tsp	dried thyme *or* tarragon	2 mL

• Lay out scallopini on work surface and divide julienned vegetables evenly between them. Sprinkle with cheese. Roll and fasten with toothpicks. Set aside.

• Combine flour with paprika and coat each turkey roll with mixture.

• Heat oil in a skillet. Add turkey rolls and cook to brown slightly. Stir in remaining ingredients, cover and let simmer about 10 minutes. Serve with the pan gravy.

* See glossary

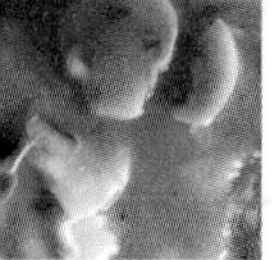

CHICKEN BIRYANI

2 SERVINGS

RICE

1 tbsp	butter	15 mL
1¾ cups	boiling water	425 mL
1	pinch salt	1
½ tsp	garam masala (see below)	2 mL
1 cup	raw basmati rice	250 mL

CHICKEN

5 tbsp	vegetable oil	75 mL
½ tsp	garam masala (see below)	2 mL
½ tsp	turmeric	2 mL
½ tsp	ground coriander	2 mL
½ tsp	ground cumin	2 mL
1 lb	boneless, skinless chicken	450 g
1	medium onion, finely chopped	1
20	raisins	20
1 tsp	minced fresh ginger	5 mL
	salt and pepper	

• In a saucepan over high heat, melt butter in boiling water. Stir in salt, garam masala and rice, lower heat to medium, cover and cook until water has almost completely disappeared. Set aside.

• Meanwhile, heat oil in a large skillet. Add garam masala, spices, chicken and onion. Cook over medium heat until chicken is cooked. Add salt and pepper to taste.

• Preheat oven to 350°F (180°C).

• Spread rice in a large baking dish and stir in raisins and ginger. Arrange chicken on top, cover and bake ½ hour.

• Just before serving, remove chicken and turn rice upside down on serving plate. Top with chicken and serve.

GARAM MASALA

10	cardamom seeds	10
1 tsp	black peppercorns	5 mL
2 tsp	cumin seeds	10 mL
½ tsp	coriander seeds	2 mL
2	small hot red peppers, seeds removed	2
2	pinches ground cinnamon	2

• Combine all ingredients in food processor. Garam masala will keep for 3 months in a tightly-closed jar.

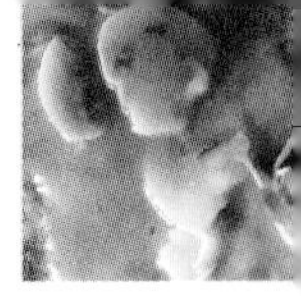

SUGGESTION

Sprinkle the biryani with slivered almonds and garnish with slices of tomato and hard-boiled egg.

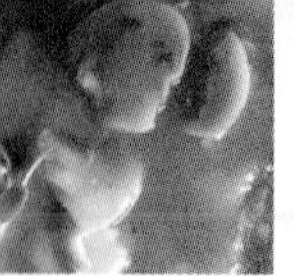

SAUTÉED TURKEY WITH HAZELNUT SAUCE

4 SERVINGS

1¼ lbs	boneless, skinless turkey breast, cut in 1-inch (2.5 cm) strips	600 g
3 tbsp	butter *or* margarine	45 mL
1 cup	whipping cream	250 mL
2 tbsp	brandy, cognac, *or* vermouth	30 mL
2 tbsp	chopped green olives	30 mL
2 tbsp	chopped fresh parsley	30 mL
¾ cup	chopped toasted hazelnuts	175 mL
1 lb	hot, cooked fettucine *or* linguini	450 g
1	pinch nutmeg	1
	pepper	
	all-purpose flour	

• Sprinkle turkey strips with pepper and small amount of flour. Toss to coat.

• Melt butter in a large skillet over medium-high heat. Add turkey and brown lightly, turning from time to time. Remove turkey and set aside.

• Add cream and brandy to skillet. Bring to a boil. Stir in olives, parsley and hazelnuts and cook 5 minutes, or until sauce thickens slightly.

• Return turkey to skillet, and simmer uncovered for 5 minutes or until meat interior is no longer pink. Season hot noodles with nutmeg and serve with turkey.

> **SUGGESTION**
>
> *Instead of mayonnaise, use plain yogurt flavored with some minced garlic.*

GREEK-STYLE CHICKEN BURGERS

4 SERVINGS

1 lb	ground chicken	450 g
⅓ cup	breadcrumbs	75 mL
1	egg	1
2 tbsp	milk	30 mL
2 tbsp	lemon juice	30 mL
½ tsp	dried mint	2 mL
½ tsp	dried oregano	2 mL
1 tbsp	vegetable oil	15 mL
¼ cup	mayonnaise	50 mL
2	pita breads, cut in half	2
4	slices red onion	4
4	slices tomato	4
8	slices cucumber	8
	pepper	

• In a bowl, combine chicken, breadcrumbs, egg, milk, 1 tbsp (15 mL) lemon juice, mint, oregano and pepper. Shape into 4 patties.

• Heat oil in a non-stick skillet. Cook patties 8 minutes over medium-high heat so that both sides are nicely browned.

• In a small bowl, combine mayonnaise with remaining lemon juice. Spread mixture in pita halves, then fill each with a chicken patty, onion slice, tomato slice and 2 cucumber slices.

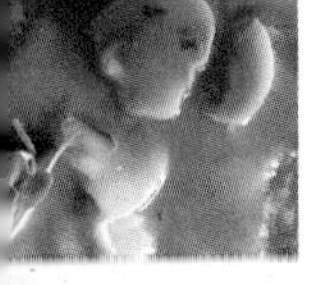

CHICKEN AND SHRIMP PAELLA

4 SERVINGS

1 tbsp	olive oil	15 mL
½ lb	boneless, skinless chicken breast, cubed	225 g
1 cup	raw long grain rice	250 mL
1	medium onion, chopped	1
1	garlic clove, thinly sliced	1
1½ cups	chicken stock	375 mL
1 cup	crushed canned tomatoes with their juice	250 mL
1 tsp	paprika	5 mL
½ lb	small *or* medium shrimp, shelled and deveined	225 g
1	red pepper, diced	1
1	green pepper, diced	1
½ cup	frozen peas	125 mL
	a few saffron threads, soaked in water (optional)	
	salt and pepper	

• Heat oil in a heavy-bottomed saucepan, add chicken and cook over high heat until lightly browned on all sides.

• Add rice, onion and garlic. Cook until onion is transparent and rice golden. Stir in chicken stock, tomatoes, paprika and saffron. Bring to a boil, then simmer, covered, 10 minutes.

• Add shrimp, red and green peppers and peas. Season and cook, covered, 10 more minutes or until liquid is absorbed and rice is tender. Serve hot.

SUGGESTION

Add some cubes of fish of your choice along with the tomatoes.

HONEY-GLAZED CHICKEN BREASTS

4 SERVINGS

4	boneless, skinless chicken breasts	4
⅓ cup	all-purpose flour	75 mL
1 tbsp	vegetable oil	15 mL
1 tbsp	butter *or* margarine	15 mL
2 tbsp	liquid honey	30 mL
1 tbsp	julienned lemon zest	15 mL
1 tbsp	chopped fresh oregano *or* tarragon	15 mL
	salt and pepper	

• Preheat oven to 350°F (180°C).

• Put flour in a plastic bag and shake chicken breasts to coat. Set aside.

• Heat oil and butter in a non-stick skillet over medium-high heat. Add chicken and cook 4 to 5 minutes, or until both sides are lightly browned. Season to taste. Arrange in baking pan and bake 10 to 15 minutes.

• Pour off excess grease from skillet and add honey, lemon zest and oregano. Cook over medium heat just until mixture bubbles. Add chicken breasts, turning so that both sides are glazed and lightly caramelized.

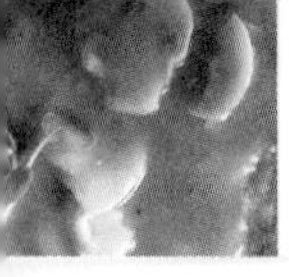

TURKEY DIVAN

4 TO 6 SERVINGS

1½ cups	béchamel sauce (see page 273)	375 mL
2 tbsp	dry white vermouth (optional)	30 mL
¼ cup	15% cream *or* plain yogurt	50 mL
1	pinch nutmeg	1
⅓ cup	grated Sbrinz *or* Parmesan cheese	75 mL
¼ cup	grated gruyère cheese	50 mL
2 cups	cooked broccoli florets	500 mL
10	slices roast turkey	10
1	pinch paprika	1
3 tbsp	chopped fresh parsley	45 mL

• Heat béchamel sauce in a saucepan over medium heat. Add vermouth, cream and nutmeg, and cook until sauce is thick and creamy.

• Stir in cheeses. Set aside.

• Preheat oven to 350°F (180°C).

• Arrange broccoli in rectangular baking dish. Arrange turkey slices on top and cover with cheese sauce. Sprinkle with paprika and parsley. Cover with a sheet of foil.

• Bake 8 to 10 minutes, or until hot through. Serve immediately.

SUGGESTION

Add grated vegetables such as carrots or turnips to the cheese sauce.

Instead of roast turkey, use sliced turkey loaf or turkey roll from the deli counter.

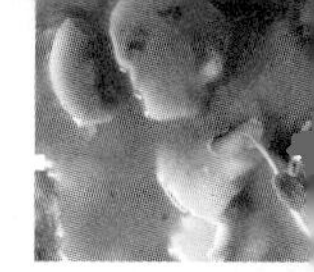

HONEY-MUSTARD CHICKEN

2 SERVINGS

1 tbsp	honey	15 mL
1½ tsp	hot mustard	7 mL
1½ tsp	lemon juice	7 mL
¼ tsp	poppy seeds	1 mL
4	small boneless chicken pieces, about 2 oz (60 g) each	4

• Preheat oven to 375°F (190°C).

• In a bowl, combine honey, mustard, lemon juice and poppy seeds. Set aside.

• Arrange chicken pieces on a baking pan and bake 10 to 12 minutes.

• Baste with reserved poppy seed mixture and continue cooking under the broiler several minutes until nicely glazed.

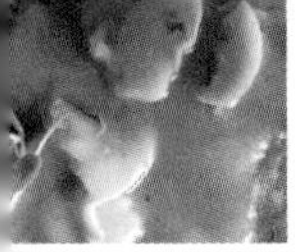

SECHUAN NOODLES WITH CHICKEN

2 SERVINGS

¼ lb	Chinese rice noodles *or* transparent vermicelli	110 g
2 tsp	sesame oil	10 mL
1	garlic clove, finely chopped	1
1 tsp	finely chopped fresh ginger	5 mL
2	green onions, chopped	2
½ lb	boneless, skinless chicken breast, in pieces	225 g
½	red pepper, sliced	½
1	carrot, sliced diagonally	1
1 cup	broccoli florets	250 mL
1 cup	cauliflower florets	250 mL
1½ cups	chicken stock	375 mL
¼ lb	snow peas	110 g
	boiling water	

Replace the spicy sauce suggested in the recipe with a mild sauce made of chicken stock, cornstarch, soy sauce and tomato paste. You can stir the soaked noodles into the skillet along with the snow peas so that they are coated with sauce.

SAUCE

2 tbsp	cornstarch	30 mL
2 tbsp	light soy sauce	30 mL
2 tbsp	hoisin sauce (optional)	30 mL
2 tsp	sesame oil	10 mL
¼ tsp	chili paste *or* tabasco sauce	1 mL

- Place noodles in a large bowl, cover with boiling water and let soak 5 to 8 minutes. Drain well and keep warm.
- Heat oil over medium-high heat in a large non-stick skillet. Add garlic, ginger, and green onions, and cook without letting them brown.
- Add chicken and cook over high heat 2 minutes. Add vegetables except snow peas, and chicken stock. Cover and cook 3 to 4 minutes or until vegetables are tender-crisp.
- Meanwhile, combine all sauce ingredients in a bowl. Set aside.
- Add snow peas to skillet. Stir in sauce and cook, stirring, 1 minute until thickened. Serve over noodles.

KALAMATA CHICKEN KEBABS

4 SERVINGS

½ cup	plain yogurt	125 mL
¼ cup	chopped fresh parsley	50 mL
¼ cup	dry white wine	50 mL
2 tbsp	chopped fresh oregano	30 mL
1 tsp	black pepper	5 mL
2	boneless, skinless chicken breasts, cubed	2
	juice of 1 lemon	
	garlic powder to taste	

• In a bowl, combine all ingredients except chicken. Set aside.

• Thread chicken cubes on wooden skewers (soaked in water first) and arrange in a single layer in a large glass dish. Cover with yogurt marinade.

• Marinate 2 hours in refrigerator, turning skewers from time to time. Drain and reserve marinade.

• Lightly oil a ridged grill pan and place over high heat. Add skewered chicken and cook 5 minutes, turning to brown all sides. Lower heat to medium and cook about 15 minutes more, or until interior is no longer pink. Meanwhile, heat the marinade.

• Serve hot with marinade.

Stir some diced cucumber, chopped black olives and paprika into the marinade. Serve over the kebabs.

SUGGESTION

You can cook these kebabs on a baking tray placed in the middle of the oven at 425°F (220°C).

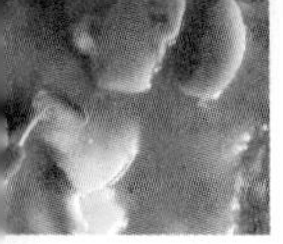

CHICKEN TAJINE WITH PRESERVED LEMONS

4 TO 6 SERVINGS

1	**grain-fed chicken, cut in serving pieces**	1
2	**large red onions, cut in strips**	2
10	**coarsely chopped green olives**	10
⅓ cup	**olive oil *or* vegetable oil**	75 mL
½ tsp	**minced garlic**	2 mL
1 tsp	**ground cumin**	5 mL
1 tsp	**ground ginger *or* small piece of fresh ginger**	5 mL
½ tsp	**turmeric**	2 mL
1	**bay leaf**	1
1	**sprig fresh thyme**	1
1	**preserved lemon**	1
	pepper	
	water	

GARNISH

whole green olives
strips of preserved lemon
fresh mint

Opened jars of lemons will keep well in refrigerator. Ready-made preserved lemons can be purchased in specialty stores which cater to mid-Eastern customers.

• Put chicken pieces in a large bowl. Add onions, olives and a little olive oil, and stir.

• In a deep skillet, heat remaining oil and add chicken. Brown on all sides. Add garlic, cumin, ginger, turmeric, bay leaf, thyme, preserved lemon and pepper.

• Add enough water to cover chicken and let simmer about 1 hour, or until chicken is cooked.

• Serve garnished with green olives, strips of preserved lemon and fresh mint leaves.

PRESERVED LEMONS

4½ lbs	**lemons (with thin rind)**	2 kg
	salt	
	water	
	white vinegar	

• Scrub lemons under running water. Split them in 4 lengthwise so that the quarters remain attached at both ends.

• Scrape out lemon pulp and salt inside of rind generously.

• Pack lemons in sterilized jars and cover completely with equal quantities of water and white vinegar. Seal with lid.

• Store jars in a cool dark place about 3 weeks before using.

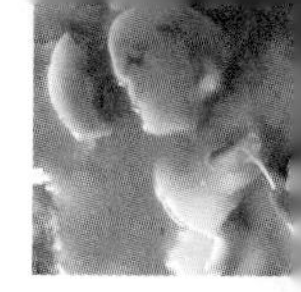

CRISPY CHICKEN BREASTS PARMENTIER

4 SERVINGS

3 tbsp	**hot mustard**	**45 mL**
2	**garlic cloves, finely chopped**	**2**
4	**boneless, skinless chicken breasts, about 4 oz (110 g) each, flattened**	**4**
1½ cups	**grated, peeled raw potatoes**	**375 mL**
1½ tsp	**olive oil**	**7 mL**
	juice of ½ lemon	
	chopped fresh chives *or* green onions	
	pepper	

• Preheat oven to 425°F (220°C).

• In a bowl, combine mustard, garlic and lemon juice. Baste chicken with this mixture. Arrange on baking pan and set aside.

• In a bowl, combine potatoes with olive oil. Cover each chicken breast with potato mixture. Sprinkle with pepper.

• Bake about 30 minutes, until potatoes are golden and interior of chicken is no longer pink.

• Place under broiler and cook another 5 minutes. Garnish with chives and serve immediately.

SUGGESTION

If you grate the potatoes in advance, keep them in cold water so they do not turn dark. Drain just before using and squeeze dry in a tea towel.

STEAMED CHICKEN PACKAGES WITH TARRAGON

4 SERVINGS

4	**boneless, skinless chicken breasts**	4
⅓ cup	**olive oil *or* vegetable oil**	75 mL
1 tbsp	**chopped fresh tarragon**	15 mL
	zest of ½ lemon, cut in thin strips	
	pepper	

• In a shallow dish, combine oil, tarragon, pepper, and lemon zest. Turn chicken breasts in mixture, then let them marinate in refrigerator at least 3 hours, covered.

• Preheat oven to 375°F (190°C).

• Drain chicken, reserve lemon zest, and discard marinade. Arrange each breast on a piece of foil, with some of the lemon zest.

• Seal packages well, place on baking pan and cook in oven 15 to 20 minutes.

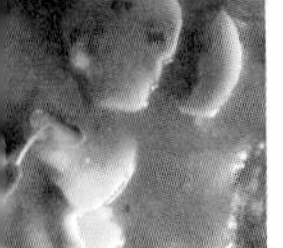

GRILLED MARINATED BREAST OF DUCK

4 SERVINGS

4	boneless duck breasts, with skin	4
1¼ cups	orange juice *or* unsweetened apple juice	300 mL
1¼ cups	water	300 mL
2 tsp	crushed garlic	10 mL
2 tsp	dried oregano	10 mL
2 tsp	ground ginger	10 mL
2 tsp	honey	10 mL
¼ tsp	ground black pepper	2 mL

- Cut slits on the diagonal through skin of each duck breast.
- Place breasts in a shallow dish, and set aside.
- In a bowl, combine remaining ingredients. Pour over duck breasts, cover, and refrigerate 6 hours.
- Cook duck on preheated barbecue grill about 20 minutes, basting often with marinade and turning every 10 minutes.
- Serve with vegetables of your choice.

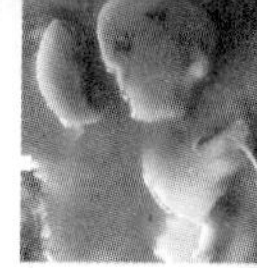

SUGGESTION

To make a tasty meal, serve turkey breast with snow peas, carrot rounds, cauliflower florets and rice.

ORIENTAL BARBECUED TURKEY BREAST

8 SERVINGS

½ cup	catsup	125 mL
¼ cup	honey	50 mL
2 tbsp	light soy sauce	30 mL
1 tsp	chopped fresh ginger	5 mL
1	garlic clove, chopped	1
4	thick raw turkey breast slices	4

• In a large bowl, combine catsup, honey, soy sauce, ginger and garlic.

• Add turkey slices and stir to coat well. Let marinate 30 minutes in refrigerator.

• Drain turkey, reserving marinade.

• Cook turkey slices on preheated barbecue grill 12 to 15 minutes, or until meat is tender and interior is no longer pink. Baste with marinade towards the end of cooking.

Like chicken, turkey breast without its skin is high in protein while low in fat.

CHICKEN À LA KING WITH YOGURT

4 SERVINGS

1 tbsp	corn oil	15 mL
2 cups	sliced mushrooms	500 mL
1	medium onion, finely chopped	1
⅓ cup	all-purpose flour	75 mL
2¼ cups	chicken stock	550 mL
2	carrots, diced	2
1	celery stalk, diced	1
1 tsp	dried thyme	5 mL
½	red pepper, diced	½
2 cups	diced cooked chicken	500 mL
1 cup	frozen peas	250 mL
¼ cup	plain yogurt	50 mL
2 tbsp	chopped fresh parsley	30 mL
4	slices whole-wheat bread, toasted	4
	pepper	
	paprika	

- Heat oil in a saucepan. Add mushrooms and onion and cook over medium heat about 3 minutes.
- Sprinkle in flour. Stir well, then gradually stir in stock. Bring to a boil and cook 3 to 5 minutes, or until sauce is smooth and creamy.
- Stir in carrots, celery and thyme.
- Lower heat. Cover and let simmer 15 minutes, stirring from time to time, until vegetables are tender.
- Add red pepper, chicken and peas.
- Heat to almost boiling. Remove from heat and stir in yogurt, parsley and pepper. Mix well.
- Serve garnished with toast points sprinkled with a little paprika.

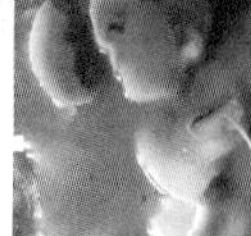

CHICKEN WITH MARINATED GREEN ONIONS

4 SERVINGS

2	boneless, skinless chicken breasts, cut in strips	2
	oil for deep frying	
	MARINADE	
4	green onions, sliced	4
2 tbsp	light soy sauce	30 mL
1 tbsp	hoisin sauce	15 mL
1 tbsp	chili pepper sauce	15 mL
1 tbsp	sherry *or* dry vermouth	15 mL
⅓ cup	cornmeal	75 mL
1	egg white	1

• In a bowl, mix all marinade ingredients well. Add chicken pieces, mix again, cover and refrigerate overnight.

• Heat oil in a wok or deep-fryer. Drain chicken pieces well and cook in oil just until tender and golden.

• Drain on paper towels.

• Serve hot, with rice and a green vegetable.

GRILLED CHICKEN AND VEGETABLES

4 SERVINGS

4	boneless chicken breasts, about 3½ oz (100 g) each	4
3 tbsp	teriyaki sauce	45 mL
1 tbsp	shredded fresh ginger	15 mL
1	red pepper, cut in wide strips	1
1	green pepper, cut in wide strips	1
2	tomatoes, cut in 4 wedges	2
1	onion, cut in 6 wedges	1
1	small eggplant, cut in rounds 1 inch (2.5 cm) thick	1
2	potatoes, peeled and cut 1 inch (2.5 cm) thick	2

SAUCE

½ cup	plain yogurt	125 mL
1 tbsp	liquid chicken stock concentrate	15 mL
3 tbsp	sunflower seeds	45 mL

- Place chicken in a shallow dish with teriyaki sauce and ginger. Cover and let marinate 2 hours in refrigerator.
- Drain chicken. Grill on preheated barbecue grill 1 to 2 minutes, then place on ovenproof serving plate. Set aside.
- Preheat oven to 350°F (180°C).
- Cover barbecue grill with aluminum foil. Cook vegetables on foil until partially cooked, then add to plate with chicken. Cook in oven about another 10 minutes, until chicken is cooked through.
- In a bowl, combine yogurt with chicken stock concentrate and sunflower seeds. Serve cold sauce with hot grilled chicken and vegetables.

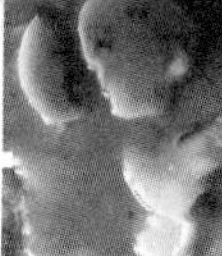

JAVANESE CHICKEN

6 SERVINGS

1 tbsp	corn oil	15 mL
3 lbs	chicken, in serving pieces	1.5 kg
2	onions, diced	2
3	tomatoes, peeled	3
2 tsp	turmeric	10 mL
4	garlic cloves	4
1 tbsp	grated fresh ginger	15 mL
3	small hot peppers, seeded (optional)	3
2 tsp	chopped fresh coriander	10 mL
1 tsp	ground cumin	5 mL
1 cup	canned coconut milk	250 mL
1 tbsp	lemon juice	15 mL
1 tbsp	shredded unsweetened coconut, lightly toasted	15 mL
2	cinnamon sticks	2
	grated zest of ½ lemon	

- Heat oil in a large skillet. Add chicken pieces and brown on all sides over medium heat.
- Remove chicken and drain on paper towels. Set aside.
- Brown onions in same skillet. Remove and set aside.
- In food processor, process tomatoes, turmeric, garlic, ginger, hot peppers, coriander, cumin, coconut milk and lemon juice until well combined.
- Pour mixture into skillet. Add reserved onions, toasted coconut, chicken, lemon zest and cinnamon, mixing well.
- Bring to a boil, lower heat and let simmer 45 minutes, or until chicken is very tender. Serve with rice.

Meats

PORK MEDALLIONS WITH PEARS

2 SERVINGS

1	pork fillet, sliced crosswise in medallions	1
1	pear, unpeeled	1
1 tbsp	olive oil *or* vegetable oil	15 mL
1	garlic clove, chopped	1
1	dry French shallot, chopped	1
3 tbsp	balsamic *or* raspberry vinegar	45 mL
¾ cup	brown sauce, homemade *or* canned	175 mL
	pepper	

• With the flat blade of a large knife, flatten each pork medallion to ½ inch (1 cm) thick. Set aside.

• Cut pear in half, remove core, cut flesh into thin slices, then the slices into long slivers. Set aside.

• Heat oil in a non-stick skillet. Cook medallions over medium heat about 3 minutes on each side, or until cooked through. Remove from skillet, sprinkle with pepper and keep warm.

• Lower heat and cook garlic and shallot in the same skillet 1 minute, then add vinegar.

• Add the slivers of pear, and cook until all liquid has evaporated. Immediately add brown sauce and simmer until heated.

• Arrange medallions on heated plates, and garnish with slivered pears and sauce. Serve with braised endive, if desired.

VEAL FILLET WITH TOMATOES AND BASIL

4 SERVINGS

1½ lbs	**veal fillet, fat trimmed**	675 g
1 tbsp	**extra virgin olive oil**	15 mL
2	**bay leaves**	2
1	**sprig fresh thyme *or* ½ tsp (2 mL) dried thyme**	1
2	**garlic cloves, chopped**	2
	salt and pepper	
	SAUCE	
6	**ripe tomatoes**	6
1 tbsp	**chopped fresh basil *or* ½ tsp (2 mL) dried basil**	15 mL
2 tsp	**chopped fresh thyme *or* ½ tsp (2 mL) dried thyme**	10 mL
2 tbsp	**extra virgin olive oil**	30 mL
	salt and pepper	

• Preheat oven to 400°F (200°C).

• Baste veal with olive oil, season with salt and pepper, and set aside.

• Heat a non-stick skillet over high heat, and brown veal on all sides.

• Place veal in a baking pan. Top with bay leaves, thyme and garlic. Roast in oven 10 to 12 minutes; the interior should remain pink.

• Remove from oven and let stand while you make the sauce.

• Drop tomatoes in a saucepan of boiling water for 30 seconds, then plunge them in cold water, slip off the skins, and cut each in 6 wedges. Remove seeds and dice flesh.

• Put tomato flesh in a saucepan with basil, thyme, and olive oil. Season and heat over low heat.

• Reheat veal in the oven 3 to 4 minutes. Slice and serve with warm sauce.

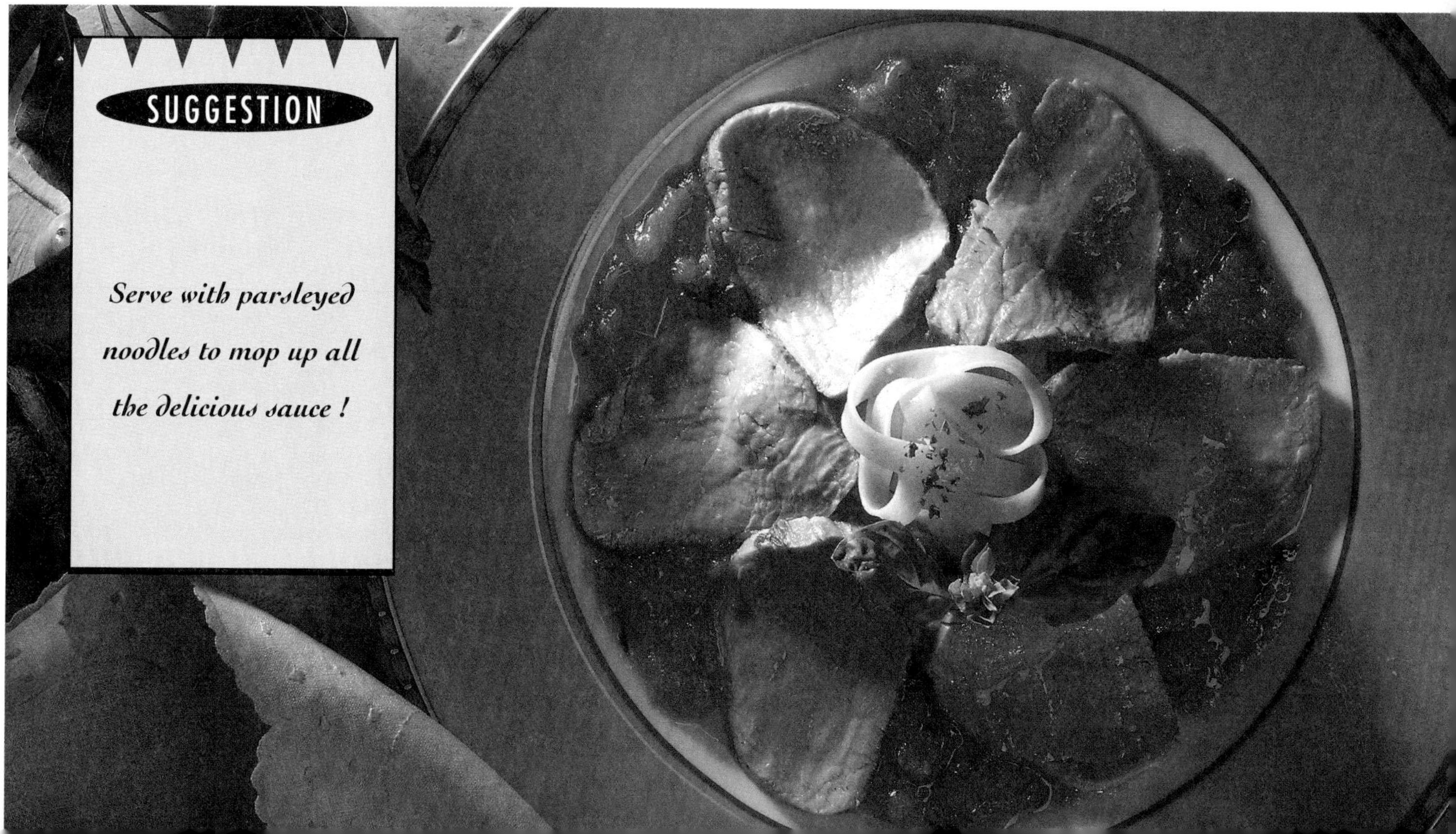

SUGGESTION

Serve with parsleyed noodles to mop up all the delicious sauce !

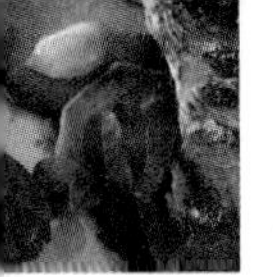

PORTUGUESE PORK AND CLAMS

4 SERVINGS

1 lb	fresh boneless pork leg, cubed	450 g
1 tsp	garlic salt	5 mL
1 tsp	paprika	5 mL
1	pinch pepper	1
1 cup	dry white wine	250 mL
2 tbsp	butter *or* margarine	30 mL
1	onion, cut in rings	1
1	red pepper, cut in strips	1
2	tomatoes, peeled, seeded and chopped	2
14 oz	can clams, drained	398 mL
2 tbsp	chopped fresh coriander	30 mL

Pork is a relatively lean meat, and most of the fat is on the surface, and easily removed. On top of that, half the fat content is monounsaturated fat.

• Sprinkle cubed pork with garlic salt, paprika and pepper. Place in a dish, Add wine, cover tightly, and let marinate in refrigerator 12 hours.

• Drain meat, reserving marinade, and dry with paper towels.

• Melt 1 tbsp (15 mL) butter in a large skillet. Brown meat on all sides about 10 minutes, then arrange in an ovenproof dish.

• Preheat oven to 350°F (180°C).

• Pour reserved marinade into same skillet and scrape bottom to blend. Cook 5 minutes to thicken. Pour sauce over meat.

• Wipe out the skillet and melt remaining butter. Add vegetables, cook 4 minutes and pour over the pork. Add clams, sprinkle with coriander, and bake 10 minutes.

1

Marinate pork. Drain and dry with paper towels.

2

Brown meat in butter, then place in ovenproof dish.

3

Deglaze pan with reserved marinade.

4

Simmer 5 minutes, then pour over pork.

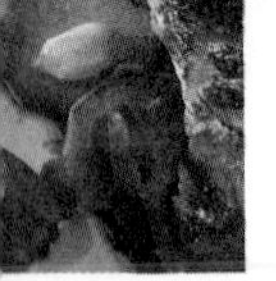

INDONESIAN SKEWERED BEEF

4 SERVINGS

1½ lbs	lean beef, cubed	675 g
½ tsp	ground cumin	2 mL
½ tsp	ground ginger	2 mL
½ tsp	cayenne pepper	2 mL
1 cup	dry white wine	250 mL
	SAUCE	
1 tbsp	dried mint	15 mL
2 tbsp	brown sugar	30 mL
1 cup	unsweetened orange juice	250 mL
¼ cup	vinegar	50 mL
1 tsp	commercial brown gravy thickener	5 mL

- Thread beef cubes on skewers, then arrange in a dish.
- Combine cumin, ginger and cayenne. Sprinkle over beef. Pour wine on top, cover and let marinate 4 hours in refrigerator.
- Preheat oven to 400°F (200°C).
- Remove kebabs from marinade (reserving marinade), drain, and bake 20 to 30 minutes, depending on degree of doneness required. Baste frequently with marinade during cooking.
- Combine sauce ingredients in a small saucepan. Heat gently, without allowing to boil, until sauce thickens.
- Serve sauce separately.

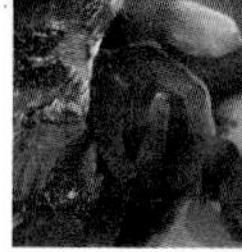

LAMB CHOPS DIJONNAISE

6 SERVINGS

12	lamb chops	12
2 tsp	Dijon mustard	10 mL
1 tsp	finely chopped garlic	5 mL
¼ tsp	crushed peppercorns	1 mL
	rosemary *or* thyme, fresh *or* dried	

- Preheat broiler.
- Trim fat from chops, then arrange in a roasting pan.
- In a small bowl, combine mustard, garlic, pepper and rosemary. Coat chops in mustard mixture.
- Broil about 6 minutes with chops 4 inches (10 cm) from broiler element. Turn chops and broil another 5 minutes. Garnish with rosemary, if desired.

SUGGESTION

Lamb chops are at their best cooked just until the interior is still slightly pink.

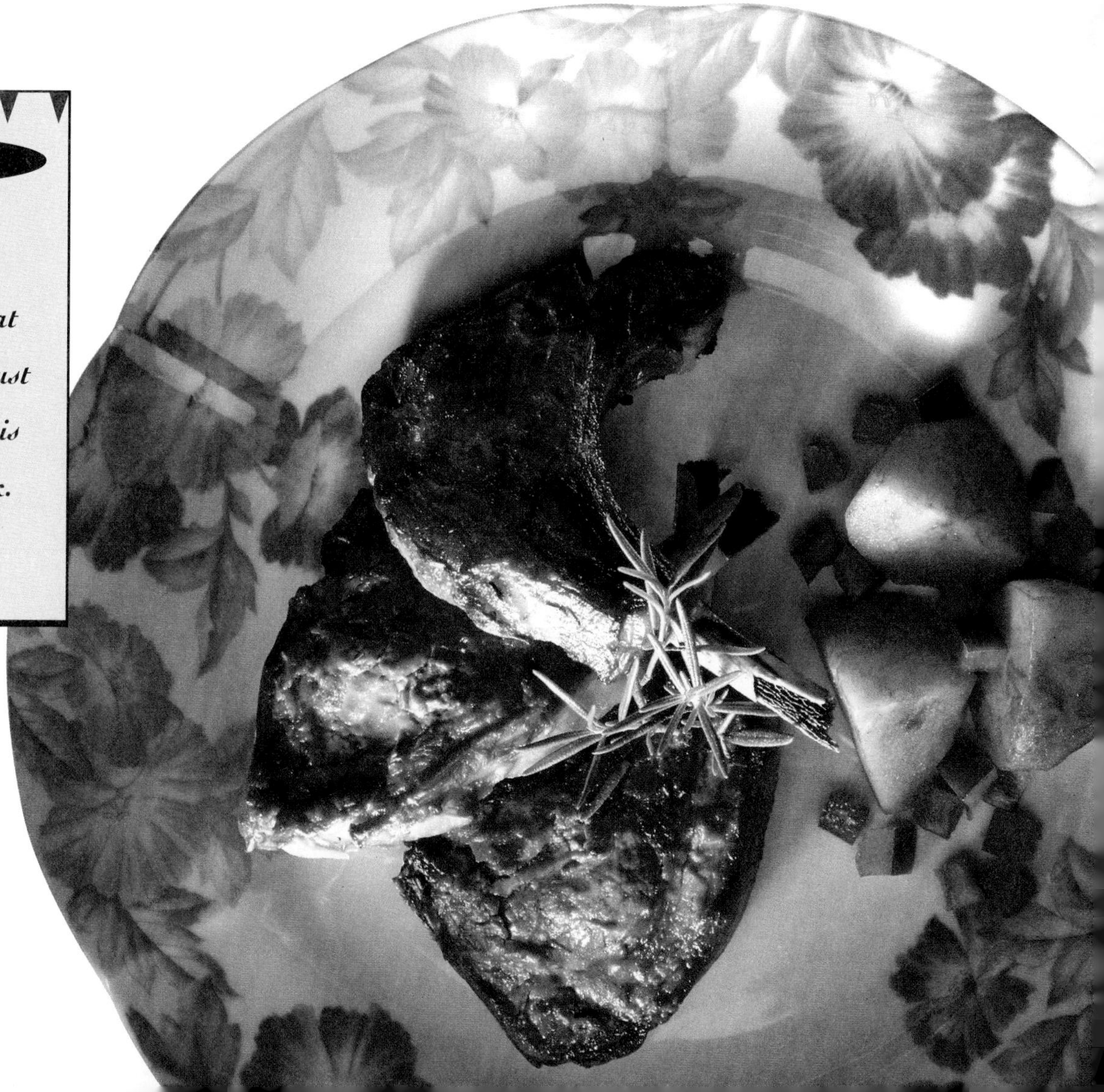

SUGGESTION

Add 2 tbsp (30 mL) grated Parmesan cheese to the herb mixture.

VEAL WITH FRESH HERBS

4 SERVINGS

1 tbsp	chopped fresh coriander	15 mL
1 tbsp	chopped fresh marjoram	15 mL
1 tbsp	chopped fresh parsley	15 mL
1 tbsp	chopped fresh tarragon	15 mL
4	veal scallopini*, about 4 oz (120 g) each	4
4	large leaves curly lettuce	4
	pepper	

- Combine herbs and pepper in a shallow bowl.
- Flatten scallopini with a mallet or flat blade of a large knife, then coat on both sides with herbs.
- Arrange each scallopini on a lettuce leaf. Roll and fasten with toothpicks.
- Place rolls on a steamer or rack over boiling water. Cover and steam 15 minutes.
- Serve with fresh pasta, if desired.

* See glossary

PORK AND TOMATOES

4 SERVINGS

2 tbsp	vegetable oil	30 mL
1¼ cups	cubed lean pork	300 mL
½ cup	chopped onion	125 mL
1	garlic clove, finely chopped	1
1 cup	chopped celery	250 mL
1 cup	sliced fresh mushrooms	250 mL
3 tbsp	thinly sliced leek	45 mL
1¾ cups	tomato sauce	425 mL
1 cup	chicken stock	250 mL
½ cup	chili sauce *or* catsup	125 mL
1 tsp	chopped fresh savory	5 mL
	pepper	

• Heat oil in a saucepan, and brown pork and onion over medium-high heat.

• Stir in garlic, celery, mushrooms and leek. Continue cooking 4 to 5 minutes over medium heat, stirring with a wooden spoon.

• Add remaining ingredients and pepper to taste, and continue cooking over medium heat 40 minutes, stirring from time to time.

• Serve with parsleyed noodles, if desired.

SUGGESTION

Just before serving, stir in 2 tbsp (30 mL) cream cheese to make the mixture rich and creamy.

BEEF SAUTÉ WITH VEGETABLES

4 SERVINGS

2 tbsp	**butter *or* margarine**	**30 mL**
1 lb	**beef (fillet, tenderized round *or* sirloin), in strips**	**450 g**
½	**onion, sliced**	**½**
½ cup	**sliced mushrooms**	**125 mL**
⅓ cup	**red wine**	**75 mL**
1	**carrot, thinly sliced**	**1**
2	**celery stalks, thinly sliced**	**2**
1	**potato, with skin, diced *or* thinly sliced**	**1**
1 cup	**canned tomatoes, crushed**	**250 mL**
1 tbsp	**coarsely chopped fresh coriander**	**15 mL**
1 cup	**prepared beef stew seasoning from envelope**	**250 mL**
	pepper	

• Heat butter in a large non-stick skillet. Add meat, onions and mushrooms, and cook over high heat 2 minutes, stirring to brown all sides. Add pepper.

• Add red wine, and cook until reduced by half. Add carrot, celery, potato, tomatoes and coriander.

• Stir in stew seasoning, and adjust salt and pepper to taste.

• Let simmer until sauce thickens and vegetables are tender.

SWISS-STYLE HAM LOAF

4 SERVINGS

1 tsp	baking powder	5 mL
1 cup	all-purpose flour	250 mL
3	eggs	3
2 tbsp	vegetable oil	30 mL
¾ cup	milk	175 mL
5 oz	grated gruyère cheese	150 g
½ lb	cooked ham, diced	225 g
	pepper	
	SAUCE	
¼ cup	butter *or* margarine	50 mL
½ cup	all-purpose flour	125 mL
2 cups	milk	500 mL
½	onion, stuck with 1 clove	½
1 tsp	salt	5 mL
1	pinch cayenne pepper	1
1	pinch nutmeg	1
¼ cup	15% cream (optional)	50 mL
1 tsp	butter *or* margarine	5 mL

• Preheat oven to 350°F (180°C).

• In food processor, combine baking powder with flour. Add eggs, oil and milk and process to combine. Mix in cheese, ham and pepper.

• Line the bottom of a loaf pan with buttered waxed paper. Pour ham mixture on top. Let stand 10 minutes.

• Bake loaf about 45 minutes.

• Meanwhile, make the sauce: melt ¼ cup (50 mL) butter in a saucepan over low heat. Stir in flour with a wooden spoon. Cook over very low heat 2 to 3 minutes, stirring often.

• Gradually stir in milk, mixing well with a wire whisk. Add onion, salt, cayenne and nutmeg. Let simmer 15 to 20 minutes, stirring often, until mixture is thick and creamy. Stir in cream and remaining butter. Remove ½ onion. Serve with ham loaf.

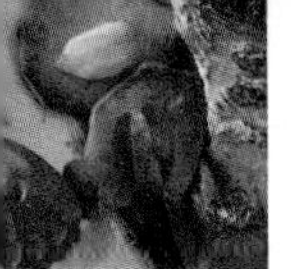

TANGY PORK CHOPS WITH PEACHES

4 SERVINGS

2 tbsp	vegetable oil	30 mL
4	large, lean pork chops	4
½ tsp	dried thyme	2 mL
2 tbsp	white vinegar	30 mL
⅓ cup	peach jam	75 mL
1 tbsp	hot mustard	15 mL
1	garlic clove, sliced	1
1	pinch crushed hot red pepper pepper	1

• Preheat oven to 350°F (180°C).

• Heat oil in a skillet. Brown pork chops on both sides. Season with pepper and thyme.

• Arrange chops in single layer in a baking pan and bake 10 to 15 minutes, until cooked through.

• Meanwhile, in a skillet, combine vinegar, jam, mustard, garlic and hot pepper flakes. Bring to a boil.

• Pour mixture over pork chops and bake 5 more minutes.

SUGGESTION

You can use this same recipe with various cuts of chicken.

PORK RAGOUT DIJONNAISE

4 SERVINGS

⅓ cup	brown sugar	75 mL
⅓ cup	all-purpose flour	75 mL
1½ lbs	lean boneless pork, in 1-inch (2.5 cm) cubes	675 g
¼ cup	Dijon mustard	50 mL
3 tbsp	vegetable oil	45 mL
1	medium onion, chopped	1
2	garlic cloves, finely chopped	2
1 cup	chicken stock	250 mL
½ cup	dry sherry *or* dry white wine	125 mL
4	potatoes, peeled, in 1-inch (2.5 cm) cubes	4
2	carrots, peeled and cut in rings	2
¼ cup	chopped fresh parsley	50 mL
	pepper	

• Preheat oven to 350°F (180°C).

• Combine brown sugar and flour in a shallow dish. Set aside.

• Brush pork cubes lightly with mustard, then roll in flour mixture.

• Heat oil in a non-stick skillet over medium heat. Brown pork cubes on all sides, remove and reserve.

• In same skillet, cook onion about 2 minutes or until soft. Add garlic, pork cubes, stock and sherry. Bring to a boil and cook 1 minute.

• Pour mixture into ovenproof dish and add potatoes and carrots. Cover and bake about 40 minutes, or until tender. Season to taste, and sprinkle with parsley before serving.

BARBECUED MARINATED FLANK STEAK

6 SERVINGS

2	garlic cloves, crushed	2
½ tsp	sugar	2 mL
4 tsp	hot mustard	20 mL
3 tbsp	chopped fresh tarragon *or* rosemary	45 mL
3 tbsp	chopped fresh coriander	45 mL
¼ cup	raspberry vinegar	50 mL
¼ cup	canola oil	50 mL
2½ lbs	flank steak	1.25 kg
1 tbsp	liquid beef stock concentrate	15 mL
	pepper	

• Combine all ingredients except beef and beef stock concentrate in a large dish.

• Arrange the beef in the dish and turn to coat all sides. Cover with plastic wrap and let marinate 3 hours at room temperature, turning often.

• Cook meat on preheated barbecue grill at high heat for 5 to 6 minutes on each side. Baste with beef concentrate during cooking. Let stand 5 minutes, covered, before slicing.

• Slice thin and arrange on plates. Serve with vegetables or a salad.

OSSO BUCCO

4 SERVINGS

4	veal shank pieces	4
¼ cup	all-purpose flour	50 mL
2 tbsp	olive oil	30 mL
1	onion, chopped	1
1	carrot, in thin rounds	1
1	celery stalk, diced	1
1	bay leaf	1
½ cup	dry white wine	125 mL
28 oz	can tomatoes, undrained	796 mL
1 tbsp	tomato paste	15 mL
1	garlic clove, finely chopped	1
2 tbsp	coarsely chopped parsley	30 mL
	grated zest of ½ lemon	
	pepper	

• Roll the veal shanks in flour.

• Heat oil in a large, heavy saucepan and brown the meat on all sides over high heat 3 to 4 minutes. Remove to a plate.

• In the same pan, cook onion, carrot, celery and bay leaf about 4 minutes, stirring from time to time.

• Add wine and let simmer until reduced by half. Stir in tomatoes with their juice, tomato paste and pepper. Bring to a boil.

• Return meat to pan, cover, and let simmer over low heat about 1 hour, or until meat is tender and falls easily from the bones.

• Arrange meat on a platter and keep warm.

• Pour the tomato mixture into food processor and purée, then pour over meat.

• Combine garlic, parsley and lemon zest and sprinkle over meat just before serving.

Fresh parsley is an excellent source of Vitamins A and C, calcium and potassium.

GERMAN-STYLE ROAST BEEF

8 SERVINGS

4 lb	cross rib roast	1.8 kg
6 tbsp	all-purpose flour	90 mL
2 tbsp	corn oil	30 mL
½ cup	chopped onion	125 mL
1	garlic clove, finely chopped	1
8	juniper berries	8
4	parsley sprigs	4
1	bay leaf	1
1 cup	beef stock	250 mL
1 cup	beer	250 mL
½ tsp	sugar	2 mL
2	carrots, chopped	2
2 tbsp	soft butter	30 mL
	pepper	

(Continued on next page)

• Wipe the roast and coat with ¼ cup (50 mL) flour, brushing off excess.

• Heat oil over medium-high heat in a casserole dish or heavy roasting pan. Brown the roast on all sides. Remove beef from pan and set aside.

• Preheat oven to 300°F (150°C).

• Put onion and garlic in roasting pan and cook until soft, stirring often.

• Tie juniper berries, parsley and bay leaf in a piece of cheesecloth, then add to roasting pan with beef stock and beer. Stir in sugar and carrots and bring to a boil.

• Return roast to pan, cover, and bake in over 2½ to 3 hours, turning halfway through. Remove roast from pan and keep warm.

• Remove bag of herbs and skim off fat. Place pan on burner.

• In a small bowl, combine butter with remaining flour. Stir mixture bit by bit into pan juices, stirring vigorously. Cook over medium heat, stirring, until sauce thickens. Add pepper to taste and serve in a gravy boat with roast.

1

Brown roast on all sides, then set aside.

2

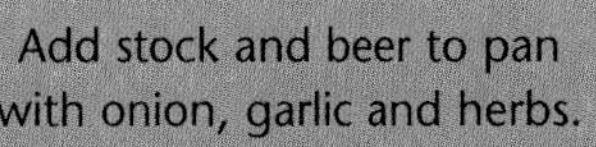

Add stock and beer to pan with onion, garlic and herbs.

3

Return roast to pan and roast in oven.

4

Remove roast and prepare gravy in roasting pan.

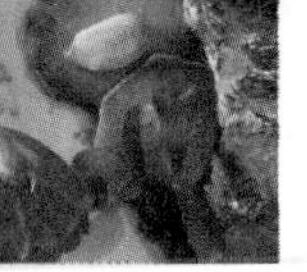

TERIYAKI PORK KEBABS

4 SERVINGS

MARINADE

⅓ cup	lemon juice *or* lemon juice concentrate	75 mL
¼ cup	soy sauce	50 mL
3 tbsp	corn oil	45 mL
2 tbsp	liquid chicken stock concentrate	30 mL
3 tbsp	chili pepper sauce	45 mL
2	garlic cloves, chopped	2
½ tsp	ground ginger	2 mL
¼ tsp	pepper	1 mL

KEBABS

1 lb	lean pork loin *or* fillet, in 1½ inch (4 cm) cubes	450 g
1	green *or* red pepper, cubed	1
1	medium onion, cubed	1
8	mushrooms, whole *or* halved	8
8	cherry tomatoes	8

SAUCE

½ cup	plain yogurt	125 mL
1	garlic clove, chopped	1
1	pinch dried oregano	1

- Combine marinade ingredients in a bowl and set aside.
- Thread meat and vegetable cubes on skewers.
- Arrange skewers in large dish with marinade. Cover.
- Let marinate in refrigerator 2 to 6 hours, turning skewers from time to time.
- Remove kebabs from marinade and cook on preheated barbecue until cooked through. Baste with marinade during cooking.
- Combine sauce ingredients in a bowl and serve with kebabs.

LAMB CHOPS WITH CITRUS

2 SERVINGS

4	lamb loin chops, medium thickness	4
1	garlic clove	1
	chopped green onions	
	pepper	
	MARINADE	
2	garlic cloves, finely chopped	2
2 tbsp	canola oil	30 mL
2 tsp	grated lemon *or* lime zest	10 mL
4 tsp	lemon juice	20 mL
2 tsp	chopped fresh thyme *or* ½ tsp (2 mL) dried thyme	10 mL
	pepper	

- Trim fat from lamb chops and rub them with garlic clove. Set aside.
- Combine all marinade ingredients in a bowl.
- Place lamb chops in a shallow dish and pour marinade on top. Cover and refrigerate 3 hours, turning chops from time to time.
- Remove chops from refrigerator 30 minutes before cooking time.
- Remove chops from marinade and cook on preheated barbecue 8 minutes on each side, or until still slightly pink inside. Season and baste with marinade during cooking.
- Arrange lamb chops on plates, garnish with chopped green onions, and serve with potatoes and vegetable of your choice.

STEAK TARTARE

2 SERVINGS

2	anchovy fillets, well drained, finely chopped (optional)	2
2	egg yolks	2
1 tbsp	oil (optional)	15 mL
½ lb	beef fillet *or* top round, finely chopped with a knife	225 g
2 tbsp	finely chopped onion	30 mL
1 tbsp	capers, drained	15 mL
2 tbsp	finely chopped fresh parsley	30 mL
	few drops of tabasco sauce	
	few drops of Worcestershire sauce	
	freshly ground pepper	

• In a wooden bowl, if you have one, combine anchovies and egg yolks. Gradually stir in oil.

• Add beef, onion, capers and parsley. Mix well.

• Stir in tabasco, Worcestershire and pepper. Shape into 2 slightly flattened balls.

• Arrange on plates garnished with capers, chopped shallots and anchovy fillets.

PORK AND MUSHROOM CASSEROLE

2 SERVINGS

4	pork chops	4
1	onion, thinly sliced	1
1 cup	sliced mushrooms	250 mL
2 tbsp	chopped fresh parsley	30 mL
10 oz	can cream of mushroom soup	284 mL
2	potatoes, peeled, cut in thick slices	2
2 tbsp	butter *or* margarine	30 mL
	pepper	

- Preheat oven to 350°F (180°C).
- Trim excess fat from chops. Grease a baking dish and spread onion and mushrooms over bottom. Arrange chops on top. Season with pepper.
- Sprinkle on ½ the parsley. Add mushroom soup and cover with sliced potatoes. Dot with butter.
- Bake about 40 minutes.
- Sprinkle with remaining parsley before serving.

LAMB FILLETS WITH ROSEMARY

2 SERVINGS

1 tbsp	butter *or* margarine	15 mL
1 tbsp	corn oil	15 mL
1	garlic clove	1
4	lamb fillets, about 4 oz (120 g) each	4
4	sprigs fresh rosemary	4
¼ cup	dry white wine	50 mL
	pepper	

• Heat butter and oil in a non-stick skillet. Add garlic and cook a few minutes to flavor oil. Remove garlic.

• Add lamb fillets and rosemary. Cook about 10 minutes over medium-high heat, turning lamb often.

• Arrange fillets on heated plate and keep warm.

• Add wine to skillet and scrape bottom. Stir in pepper and cook until sauce is creamy.

• Return lamb to pan and turn quickly to coat with sauce.

• Slice fillets to serve. Accompany with potatoes and a green vegetable.

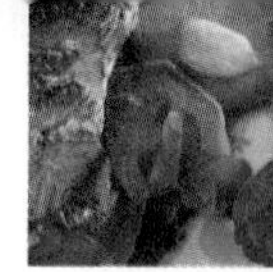

VEAL CHOPS WITH MUSHROOMS

2 SERVINGS

2	**veal chops**	**2**
2 tbsp	**butter *or* margarine**	**30 mL**
2 cups	**sliced fresh mushrooms**	**500 mL**
½ cup	**sliced onion**	**125 mL**
1	**garlic clove, finely chopped**	**1**
¾ cup	**dry white wine**	**175 mL**
1¼ cups	**beef *or* chicken stock**	**300 mL**
3 tbsp	**commercial brown gravy thickener**	**45 mL**
1 to 2	**pinches dried thyme *or* tarragon**	**1 to 2**
	pepper	

• Trim excess fat from chops.

• Melt 1 tbsp (15 mL) butter in a large saucepan. Add mushrooms, onion and garlic and cook over high heat about 5 minutes.

• Add wine and beef stock. Stir in gravy thickener. Let simmer over low heat a few minutes. Season with pepper and thyme.

• Heat remaining butter in a large skillet. Cook chops over high heat, turning to brown both sides, until cooked through. Pour mushroom sauce over to serve.

ROAST LEG OF LAMB

10 SERVINGS

1	leg of lamb	1
4 to 6	garlic cloves, halved	4 to 6
1	carrot, coarsely chopped	1
1	onion, coarsely chopped	1
1	celery stalk, coarsely chopped	1
1	sprig fresh thyme, finely chopped	1
3 tbsp	butter *or* margarine	45 mL
2 tbsp	hot mustard	30 mL
2 tbsp	fine breadcrumbs	30 mL
½ cup	water, white grape juice *or* chicken stock	125 mL
	pepper	

- Preheat oven to 450°F (230°C).
- Trim excess fat from lamb, then rub and stud with garlic.
- Arrange vegetables in baking pan with leg of lamb on top. Pepper and set aside.
- In a bowl, combine thyme, butter, mustard and breadcrumbs. Baste lamb with butter mixture. Roast in oven 50 to 60 minutes, basting with cooking juices from time to time.
- Turn lamb after 30 minutes cooking.
- When done to taste, remove lamb from pan, slice thinly and keep warm.
- Skim fat from cooking juices and pour a little over lamb slices. Serve with pan-roasted potatoes.

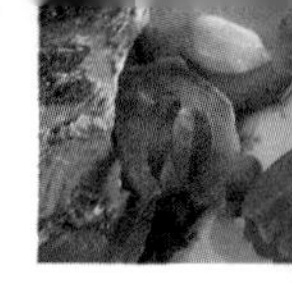

SUGGESTION

Flavor the cooking juices with fresh mint. Be sure to skim off excess fat before serving.

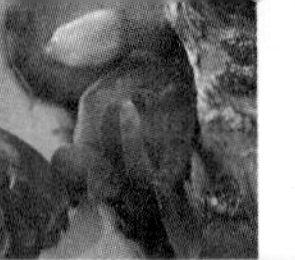

SUGGESTION

Skim fat from top of sauce before serving.

Slice the roast with a very sharp knife.

BRAISED BEEF WITH SPANISH ONIONS

4 SERVINGS

14 oz	**can tomatoes**	**398 mL**
2 cups	**thinly sliced Spanish onions**	**500 mL**
2	**garlic cloves, finely chopped**	**2**
1¾ lbs	**lean beef roast (eg. top round)**	**750 g**
¼ cup	**water**	**50 mL**
2	**potatoes, with peel, sliced**	**2**
1 tbsp	**cornstarch dissolved in 1 tbsp (15 mL) cold water**	**15 mL**
	pepper	

• Preheat oven to 325°F (160°C).

• In a baking dish, spread the tomatoes and half the onions and garlic. Place roast on top. Cover with remaining onions and garlic. Season with pepper, add water and cover.

• Cook in oven 2½ to 3 hours, or until meat is tender. Add potatoes 15 minutes before end of cooking.

• Arrange beef and vegetables on a serving plate, cover with foil, and let stand 10 minutes.

• Meanwhile, add enough water to cooking juices remaining in pan to make about 1 cup (250 mL). Dissolve cornstarch in 1 tbsp (15 mL) cold water and stir into cooking juices. Cook over medium-high heat 2 to 3 minutes to thicken slightly.

• Slice the roast thinly, and serve with sauce.

GAUCHO GRILL

8 SERVINGS

1 lb	flank steak (scored on both sides)	450 g
1 lb	skinless chicken, in pieces	450 g
1 lb	smoked sausages	450 g
	MARINADE	
½ cup	corn oil	125 mL
¼ cup	wine vinegar *or* raspberry vinegar	50 mL
⅓ cup	chopped fresh parsley	75 mL
¼ cup	chopped onion	50 mL
½ cup	prepared onion sauce from packaged mix	125 mL
4	garlic cloves, chopped	4
2 tsp	dried oregano	10 mL
2	bay leaves	2
½ tsp	cayenne pepper	2 mL
1	pinch pepper	1

• Combine marinade ingredients in a bowl. Place meats in marinade, cover and refrigerate 1 hour.

• Cook meats on preheated barbecue to desired degree of doneness. Baste with marinade at end of cooking time. Serve with grilled vegetables.

LAMB SAUTÉ WITH GARLIC

4 SERVINGS

2 tbsp	**olive oil**	**30 mL**
1½ lbs	**boneless lamb shoulder, cubed**	**675 g**
1 tbsp	**butter *or* margarine**	**15 mL**
½ cup	**breadcrumbs**	**125 mL**
3	**garlic cloves, chopped**	**3**
3 tbsp	**chopped fresh parsley**	**45 mL**
2 cups	**chicken stock**	**500 mL**

• Heat oil in a skillet. Add meat and sear on all sides, but do not let brown. Remove from heat and set aside.

• Melt butter in a saucepan. Add breadcrumbs and cook until browned, stirring. Add meat and stir well to coat with breadcrumbs.

• Combine garlic and parsley, and sprinkle over lamb.

• Add chicken stock, and let simmer over low heat 45 minutes, stirring from time to time, so that meat is evenly coated with breadcrumbs and garlic mixture. Add a little water if the mixture seems dry.

1

Heat oil in skillet and add lamb.

2

Brown breadcrumbs in melted butter. Add lamb.

3

Combine garlic and parsley; sprinkle over lamb.

4

Add chicken stock and let simmer, stirring occasionally.

SUGGESTION

Always soak wooden skewers for a few minutes in cold water before using, or they tend to burn.

BEEF KEBABS LEBANESE-STYLE

5 SERVINGS

2 lbs	filet mignon, trimmed and cubed	900 g
1 tsp	salt	5 mL
1 tsp	ground black pepper	5 mL
2 tsp	ground allspice	10 mL
1 tsp	sumac*	5 mL
1 tsp	dried hot red pepper	5 mL
5	garlic cloves, crushed	5
1 tsp	lemon juice	5 mL
1 tbsp	tomato paste	15 mL
1 tbsp	olive oil	15 mL
1	red pepper, cubed	1
1	Spanish onion, cubed	1

- Salt and pepper the meat cubes. Set aside.
- Combine all remaining ingredients except red pepper and onion in a shallow bowl, add meat cubes, and turn so they are well coated.
- Cover and let marinate in refrigerator 1 hour.
- Remove meat from marinade and thread on 5 presoaked wooden skewers, alternating meat with pepper and onion pieces.
- Cook on preheated barbecue to taste.
- Serve with pita bread spread with softened butter and leftover marinade, then grilled on barbecue.

* See glossary

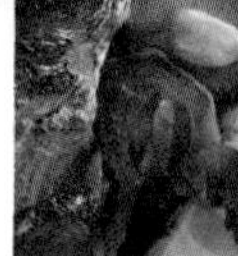

FEATHER-LIGHT SCALLOPINI

2 SERVINGS

¼ cup	all-purpose flour	50 mL
2	large veal scallopini, about 4 oz (120 g) each	2
1	egg	1
¼ cup	milk	50 mL
¼ cup	grated gruyère *or* Emmenthal cheese	50 mL
2 tbsp	corn oil	30 mL
	paprika	
	nutmeg	
	pepper	
	lemon slices	

- Put flour in a shallow plate. Coat veal on both sides with flour. Set aside.
- In a bowl, combine egg, milk, cheese, paprika, nutmeg and pepper.
- Dip scallopini in egg mixture.
- Heat oil in a non-stick skillet and brown scallopini on both sides over medium-high heat.
- Garnish with lemon and serve with pasta.

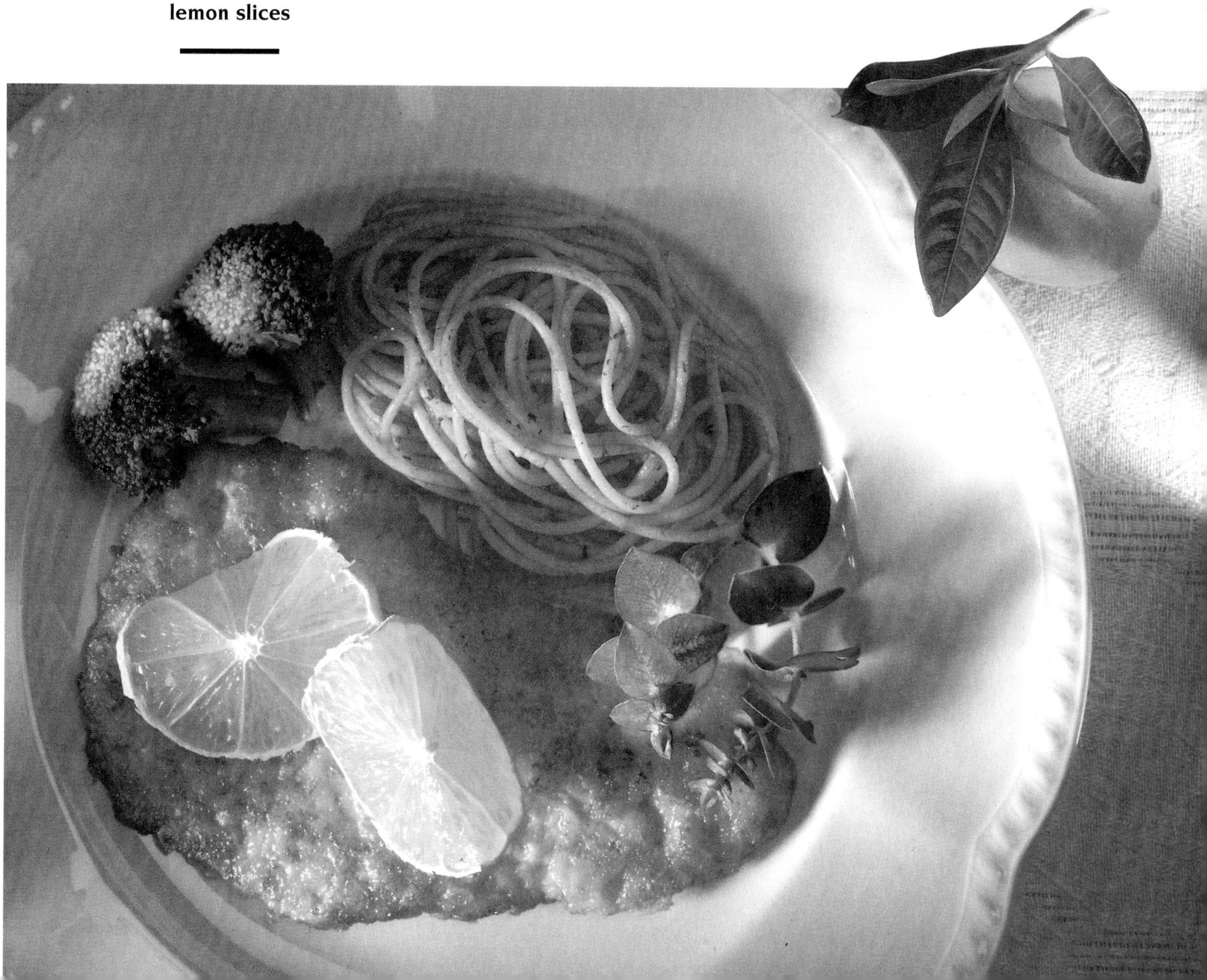

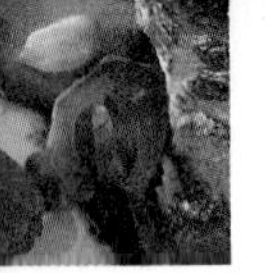

NUTTY PORK CHOPS

4 SERVINGS

4	lean, boneless pork chops	4
4 tsp	hot mustard	20 mL
⅓ cup	ground pecans	75 mL
4 tsp	soft butter	20 mL
½ tsp	dried basil	2 mL
½ tsp	dried thyme	2 mL
2 tbsp	sesame seeds	30 mL

- Trim excess fat from chops and coat on both sides with mustard. Set aside.
- In a bowl, combine remaining mustard, nuts, butter, basil and thyme. Set aside.
- Arrange chops on oiled, preheated barbecue grill and cook 10 to 12 minutes. Turn over and cook another 5 minutes.
- Baste chops with nut mixture and cook another 3 minutes, or until meat interior is no longer pink.
- Sprinkle with sesame seeds and serve with vegetable of your choice.

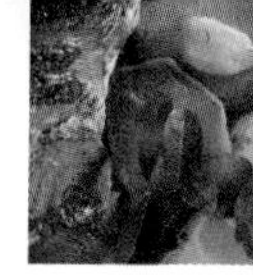

CARIBBEAN BURGERS

12 SERVINGS

2 tsp	corn oil	10 mL
1	onion, finely chopped	1
1	garlic clove, chopped	1
1	green pepper, cut in thin strips	1
2 lbs	lean ground beef	900 g
1 tsp	dried fines herbes*	5 mL
2	eggs, beaten	2
2 cups	whole-wheat breadcrumbs	500 mL
½ cup	grated cheddar cheese	125 mL
1 tbsp	tomato paste	15 mL
12	pineapple slices	12
12	hamburger buns	12
	melted butter	
	pepper	

• Heat oil in a large saucepan. Add onion, garlic and green pepper, and cook over medium heat 5 minutes. Let cool.

• In a bowl, combine sautéed vegetables with meat, herbs, eggs, breadcrumbs, cheese, tomato paste and pepper. Shape into 12 patties.

• Cook patties on oiled, preheated grill 8 to 10 minutes on each side.

• Baste pineapple slices with melted butter and grill on barbecue 4 minutes, turning halfway through. Lightly grill hamburger buns.

• Place 1 patty and 1 pineapple slice in each bun to serve.

* See glossary

GINGER-HONEY PORK RIBS

4 TO 6 SERVINGS

3 lbs	pork ribs	1.3 kg
1 inch	piece fresh ginger, finely chopped	2.5 cm
⅔ cup	honey	150 mL
1 tsp	liquid vegetable stock concentrate	5 mL
2 tsp	hot mustard	10 mL
1 tsp	ground allspice	5 mL
	juice and zest of 1 orange	

ACCOMPANIMENT

4 to 6	potatoes	4 to 6
2 tbsp	plain yogurt	30 mL
2 tbsp	chopped green onions	30 mL

- Put ribs in a large saucepan and cover with water. Bring to a boil, lower the heat, and simmer 30 to 35 minutes. Drain and set aside.
- Combine remaining ingredients (except accompaniments) in a bowl. Pour this mixture into a saucepan, bring to a boil, and cook until slightly thickened.
- Wrap potatoes in foil and bake on barbecue grill 35 to 40 minutes with the barbecue cover closed.
- Put the ribs on the barbecue grill and cook 3 to 4 minutes on each side, basting often with sauce.
- Serve ribs with potatoes topped with yogurt and chopped green onions.

BARBECUED BURGERS WITH PINE NUTS

4 TO 6 SERVINGS

1½ lbs	lean ground beef	675 g
1	onion, finely chopped	1
1	garlic clove, crushed	1
½ cup	soft breadcrumbs	125 mL
½ cup	grated Romano *or* Parmesan cheese	125 mL
4 oz	pine nuts	120 g
½ cup	finely chopped parsley	125 mL
2	eggs	2
1 tsp	pepper	5 mL
	corn oil	

• Preheat barbecue grill.

• Combine all ingredients except corn oil in a bowl.

• Shape meat mixture into patties. Baste with oil.

• Cook patties over high heat about 5 minutes on each side, or until exterior is browned and crispy.

• Serve with tomato sauce and a green vegetable, if desired.

PORK WITH VERMOUTH

6 SERVINGS

3	pork fillets, cut crosswise in ½-inch (1 cm) thick medallions	3
½ tsp	paprika	2 mL
¼ cup	all-purpose flour	50 mL
2 tbsp	corn oil	30 mL
1 tbsp	butter *or* margarine	15 mL
1 tsp	chopped dry French shallot	5 mL
1 tsp	tomato paste	5 mL
¼ cup	red wine	50 mL
1 cup	chicken stock	250 mL
2 tbsp	dry white vermouth	30 mL
	pepper	

- Place pork slices between 2 sheets waxed paper and flatten slightly with side of a large knife.
- Pepper lightly, and sprinkle with paprika and flour.
- Heat oil in a skillet. Brown pork on both sides over medium-high heat. Remove pork and drain on paper towels.
- Arrange pork on serving plate and keep warm.
- Melt butter in the hot skillet, add chopped shallot and cook until soft. Sprinkle in 1 tbsp (15 mL) flour and stir until browned.
- Add tomato paste, remove pan from heat and mix well. Add wine and continue cooking over medium heat until reduced by half.
- Add chicken stock and cook a few more minutes. Stir in vermouth, then strain sauce.
- Pour sauce over pork medallions and serve with parsleyed thin noodles.

VEAL SCALLOPINI WITH MUSHROOM SAUCE

2 SERVINGS

2	**veal scallopini, about 5 oz (150 g) each, fat trimmed**	2
2 tbsp	**butter *or* margarine**	30 mL
1 cup	**sliced mushrooms**	250 mL
½ tsp	**dried thyme**	2 mL
3 tbsp	**dry white wine *or* dry white vermouth (optional)**	45 mL
1 cup	**béchamel sauce (see page 273)**	250 mL
	pepper	

- Sprinkle meat with pepper.
- Heat butter in a skillet. Brown veal on both sides until nice and brown. Put meat on serving plate and keep warm.
- Cook mushrooms in same skillet 4 to 5 minutes.
- Add thyme and wine, and cook a few minutes to reduce wine.
- Stir in béchamel sauce and cook over low heat until thick.

Pour mushroom sauce over veal and serve with vegetables of your choice.

LAMB CHOPS WITH CUMIN

2 SERVINGS

1 tbsp	**cumin seeds, toasted and crushed**	**15 mL**
¼ tsp	**ground cinnamon**	**1 mL**
3	**garlic cloves, crushed**	**3**
3 tbsp	**unsweetened orange juice**	**45 mL**
2 tbsp	**canola oil**	**30 mL**
4	**lamb chops**	**4**

• In a bowl, combine toasted cumin, cinnamon, garlic, orange juice and oil.

• Add lamb chops and turn to coat with marinade. Cover and let marinate at room temperature 2 hours, turning chops from time to time.

• Preheat oven to 500°F (260°C).

• Arrange lamb chops on baking pan. Bake about 8 minutes each side, basting often with leftover marinade. Adjust cooking time if chops are very thick or very thin. Let stand 3 minutes before serving.

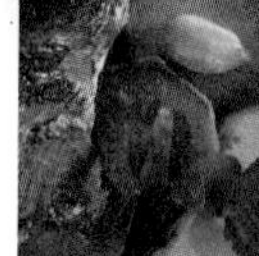

PORK FILLET AND MUSHROOM PACKAGES

2 SERVINGS

2	small pork fillets	2
1	garlic clove, halved	1
½ tsp	chopped fresh thyme	2 mL
2 tbsp	butter *or* margarine	30 mL
1	onion, finely chopped	1
2	celery stalks, chopped	2
1½ cups	sliced mushrooms	375 mL
¼ cup	whipping cream	50 mL
	chopped fresh parsley	
	pepper	

• Preheat oven to 450°F (230°C).

• Wipe fillets and rub with garlic, pepper and thyme.

• Cut 2 circles of aluminum foil large enough to wrap fillets; set aside.

• Melt 1 tbsp (15 mL) butter in a non-stick skillet. Brown fillets on all sides 3 or 4 minutes. Remove from skillet and arrange one on each of 2 foil circles. Set aside.

• Add remaining butter to skillet, if necessary, and cook onion and celery 1 minute over high heat. Add mushrooms and cook until all liquid has evaporated, stirring from time to time.

• Divide mushroom mixture over fillets, add 2 tbsp (30 mL) cream to each, sprinkle with parsley and wrap packages to seal well.

• Bake packages on the middle shelf of oven 18 to 20 minutes. Serve at once.

SUGGESTION

Make chicken packages using skinless chicken breasts instead of pork.

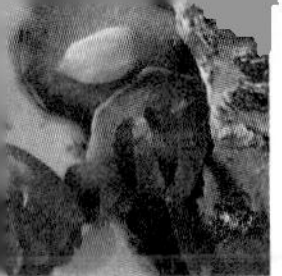

BEEF WITH CHINESE CABBAGE

4 SERVINGS

1 tbsp	soy sauce	15 mL
1 tbsp	rice vinegar	15 mL
2 tbsp	corn oil	30 mL
1 tsp	sugar	5 mL
1 tbsp	cornstarch	15 mL
1	pinch salt	1
½ lb	flank steak, thinly sliced across grain	225 g
4 cups	shredded Chinese cabbage	1 liter
½ cup	sliced green onions	125 mL
1 cup	sliced celery	250 mL
½ cup	sliced carrot (cut diagonally)	125 mL
1 tbsp	finely chopped fresh ginger	15 mL
½ cup	chicken stock	125 mL
3 tbsp	sesame seeds, toasted	45 mL

• Combine soy sauce and vinegar in a large bowl. Stir in 1 tbsp (15 mL) corn oil, sugar, 1 tsp (5 mL) cornstarch and salt. Put meat in this marinade. Cover and refrigerate overnight, or let marinate 2 to 3 hours at room temperature.

• Remove meat from marinade just when ready to cook. Stir remaining cornstarch into marinade and set aside.

• Heat remaining oil in a wok over high heat. Cook meat 2 to 3 minutes, stirring, or until browned.

• Add Chinese cabbage, green onions, celery, carrot and ginger. Cook 1 more minute, stirring. Stir in chicken stock and marinade. Cover and cook 2 to 3 minutes.

• Adjust salt and pepper to taste. Sprinkle with toasted sesame seeds to serve.

1

Prepare marinade and add meat.

2

Cook meat in oil 2 to 3 minutes over high heat.

3

Add vegetables.

4

Stir in stock and marinade.

PORK FILLET WITH BLACK OLIVE SAUCE

2 SERVINGS

1	**pork fillet**	1
2	**sprigs fresh thyme *or* oregano**	2
2	**garlic cloves, halved**	2
½ cup	**olive oil *or* vegetable oil**	125 mL
1 tbsp	**butter *or* margarine**	15 mL
	pepper	
	SAUCE	
2 tbsp	**brandy *or* cognac**	30 mL
1	**dry French shallot, chopped**	1
¼ cup	**dry white wine**	50 mL
¼ cup	**chicken stock *or* beef stock**	50 mL
¼ cup	**whipping cream *or* cream cheese**	50 mL
2 oz	**black olives, pitted and puréed**	60 g
	cooking juices from pork	
	pepper	

• Sprinkle pork with pepper and place in dish with thyme and garlic. Coat with olive oil, cover with plastic wrap, and refrigerate about 3 hours.

• Remove pork from dish and slice crosswise into 1 inch (2.5 cm) medallions. Flatten each medallion slightly with flat edge of a large knife.

• Preheat oven to 400°F (200°C).

• Heat butter in a skillet. Brown pork on both sides over medium-high heat.

• Arrange pork in baking dish and cook another 4 minutes in oven. Remove from oven and set aside.

• Discard excess fat in skillet. Pour in brandy and cook over medium heat until liquid is almost completely evaporated.

• Add shallot and white wine; cook 1 minute. Stir in pork cooking juices and stock. Cook until reduced by half.

• Stir in cream, puréed olives and pepper to taste. Cook to thicken slightly.

• Arrange pork medallions on heated plates and pour sauce over. Serve with potatoes.

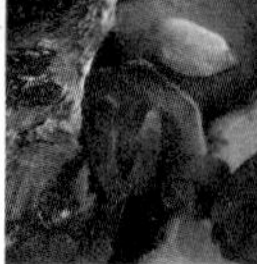

VEAL LIVER WITH RAISINS

4 SERVINGS

½ cup	raisins	125 mL
1 cup	lukewarm tea	250 mL
2 tbsp	canola oil	30 mL
1	onion, sliced	1
1½ lbs	veal liver, cubed	675 g
½ cup	dry white wine	125 mL
	salt and pepper	

• Soak raisins in tea about 1 hour.

• Heat oil in a large skillet. Add onion and cook over medium heat until golden.

• Add liver and cook over medium-high heat to brown all sides.

• Remove liver from skillet. Add wine to pan and cook 1 to 2 minutes over medium heat, scraping bottom of pan. Drain raisins and add to skillet.

• Return liver to skillet and simmer 5 minutes over low heat. Season to taste before serving.

SUGGESTION

Replace the raisins with canned peaches; you will not need the tea.

PORK FILLET STUFFED WITH SUN-DRIED TOMATOES

4 SERVINGS

½ cup	corn kernels, drained	125 mL
½ cup	diced red pepper	125 mL
½ cup	sultana raisins	125 mL
½ cup	rehydrated and drained Hijaki seaweed	125 mL
1	apple, peeled, cored and diced	1
2 tsp	ground cardamom	10 mL
2	pork fillets, 12 oz (375 g) each	2
1 tbsp	corn oil	15 mL
1	dry French shallot, minced	1
⅓ cup	dry white vermouth *or* dry white wine	75 mL
2 cups	chicken stock	500 mL
½ cup	sun-dried tomatoes, drained and chopped	125 mL
⅓ cup	sour cream	75 mL

• Preheat oven to 350°F (180°C).

• In a bowl, combine corn, red pepper, raisins, seaweed, apple and cardamom. Set aside.

• Slice pork fillets lengthwise with a sharp knife to make a deep pocket. Stuff with corn mixture and fasten closed with toothpicks.

• Heat oil in a non-stick skillet over high heat and brown the pork on both sides. Arrange pork in baking dish and bake in oven 15 minutes.

• Meanwhile, put the chopped shallot in the skillet and cook, stirring, 1 minute over medium-high heat. Add vermouth and scrape bottom. Stir in chicken stock and sun-dried tomatoes; simmer until reduced by half.

• Purée tomato mixture and return to skillet. Stir in sour cream.

• Pour tomato sauce on plates, and top with sliced pork fillets.

RABBIT KEBABS MARTINIQUE

4 TO 6 SERVINGS

1	rabbit, deboned and cubed	1
½ lb	bacon, cut in strips	225 g
2	large onions, cubed	2
1	green pepper, cubed	1
1	red pepper, cubed	1
24	mushrooms, stems removed	24
12	cherry tomatoes	12

MARINADE

3	dry French shallots, chopped	3
2	garlic cloves, finely chopped	2
1	hot pepper, finely chopped	1
4	green onions, chopped	4
1	bay leaf	1
1	pinch dried thyme	1
1	pinch dried rosemary	1
1	pinch ground allspice	1
¼ cup	amber rum	50 mL
½ cup	corn oil	125 mL
	juice of 2 limes	
	grated zest of 1 lime	
	carrot and onion rings	
	salt and pepper	

• Combine all marinade ingredients in a large bowl.

• Add rabbit pieces, cover and refrigerate 3 to 4 hours.

• Remove rabbit from marinade, drain, and wrap each cube in bacon.

• Thread cubes on skewers, alternating with vegetables.

• Cook on oiled, preheated barbecue grill, basting with remaining marinade from time to time.

FLANK STEAK MARINATED IN BEER

4 SERVINGS

1 lb	flank steak, tenderized	450 g
	MARINADE	
1	large onion, in rings	1
2	garlic cloves, chopped	2
¼ cup	corn oil	50 mL
1 cup	beer	250 mL
⅓ cup	lemon juice	75 mL
2 tbsp	brown sugar	30 mL
2 tbsp	Worcestershire sauce	30 mL

(Continued on next page)

• Combine marinade ingredients in a bowl.

• Lay steak in a shallow glass dish and cover with marinade, turning to coat all sides. Cover with foil and refrigerate at least 6 hours. Turn meat from time to time.

• Remove steak from marinade. Drain well and grill on preheated barbecue grill or in a heavy skillet to the desired degree of doneness, basting often with marinade during cooking.

TO MARINATE FLANK STEAK

Combine marinade ingredients in a bowl.

Arrange steak in shallow glass dish and cover with marinade.

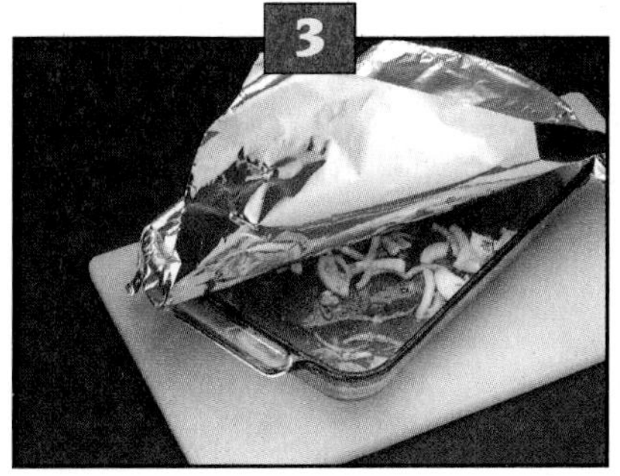

Cover with foil and refrigerate at least 6 hours, turning meat from time to time.

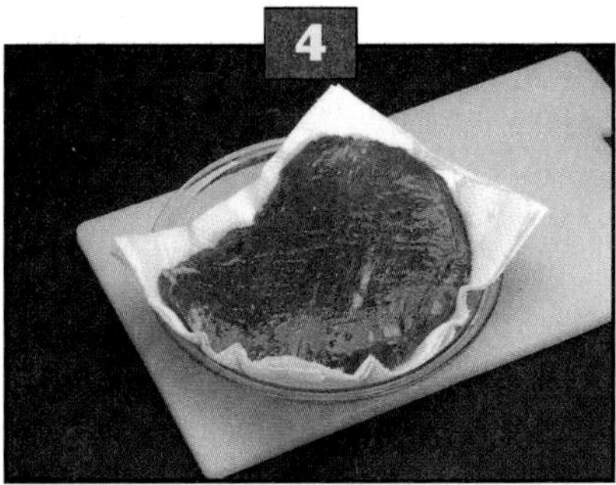

Remove steak from marinade and drain well before cooking.

SUGGESTION

Serve in deep plates, and sprinkle with grated cheese, if desired.

EASY BEEF AND VEGETABLE STEW

4 SERVINGS

1 tbsp	butter *or* margarine	15 mL
½	onion, finely chopped	½
½ lb	lean ground beef	225 g
½ lb	lean ground veal	225 g
1	garlic clove, sliced	1
19 oz	can tomatoes, with juice, coarsely chopped	540 mL
4 cups	beef stock	1 liter
½ tsp	dried thyme	2 mL
2 cups	chopped mixed vegetables	500 mL
	chopped fresh parsley	
	pepper	

• In a casserole dish or large, heavy saucepan, melt butter over high heat.

• Add onion, beef, veal and garlic. Cook 4 to 5 minutes over high heat, stirring, until meat is browned.

• Stir in tomatoes with their juice, beef stock and thyme.

• Bring to a boil, partially cover, and let simmer 30 minutes over low heat.

• Add chopped vegetables, parsley and pepper. Cook another 20 to 30 minutes over low heat.

PORK FILLET WITH ONION PURÉE

4 SERVINGS

1 to 2	**pork fillets, about 1½ lbs (675 g) in total**	1 to 2
1	**garlic clove, halved**	1
4 tsp	**butter *or* margarine**	20 mL
1	**large onion, finely chopped**	1
½ cup	**raspberry vinegar *or* dry white wine**	125 mL
2 cups	**water**	500 mL
½ cup	**15% cream**	125 mL
2 tbsp	**chopped fresh chives**	30 mL
	pepper	

• Slice fillets crosswise into medallions about 1 inch (2.5 cm) thick. Rub with garlic and set aside.

• Heat ½ the butter in a non-stick skillet. Add onion and cook over medium-high heat until golden.

• Add vinegar and water, scraping bottom. Cook over low heat until liquid has almost all evaporated.

• Purée onion mixture in food processor. Return to skillet and heat gently. Stir in cream.

• Add chives and pepper and keep warm.

• Heat remaining butter in a second skillet. Cook pork medallions over medium-high heat 8 to 10 minutes or until cooked to taste, turning halfway through. Serve with onion purée.

If you prefer, brown the pork on both sides in a skillet, then complete the cooking for about 5 minutes in a 400°F (200°C) oven.

BEEF TOURNEDOS WITH AVOCADO MOUSSE

2 SERVINGS

Avocados are ripe when they yield to slight finger pressure. Pick those that are heavy for their size, and without black spots or blemishes. Avocados are rich in potassium and Vitamins A and C.

1	**avocado**	1
1 tbsp	**chopped fresh parsley**	15 mL
1 tsp	**mayonnaise**	5 mL
½	**dry French shallot**	½
1	**pinch cayenne pepper**	1
2	**beef tournedos* *or* beef fillet slices, about 4 oz (120 g) each**	2
1 tbsp	**corn oil**	15 mL
1	**orange, in segments, pith and membranes removed**	1
	juice of ¼ lemon	
	pepper	

• Slice avocado in half, remove pit, and spoon out flesh.

• In food processor, purée avocado flesh with parsley, mayonnaise, shallot, cayenne and lemon juice. Set aside.

• Brush beef with oil and sprinkle with pepper. Cook on preheated barbecue grill to desired doneness.

• Just before serving, garnish each tournedos with avocado mousse and orange segments.

* See glossary

SUGGESTION

Serve with steamed new potatoes and cherry tomatoes for an easy summer meal.

HERB AND GINGER PORK FILLETS

4 SERVINGS

½ tsp	dried thyme	2 mL
½ tsp	dried rosemary	2 mL
4	garlic cloves, crushed	4
1 tbsp	chopped fresh ginger	15 mL
1 tbsp	olive oil	15 mL
3 to 4 tsp	honey	15 to 20 mL
3 tbsp	butter *or* margarine	45 mL
¾ lb	pork fillet, fat trimmed	375 g
	grated zest of ½ lemon	
	juice of 1 lemon	
	julienne strips of lemon zest	
	pepper	

- In food processor, combine thyme, rosemary, grated lemon zest and lemon juice, garlic, ginger, oil, honey and pepper.
- Add butter and process until smooth.
- Baste pork fillet with herb mixture, arrange in a glass dish, and cover with remaining herb mixture.
- Cover and refrigerate at least 4 hours.
- Drain the fillet, reserving marinade, and cook on preheated barbecue grill until done to taste.
- Pour marinade in a small saucepan and heat.
- Slice the fillet and arrange on plates garnished with strips of lemon zest. Serve with heated marinade.

Thyme contains iron and Vitamin A. Rosemary is a source of Vitamin C, and is delicious with grilled meats.

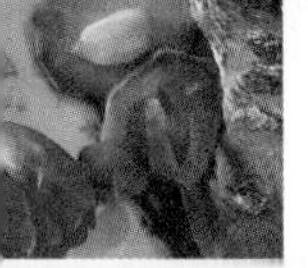

VEAL PARMIGIANA

4 SERVINGS

3 tbsp	**breadcrumbs**	**45 mL**
⅓ cup	**grated Parmesan cheese**	**75 mL**
1 lb	**veal scallopini**	**450 g**
1	**egg, beaten**	**1**
2 tbsp	**vegetable oil**	**30 mL**
1 tbsp	**butter *or* margarine**	**15 mL**
¼ cup	**dry white vermouth *or* dry white wine**	**50 mL**
1 cup	**tomato sauce**	**250 mL**
1 cup	**grated mozzarella cheese**	**250 mL**
	dried oregano	
	pepper	

• Combine breadcrumbs, Parmesan, oregano and pepper in a shallow dish. Set aside.

• Flatten the scallopini with the flat edge of a large knife. Dip them in egg, then in breadcrumb mixture to coat. Set aside.

• Heat oil and butter in a non-stick skillet. Brown veal on both sides 5 to 6 minutes over high heat. Continue cooking until interior is no longer pink. Remove veal from skillet and arrange in a single layer in a baking pan.

• Return skillet to burner and add vermouth, scraping the bottom. Stir in tomato sauce and heat through. Cover scallopini with tomato sauce and mozzarella.

• Place under hot broiler until cheese melts and browns slightly. Serve with parsleyed noodles, if desired.

OLD-FASHIONED BOILED HAM

6 TO 8 SERVINGS

3 tbsp	**whole pickling spice**	**45 mL**
1	**bay leaf**	**1**
1 tbsp	**dry mustard**	**15 mL**
¼ cup	**molasses**	**50 mL**
3 tbsp	**brown sugar**	**45 mL**
¼ cup	**white vinegar**	**50 mL**
2 to 4½ lb	**smoked ham, bone-in *or* smoked pork shoulder, bone-in**	**900 g to 1.8 kg**

• In a bowl, mix together pickling spice, bay leaf, mustard, molasses, brown sugar and vinegar. Set aside.

• Place ham in a large saucepan and cover with water.

• Add spice mixture.

• Cook over low heat 1 to 2 hours. Let ham cool in its cooking liquid.

SUGGESTION

Instead of boiling the ham, coat it with the spice mixture, cover with foil, and bake in a 375°F (190°C) oven 50 to 60 minutes.

CHEESY LAMB CHOPS IN CABBAGE LEAVES

4 SERVINGS

1½ cups	**béchamel sauce (see page 273)**	**375 mL**
4 tbsp	**blue cheese**	**60 mL**
½ cup	**virgin olive oil**	**125 mL**
2	**pinches dried thyme**	**2**
1	**garlic clove, finely chopped**	**1**
8	**Frenched rib lamb chops***	**8**
8	**large cabbage leaves, blanched**	**8**
1	**medium onion, sliced**	**1**
¼ cup	**chicken stock**	**50 mL**
	pepper	

- Preheat oven to 375°F (190°C).
- Prepare béchamel sauce and stir in blue cheese. Let cool.
- Combine olive oil, thyme, garlic and pepper in a shallow dish. Arrange lamb chops in marinade, cover and refrigerate about 30 minutes.
- Remove chops from marinade and brown them on both sides over high heat in a non-stick skillet.
- Arrange one chop on each cabbage leaf, and cover with béchamel sauce and an onion slice. Wrap cabbage around chop, letting the bone stick out.
- Arrange cabbage packages in a baking dish, and pour chicken stock over. Bake 6 to 10 minutes, or to taste.
- Arrange on heated plates. Serve with bulgar and vegetables of your choice.

* If your butcher does not carry Frenched rib lamb chops, buy ordinary lamb rib chops and trim all tissue from about 1 inch (2.5 cm) of the bone end.

1

Combine béchamel sauce and blue cheese.

2

Marinate lamb chops.

3

Top chops with sauce and onion, and wrap in cabbage leaf.

4

Pour chicken stock over and bake.

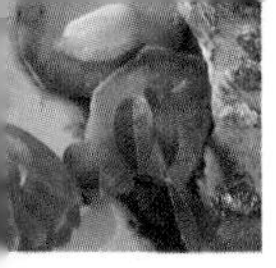

BEEF WITH CARROTS

4 SERVINGS

2 tbsp	all-purpose flour	30 mL
½ tsp	paprika	2 mL
1 lb	boneless beef, trimmed of fat and cubed	450 g
2 tbsp	vegetable oil	30 mL
3 tbsp	butter *or* margarine	45 mL
1	celery stalk, thickly sliced	1
2 cups	thickly sliced carrots	500 mL
½ cup	chopped onion	125 mL
¼ cup	dry white wine *or* unsweetened apple juice	50 mL
½ cup	beef stock *or* chicken stock	125 mL
1 tbsp	chopped fresh parsley	15 mL
	pepper	

• Preheat oven to 350°F (180°C).

• Combine flour, paprika and pepper in a bowl.

• Toss beef cubes in flour, shaking off excess, and set aside.

• Heat oil and 2 tbsp (30 mL) butter in a non-stick skillet. Brown beef on all sides over medium-high heat, than place cubes in a baking dish and set aside.

• Add remaining butter to skillet. Add celery, carrots and onion and cook over medium heat 3 to 4 minutes, stirring often with a wooden spoon.

• Add white wine and scrape bottom. Stir in stock and bring to a boil. Pour carrot mixture over beef, cover and bake 40 to 45 minutes or until meat and vegetables are tender. Sprinkle with parsley before serving.

SUGGESTION

Instead of beef, make this dish using skinless cubed chicken.

PORK LOIN WITH GINGER AND MANGO CHUTNEY

4 SERVINGS

1½ lbs	boneless pork loin roast, trimmed of fat	675 g
	MARINADE	
¼ cup	lemon marmalade *or* orange marmalade	50 mL
2 tbsp	sherry	30 mL
2 tbsp	chopped fresh ginger	30 mL
2 tsp	chopped garlic	10 mL
2 tsp	hot mustard	10 mL
2 tsp	light soy sauce	10 mL
2 tsp	sesame oil *or* vegetable oil	10 mL
1 tsp	grated lemon zest	5 mL
	CHUTNEY	
1	mango, peeled and diced	1
½ cup	diced red onion	125 mL
½ cup	diced cucumber	125 mL
2 tbsp	lime juice	30 mL
½ tsp	grated lime zest	2 mL
¼ tsp	ground cumin *or* curry powder	1 mL

• Combine all marinade ingredients in a glass baking dish.

• Place pork in marinade, turning to coat all sides. Cover and refrigerate at least 4 hours, turning the meat from time to time.

• Meanwhile, combine chutney ingredients in a small bowl. Cover and let flavors combine 1 to 2 hours.

• Preheat oven to 350°F (180°C).

• Place pork in a baking dish and roast, uncovered, 1½ to 2 hours, basting from time to time with marinade.

• Let roast stand several minutes before slicing. Serve with mango chutney.

SUGGESTION

Replace the pork roast with two pork fillets, and reduce the roasting time just until done to taste.

SUGGESTION

Instead of using the oven, cook the lamb chops 10 minutes on each side over medium heat in a lightly greased skillet.

LAMB CHOPS MARINATED WITH ROSEMARY

2 SERVINGS

2 tbsp	olive oil *or* vegetable oil	30 mL
2 tsp	grated lemon zest	10 mL
¼ cup	dry red wine	50 mL
2	garlic cloves, finely chopped	2
½ tsp	dried rosemary	2 mL
4 to 6	lean lamb chops	4 to 6
	pepper	
	sprigs of fresh rosemary (to garnish)	

• Combine oil, lemon zest, wine, garlic and rosemary in a dish. Add chops and turn to coat all sides.

• Cover and refrigerate 1½ to 2 hours, turning chops from time to time.

• Preheat oven to 400°F (200°C).

• Remove chops from marinade and arrange in a baking dish. Place on top rack of oven and cook 5 to 6 minutes on each side, or until browned but still pink inside. Sprinkle with pepper before serving. Garnish with fresh rosemary.

MEAT AND EGGPLANT TURNOVERS

4 SERVINGS

½	**eggplant, unpeeled, coarsely chopped**	½
2	**dry French shallots, finely chopped**	2
2	**garlic cloves, chopped**	2
1 tbsp	**butter *or* margarine**	15 mL
5 oz	**lean pork *or* chicken, thinly sliced**	150 g
1	**green pepper, diced**	1
1	**potato, unpeeled, diced**	1
1½ cups	**tomato sauce**	375 mL
1	**pinch curry powder**	1
4 to 5	**filo pastry sheets**	4 to 5
2 to 3 tbsp	**melted butter**	30 to 45 mL
	pepper	

• In a food processor, purée the eggplant, shallots and garlic. Set aside.

• Melt butter in a non-stick skillet. Add meat and cook 2 to 3 minutes, then stir in eggplant mixture.

• Add green pepper, potato, and ½ cup (125 mL) tomato sauce. Simmer about 5 minutes, and season with pepper and curry. Let cool to room temperature.

• Preheat oven to 450°F (230°C).

• Stack 4 to 5 sheets of filo, and baste with melted butter. Cut into 4 equal squares.

• Divide eggplant mixture between filo stacks. Fold over to form turnovers.

• Brush edges with melted butter and seal. Arrange on a baking sheet. Bake 15 minutes or until golden-brown.

• Heat remaining tomato sauce, and pour a little onto 4 heated plates. Arrange a turnover on each.

> SUGGESTION
>
> *You can use just about any cut of pork for this recipe, adjusting the cooking time.*

PORK CHOPS WITH THYME AND HONEY

4 SERVINGS

4	pork chops, about 5 oz (150 g) each	4
2 tbsp	canola oil	30 mL
2 tbsp	lemon juice	30 mL
4 tsp	honey	20 mL
2 tsp	hot mustard	10 mL
1 tsp	dried thyme	5 mL
	salt and pepper	

• Trim fat from pork chops and arrange them in a shallow dish.

• In a bowl, whisk together oil, lemon juice, honey, mustard and thyme. Pour over chops, cover, and let marinate 8 hours refrigerated, turning meat often.

• Preheat oven to 350°F (180°C).

• Drain pork chops (reserving marinade) and arrange in a baking dish. Cook in oven 15 minutes.

• Turn chops and cook another 20 minutes. Baste with marinade from time to time. Season just before serving.

VEAL AND MUSHROOM MEATBALLS

4 SERVINGS

1 tsp	butter *or* margarine	5 mL
1 cup	chopped mushrooms	250 mL
1 cup	chopped fresh spinach	250 mL
1½ lbs	lean ground veal	675 g
1	egg	1
8	crackers, crumbled	8
1	pinch dried sage	1
1	envelope stew seasoning mix, prepared	1
½ cup	buttermilk *or* 10% cream	125 mL
1	bay leaf	1
	pepper	

• Melt butter in a non-stick skillet over high heat, add mushrooms and cook until liquid has completely evaporated.

• Stir in spinach, remove from heat and let cool.

• In a bowl, combine ground veal, egg, cracker crumbs, mushrooms mixture, sage and pepper.

• Shape into balls 1 to 1½ inch (3.5 to 3.5 cm) in diameter and brown them in the skillet over medium-high heat.

• Add stew seasoning prepared according to package directions, buttermilk, and bay leaf. Simmer over low heat 30 to 40 minutes. Serve with steamed potatoes.

VEAL ROLLS WITH PAPRIKA

4 SERVINGS

2	**red peppers**	**2**
1 tbsp	**paprika**	**15 mL**
⅓ cup	**breadcrumbs**	**75 mL**
1 lb	**veal scallopini**	**450 g**
2 tbsp	**teriyaki sauce**	**30 mL**
1	**egg, beaten**	**1**
1 tbsp	**corn oil**	**15 mL**
1 tbsp	**butter *or* margarine**	**15 mL**
¼ cup	**dry white vermouth**	**50 mL**
1½ cups	**vegetable stock**	**375 mL**
1 tsp	**paprika**	**5 mL**
¼ cup	**creamy-style peanut butter**	**50 mL**
1 tbsp	**sour cream**	**15 mL**

• Broil red peppers on all sides until skin blackens, then place in a paper bag 10 minutes to steam.

• Rub off skin, cut in half and seed peppers. Set aside.

• Combine paprika and breadcrumbs in a bowl. Set aside.

• Marinate veal in teriyaki sauce 30 minutes.

• Preheat oven to 350°F (180°C).

• Remove veal from marinade and drain. Dip one side only in egg, then in crumb mixture. Roll veal with crumb side out and set aside.

• Heat oil and butter in a non-stick skillet. Add veal rolls and brown over high heat on all sides 3 to 4 minutes. Place veal rolls in a baking dish and bake another 15 to 20 minutes.

• Meanwhile, cook the red pepper in the same skillet 1 minute, then stir in vermouth. Add vegetable stock, paprika and peanut butter. Cook 5 minutes over high heat.

• Purée peanut butter mixture in food processor, return to skillet, and stir in sour cream.

• Pour sauce onto heated plates and arrange veal rolls on top.

MARITIME STEAK

4 SERVINGS

1 tbsp	butter *or* margarine	15 mL
3	green onions, finely chopped	3
2	kiwis, peeled and diced	2
1 cup	small shrimp *or* imitation crabmeat	250 mL
¼ cup	breadcrumbs	50 mL
2 tbsp	lemon juice	30 mL
2 tbsp	dry white vermouth	30 mL
4	rib eye steaks, 1¼ inch (3 cm) thick	4
1 tbsp	liquid beef stock concentrate	15 mL
	pepper	
	chopped fresh parsley	
	corn oil	

• In a bowl, combine all ingredients except steaks, beef stock concentrate and corn oil. Set aside.

• Cut a deep slit lengthwise in each steak to make a pocket.

• Fill slit with shrimp mixture and fasten shut with toothpicks or wooden skewers.

• Baste steaks with corn oil and cook on oiled, preheated barbecue grill over medium-high heat 10 to 18 minutes, or to taste.

• Baste steaks with beef stock concentrate during cooking.

• Serve with a tomato cucumber salad.

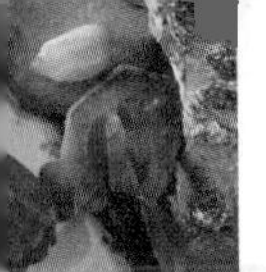

STUFFED VEAL ROLLS

8 SERVINGS

3 tbsp	soft butter	45 mL
12	green olives, pitted and chopped	12
½ cup	finely chopped pine nuts	125 mL
1¼ cups	whole-wheat breadcrumbs	300 mL
8	veal scallopini, well flattened	8
14 oz	can tomatoes	396 mL
1	garlic clove	1
1	pinch chopped fresh parsley	1
⅓ cup	dry red wine	75 mL
	pepper	

• Combine together in a bowl the butter, olives, pine nuts, breadcrumbs and pepper.

• Divide breadcrumb mixture between scallopini, placing it on one end of each veal piece; roll up the scallopini.

• Wrap each veal roll in foil and cook on preheated barbecue grill, with cover closed, 20 minutes, or until veal is tender. Turn rolls halfway through.

• Combine remaining ingredients in a food processor. Strain mixture into a saucepan, and cook over medium heat, stirring constantly, until slightly thickened. Serve sauce with veal rolls, and accompany with rice.

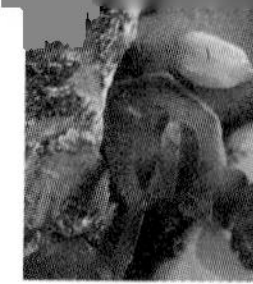

BEEF ROULADE

8 SERVINGS

1 tbsp	butter *or* margarine	15 mL
1 lb	lean ground beef	450 mL
1	onion, sliced	1
¼ cup	catsup	50 mL
¼ tsp	garlic salt	1 mL
¼ tsp	pepper	1 mL
¾ cup	canned condensed cream of asparagus soup (*or* other cream soup)	175 mL
	PASTRY	
2 ¾ cups	all-purpose flour	675 mL
2 tbsp	baking powder	30 mL
½ tsp	salt	2 mL
1 tsp	curry powder	5 mL
⅓ cup + 2 tbsp	vegetable shortening	105 mL
¾ cup	skim milk	175 mL

• Melt butter in a non-stick skillet. Add beef and onion, and cook over medium-high heat until browned.

• Stir in catsup, garlic salt, pepper, and soup. Let cool and set aside.

• Preheat oven to 400°F (200°C).

• In a food processor, mix together the flour, baking powder, salt and curry. Add shortening bit by bit, processing between each addition.

• Gradually add enough milk to make a firm ball of dough. Turn out onto floured board and knead 10 seconds.

• Roll out dough to make a square 12 inches (30 cm) on each side; spread dough with cooled meat mixture. Shape into a roll, and seal edges with a little water.

• Cut roll into 8 slices 1½ inch (3 cm) thick. Arrange slices in a ring on a lightly greased and floured baking sheet, with one slice in the middle.

• Bake 20 to 25 minutes. Serve hot, with tomato sauce if desired.

GYPSY-STYLE RIB ROAST

8 SERVINGS

4 lb	cross-rib roast	1.8 kg
2 tbsp	corn oil	30 mL
1 cup	chopped onion	250 mL
1 cup	chopped carrots	250 mL
1 cup	chopped celery	250 mL
1 cup	chopped parsnips	250 mL
1 cup	unsweetened white grape juice	250 mL
1 cup	beef stock	250 mL
½ cup	chopped ham	125 mL
1 tbsp	cornstarch, dissolved in a little cold water	15 mL
	pepper	

- Preheat oven to 300°F (150°C).
- Wipe off surface of roast and set aside.
- In a large casserole dish, heat oil over medium-high heat. Add roast and brown well on all sides. Remove from pan and set aside.
- Add onion to cooking juices in pan and brown over medium-high heat, stirring often. Add carrots, celery, parsnips, grape juice, beef stock and ham. Bring to a boil.
- Return roast to pan, cover and bake 2½ to 3 hours. Turn halfway through. Remove roast from pan, cover and set aside.
- Skim fat from cooking juices and stir in cornstarch mixture. Cook on stove-top over low heat, stirring constantly, 1 to 2 minutes or until sauce thickens. Season with pepper.
- Serve roast with vegetable sauce.

SUGGESTION

Broccoflower is a hybrid of broccoli and cauliflower. If you cannot find it, use broccoli instead.

LAMB WITH GARLIC AND VEGETABLES

4 SERVINGS

1 cup	thinly sliced carrots	250 mL
1 cup	diced zucchini	250 mL
1 cup	diced turnip	250 mL
1 cup	broccoflower florets	250 mL
1 cup	snow peas	250 mL
1	egg	1
3 tbsp	vegetable oil	45 mL
16	garlic cloves, peeled	16
3 tbsp	breadcrumbs	45 mL
1 cup	vegetable oil	250 mL
2½ tbsp	butter *or* margarine	35 mL
4	pieces lamb loin, 4 oz (120 g) each	4
1 cup	dry white wine	250 mL
1½ tbsp	chopped fresh mixed thyme, rosemary, tarragon, chives, and mint	20 mL
	salt and pepper	

• Cook vegetables individually in a steamer or in boiling salted water, until just tender-crisp. Plunge immediately in ice water to halt cooking; drain and set aside.

• Beat egg with 3 tbsp (45 mL) oil. Dip garlic cloves in egg mixture, then in breadcrumbs.

• Heat remaining vegetable oil in a heavy saucepan. Fry breaded garlic in oil until golden. Drain and keep warm.

• Melt a little butter in a skillet. Add lamb and brown on all sides. Season to taste.

• Remove lamb from skillet and keep warm.

• Skim fat from pan juices, add wine, and stir over medium-high heat, scraping bottom. Add reserved vegetables and chopped herbs, season to taste, and cook another 5 minutes. Dot with remaining butter.

• Arrange vegetables on heated plates. Thinly slice the lamb and arrange on top. Top with deep-fried garlic.

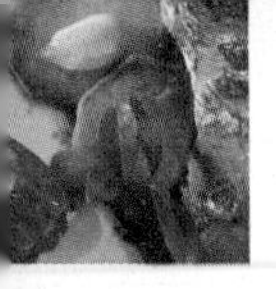

CREAMY VEAL AND MUSHROOMS

4 SERVINGS

6 tbsp	**all-purpose flour**	**90 mL**
1½ lbs	**veal scallopini, cut in thin strips**	**675 g**
6 tbsp	**butter *or* margarine**	**90 mL**
¼ cup	**finely chopped onion**	**50 mL**
⅔ cup	**sliced mushrooms**	**150 mL**
⅓ cup	**dry white wine *or* dry white vermouth**	**75 mL**
½ cup	**whipping cream**	**125 mL**
¼ tsp	**paprika**	**1 mL**
	pepper	
	parsley	

• Combine flour and pepper in a shallow dish. Coat veal strips lightly on both sides.

• Melt 4 tbsp (60 mL) butter in a non-stick skillet. Add veal and cook over medium heat 7 to 10 minutes, turning often.

• Remove veal from skillet and keep warm.

• Melt remaining butter in the skillet and add onions. Cook over medium heat, stirring often with a wooden spoon, until soft. Add mushrooms and cook another 2 minutes, stirring constantly. Add wine and bring to a boil.

• Lower heat and let simmer about 1 minute. Stir in cream, paprika and reserved veal; cook another 4 to 5 minutes.

• Serve on heated plates sprinkled with parsley, with noodles and a vegetable.

MARINATED FLANK STEAK

4 SERVINGS

2 lbs	lean flank steak	900 g
1¼ cups	canned tomatoes, crushed	300 mL
1¼ cups	beef stock	300 mL
¾ cup	dry red wine	175 mL
1	onion, sliced	1
1	garlic clove, thinly sliced	1
1 tbsp	Worcestershire sauce	15 mL
1 tsp	dried thyme	5 mL
1	bay leaf	1
2 tbsp	butter *or* margarine	30 mL
1	envelope pepper sauce mix	1

• Combine all ingredients, except steak, in a glass dish. Arrange steak in mixture and turn to coat well.

• Cover and let marinate refrigerated 12 hours, turning the steak once or twice.

• Preheat broiler.

• Remove meat from marinade. Dry surface with paper towels, then place in a baking pan and cook under the broiler to desired degree of doneness, turning once.

• Meanwhile, pour marinade into a saucepan and cook over medium-high heat until slightly thickened.

• Serve steak thinly sliced across the grain with marinade sauce and julienned carrots.

RABBIT STEW

4 SERVINGS

1 tsp	salt	5 mL
½ cup	all-purpose flour	125 mL
2 lbs	rabbit, cut in serving pieces	900 g
3 tbsp	butter *or* margarine	45 mL
1	slice bacon, cut in strips (optional)	1
1	onion, quartered	1
1	celery stalk, coarsely chopped	1
2	carrots, cut in rings	2
½ cup	marsala wine *or* dry white wine	125 mL
1 cup	chicken stock	250 mL
1	bay leaf	1
3	sprigs fresh oregano *or* thyme	3
	pepper	

• Salt and flour the rabbit pieces.

• Heat butter in a casserole dish or large, heavy saucepan. Add rabbit and brown on all sides over high heat. Remove rabbit from pan and set aside.

• Lower heat and add bacon, onion, celery and carrots. Cook, stirring, 2 to 3 minutes.

• Add marsala and chicken stock.

• Add rabbit pieces, bay leaf and oregano. Season to taste, bring to a boil, then simmer over low heat, covered, 1½ to 2 hours.

SUGGESTION

If you wish, garnish with chopped fresh parsley and sliced stuffed olives or black olives.

ITALIAN-STYLE PORK CHOPS

4 SERVINGS

¼ cup	all-purpose flour	50 mL
½ tsp	dried oregano	2 mL
½ tsp	dried thyme	2 mL
4	lean pork chops, medium thickness	4
1 tbsp	vegetable oil	15 mL
3 tbsp	butter *or* margarine	45 mL
1	envelope vegetable *or* minestrone soup mix	1
2 cups	hot water	500 mL
3 tbsp	grated Sbrinz *or* Parmesan	45 mL
	pepper	

• Preheat oven to 350°F (180°C).

• In a bowl, combine flour, pepper and herbs. Coat each chop with flour mixture.

• Heat oil and butter in a skillet. Cook pork chops over medium heat 8 to 10 minutes, turning halfway through. Arrange chops in a baking pan.

• In a bowl, stir soup mix into hot water; pour over pork chops. Sprinkle with cheese and bake 20 to 30 minutes.

• Serve with noodles, if desired.

STEAK WITH SHALLOTS

4 SERVINGS

4 tbsp	butter *or* margarine	60 mL
6	dry French shallots, finely chopped	6
½	celery stalk, finely chopped	½
1	pinch dried thyme	1
1	bay leaf	1
3 tbsp	chopped fresh parsley	45 mL
1	tomato, chopped	1
1 tsp	tomato paste	5 mL
1½ tbsp	crushed black peppercorns	25 mL
1¼ cups	full-bodied red wine	300 mL
2 tbsp	red wine vinegar	30 mL
1¼ cups	beef stock	300 mL
1	boneless broiling steak of your choice, about 1 lb (450 g)	1
2 tbsp	vegetable oil	30 mL
	pepper	

• Preheat oven to 425°F (220°C).

• Melt 2 tbsp butter (30 mL) in a heavy saucepan. Add ½ of shallots and all the celery, and cook until tender.

• Add herbs, tomato, tomato paste, peppercorns and wine. Cook over medium heat until reduced to ⅓.

• Add vinegar and beef stock. Cook to reduce by ½.

• Strain mixture through a fine sieve. Keep warm.

• Sprinkle steak with pepper.

• Heat 2 tbsp (30 mL) oil in an ovenproof skillet. Brown steak on both sides. Continue cooking in oven until done to taste.

• Melt remaining butter in a small saucepan. Add remaining shallots and cook until soft. Stir into wine sauce.

• Serve steak with shallot sauce, and vegetables of your choice.

OLD-FASHIONED MEATBALLS

4 SERVINGS

1 lb	lean ground beef	450 g
⅓ cup	Italian-flavored breadcrumbs	75 mL
2 tbsp	milk	30 mL
2 tbsp	grated Parmesan	30 mL
1	garlic clove, finely chopped	1
1 tbsp	vegetable oil	15 mL
3 tbsp	butter *or* margarine	45 mL
1	envelope onion soup mix	1
2 cups	hot water	500 mL
	pepper	

• In a bowl, combine beef, breadcrumbs, milk, Parmesan, garlic and pepper. Shape into 16 equal balls.

• Heat oil and butter in a non-stick skillet. Brown meatballs on all sides, turning often. Remove from heat.

• In a bowl, stir soup mix into hot water. Pour mixture over meatballs. Continue cooking 20 minutes over medium heat, stirring from time to time.

• Serve with rice, if desired.

SHABU SHABU

4 SERVINGS

1 lb	thinly sliced beef (fondue beef)	450 g
10 cups	water	2.5 liters
½ lb	transparent rice noodles	225 g
2	pieces konbu seaweed	2
20	mushrooms, cleaned and halved	20
4	leaves Chinese cabbage, coarsely chopped	4
4	medium carrots, cut in thin rings	4
⅓ cup	chopped green onions	75 mL
⅓ cup	grated daikon radish	75 mL
12 oz	tofu, drained and diced	300 g
½ lb	Japanese buckwheat noodles (udon)	225 g

• Keep meat refrigerated until ready to serve.

• Boil 4 cups (1 liter) water and cook rice noodles about 2 minutes; drain, reserving stock. Chop noodles into about 4 inch (10 cm) lengths.

• Wipe seaweed with a damp cloth. Place in a saucepan with 6 cups (1.5 liters) water and bring to a boil. As soon as water reaches a boil, remove seaweed and pour liquid into a fondue pot.

• Arrange beef, vegetables, rice noodles and tofu on a platter or 4 plates.

• Cook buckwheat noodles in stock leftover from rice noodles.

• Heat liquid in fondue pot to boiling. Cook vegetables and beef in liquid, and use it to warm tofu and rice noodles. Serve with buckwheat noodles, sesame seed sauce for beef, and Ponzu sauce for vegetables.

PONZU SAUCE

½ cup	lemon juice	125 mL
½ cup	soy sauce	125 mL
2 tbsp	mirin sauce	30 mL
1	pinch dried bonito flakes	1

• Combine all ingredients. Will keep 2 days refrigerated in a sealed container.

SESAME SEED SAUCE

¾ cup	sesame seeds	175 mL
1 tbsp	miso paste	15 mL
1 tbsp	sugar	15 mL
2 tbsp	soy sauce	30 mL
2 tbsp	rice vinegar	30 mL
6 tbsp	soy sauce	90 mL

• Toast sesame seeds a few minutes in a hot, dry skillet. When golden, remove from heat, let cool, and pound to a paste with a mortar and pestle.

• Combine sesame paste with remaining ingredients in a bowl. Will keep 2 days refrigerated in a sealed container.

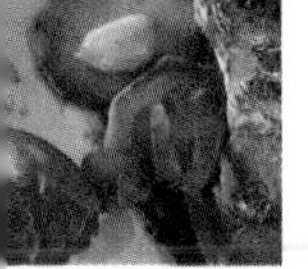

MANDARIN PORK KEBABS

4 SERVINGS

10 oz	pork loin, cut in strips	300 g
2 tbsp	sesame seeds	30 mL
	MARINADE	
3 tbsp	vegetable oil	45 mL
½ tsp	chopped garlic	2 mL
2 tbsp	chopped fresh ginger	30 mL
¼ cup	chopped fresh coriander	50 mL
3 tbsp	soy sauce *or* hoisin sauce	45 mL
3 tbsp	honey	45 mL
	a few shreds of orange zest	
	pepper	

• In a small bowl, combine all marinade ingredients.

• Place meat in marinade, cover, and refrigerate 2 to 3 hours.

• Preheat barbecue grill or oven to 350°F (180°C). Thread pork strips in zig-zag pattern onto presoaked wooden skewers.

• Cook kebabs about 2 minutes on each side, basting often with marinade. Season to taste and sprinkle with sesame seeds just before removing from grill.

• Garnish with orange zest from marinade, and serve with rice and vegetables.

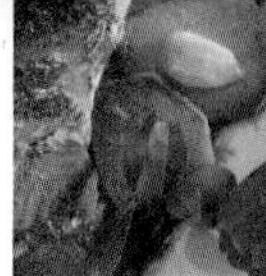

STEWED VEAL WITH PEPPERS

2 SERVINGS

¼ cup	olive oil	50 mL
½	red onion, diced	½
1	garlic clove, finely chopped	1
2 tbsp	all-purpose flour	30 mL
1 lb	lean veal, cubed	450 g
⅓ cup	dry red wine	75 mL
½	envelope brown sauce mix, prepared	½
1 cup	chopped tomatoes	250 mL
1 tsp	dried thyme	5 mL
1	bay leaf	1
½	green pepper, sliced	½
2 tbsp	chopped fresh parsley	30 mL
	pepper	

• Heat 2 tbsp (30 mL) oil in a heavy saucepan or casserole dish. Add onion and garlic and cook 2 to 3 minutes. Set aside in a bowl.

• Lightly flour the veal cubes. Heat remaining oil in the same pan and brown veal on all sides. Put meat in bowl with onion.

• Add wine to pan and cook, scraping bottom, until reduced by half.

• Return meat and onion to pan, add remaining ingredients, and simmer about 1 hour, or until meat falls apart to a fork.

• Serve with potatoes.

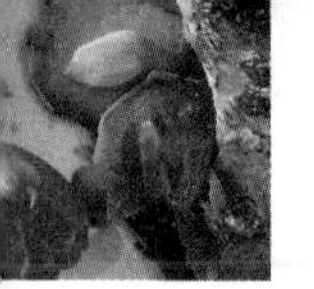

ORIENTAL FONDUE WITH TANGY HONEY SAUCE

4 SERVINGS

1 lb	fondue meat (turkey *or* beef) thinly sliced	450 g
8 oz	mushrooms, cut in strips	225 g
1	carrot, thinly sliced diagonally	1
1 cup	broccoli *or* cauliflower florets	250 mL
1	zucchini, cut in rounds	1
½ cup	commercial concentrated Chinese fondue flavoring	125 mL
4 cups	water	1 liter
	SAUCE	
3 tbsp	honey	45 mL
1½ cups	catsup	375 mL
3 tbsp	white vinegar	45 mL
1 tbsp	chopped chives *or* green onions	15 mL
1 tbsp	finely chopped fresh coriander (optional)	15 mL
1 tbsp	finely chopped fresh parsley	15 mL
2	garlic cloves, finely chopped	2
1	hot pepper, finely chopped	1
½ tsp	curry powder	2 mL
	pepper	

• Combine sauce ingredients in a small bowl.

• Adjust seasoning to taste, pour into a jar with tight-fitting lid, and refrigerate until serving time.

• Arrange meat and vegetables on a platter. Cover and refrigerate.

• Pour fondue flavoring and water into a fondue pot, and bring to a boil.

• Guests spear and cook meat and vegetables with fondue forks. Serve with Tangy Honey Sauce or other dipping sauces.

GRILLED MARINATED SIRLOIN

4 SERVINGS

1	sirloin steak, about 1 lb (450 g)	1
2 tbsp	corn oil	30 mL
1 tbsp	chopped fresh coriander	15 mL
⅓ cup	orange juice	75 mL
1 tbsp	lime juice	15 mL
2 tsp	cider vinegar	10 mL
1 tbsp	liquid beef stock concentrate	15 mL
	orange segments	
	pepper	

- Place steak in a shallow dish.
- Combine oil, coriander, orange juice, lime juice, vinegar, beef concentrate and pepper in a bowl. Pour over steak, cover and refrigerate overnight.
- Let steak stand at room temperature 45 minutes.
- Cook on preheated barbecue grill 5 minutes on each side, basting with marinade. Garnish with orange segments to serve.

VEAL WITH JUNIPER BERRIES

2 SERVINGS

1 lb	veal fillet, sliced crosswise in 1-inch (2.5 cm) thick medallions	450 g
1 tsp	butter *or* margarine	5 mL
2 tsp	corn oil	10 mL
3 tbsp	gin (optional)	45 mL
¾ cup	chicken stock	175 mL
6	juniper berries	6
2 tbsp	whipping cream	30 mL
	pepper	
	chopped fresh parsley	

• Lightly flatten veal medallions with flat edge of a large knife.

• Heat butter and oil in a non-stick skillet. Cook veal 5 minutes on each side over medium-high heat; set aside.

• Pour gin into pan and scrape bottom. Stir in chicken stock, juniper berries and parsley. Cook over medium heat several minutes to reduce slightly, then stir in cream and pepper.

• Pour sauce on heated plates, and arrange veal on top.

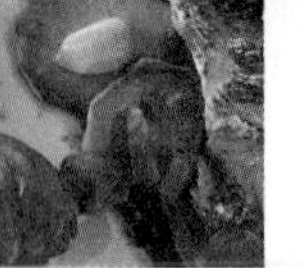

PORK WELLINGTON

2 SERVINGS

2 tbsp	butter *or* margarine	30 mL
⅓ cup	finely chopped onion	75 mL
1½ cups	chopped mushrooms	375 mL
¼ cup	dry white wine	50 mL
¼ cup	15% cream	50 mL
⅓ cup	mild-flavored paté	75 mL
1	pork fillet, about 5 oz (150 g)	1
1	pinch nutmeg	1
1	rectangle puff pastry, about 5 x 8 inches (12 x 20 cm)	1
½ cup	blanched chopped spinach	125 mL
1	egg yolk	1
2 tbsp	milk	30 mL
	pepper	

(Continued on next page)

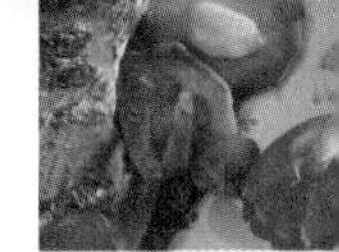

• Heat 1 tbsp (15 mL) butter in a skillet. Brown onion and mushrooms 5 minutes.

• Add wine and cook over low heat until liquid has completely evaporated. Stir in cream and cook until thick. Set aside to cool.

• Add paté to mixture, stirring well.

• Season pork with pepper and nutmeg. Brown on all sides in remaining butter in same skillet over medium-high heat.

• Preheat oven to 400°F (200°C).

• Spread pastry on work surface. Spread center with spinach, then with mushroom mixture. Arrange pork fillet on top.

• Fold pastry around meat, and seal with egg yolk beaten together with milk. Baste entire surface with yolk mixture.

• Arrange pastry package on baking pan. Bake in oven 15 to 20 minutes.

• Slice just before serving, and accompany with a green vegetable and sauce of your choice.

FILLET COOKED IN PASTRY

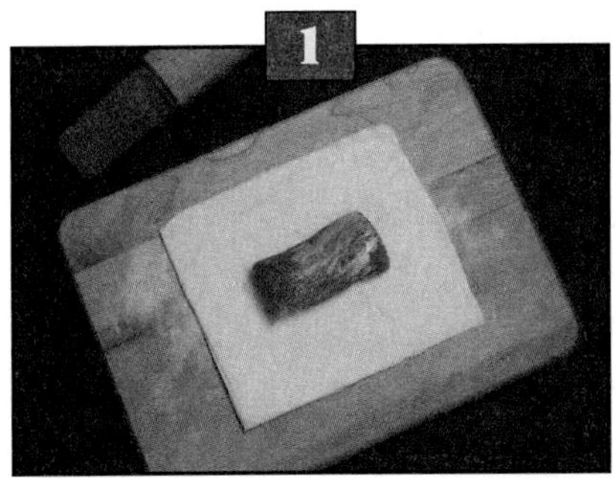

Spread out a rectangle of pastry large enough so that it extends at least 3 inches (7.5 cm) beyond each side of the fillet.

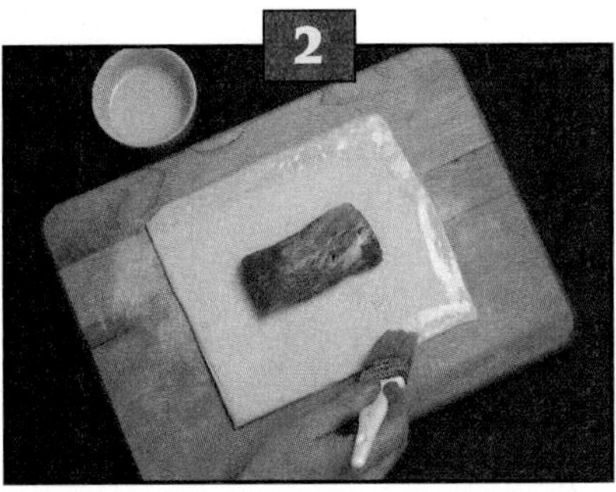

Baste pastry edges with egg yolk and milk mixture to seal.

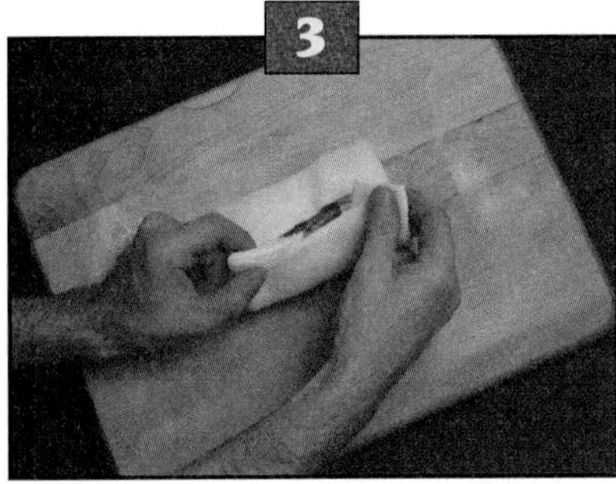

Fold in the pastry ends, then the sides.

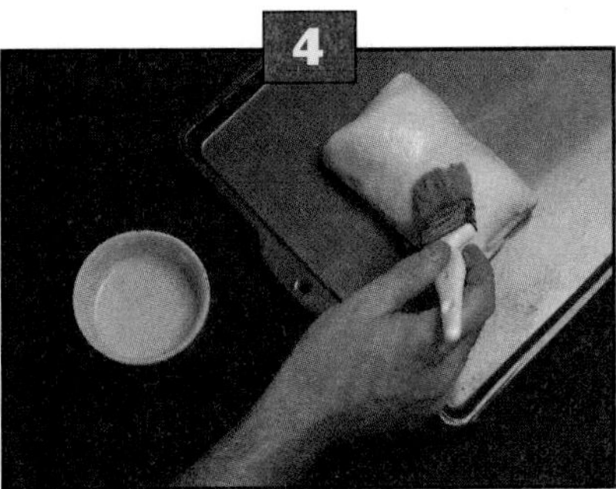

Place pastry on baking sheet and baste with egg yolk mixture.

Fish & SEAFOOD

SUGGESTION

Replace the fresh ginger with 1 tsp (5 mL) ground ginger.

ORIENTAL FISH

6 SERVINGS

2 lbs	turbot *or* other white fish, in thick slices	900 g
	corn oil	
	MARINADE	
3 tbsp	dry white vermouth	45 mL
2 tbsp	light soy sauce *or* tamari	30 mL
2 tbsp	water	30 mL
1 tbsp	grated fresh ginger	15 mL
	SAUCE	
½ cup	plain yogurt	125 mL
5	drops tabasco sauce	5
5	sweet gherkins, chopped	5

Soy sauce and tamari sauce are both high in sodium; 1 tbsp (15 mL) soy sauce contains ½ tsp (2 mL) salt.

• Combine all marinade ingredients in a bowl. Arrange fish in a dish and cover with marinade. Cover with foil and refrigerate at least 2 hours, turning fish twice.

• Preheat oven to 325°F (160°C) and oil a roasting pan, or oil and heat the barbecue grill.

• Bake fish in oven about 4 minutes on each side, or cook on barbecue until flesh is opaque.

• Mix together sauce ingredients and serve with cooked fish.

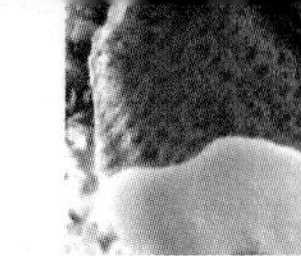

SCALLOPS WRAPPED IN BACON

4 SERVINGS

32	large scallops	32
16	bacon slices	16
1 tsp	oil	5 mL
1 tsp	butter	5 mL
1	large dry French shallot, finely chopped	1
6	Belgian endives, sliced	6
2 cups	whipping cream	500 mL
	juice of 2 lemons	
	salt and pepper	

• Wrap each scallop in ½ slice bacon.

• Heat oil and butter in a skillet. Cook a few scallops at a time over high heat for 2 to 3 minutes or until flesh is opaque through. Remove scallops from skillet and keep warm.

• Cook shallots and endives in same skillet over medium-high heat until tender. Add lemon juice and cook another minute or two.

• Stir in cream, and cook to thicken slightly. Salt and pepper to taste.

• Pour endive sauce onto plates and arrange scallops in a circle on top.

GRILLED GINGER SHRIMP

4 SERVINGS

10	raw medium shrimp, peeled except for tail end and deveined	10
3 tbsp	corn oil	45 mL
3 tbsp	lemon juice	45 mL
½	onion, coarsely chopped	½
2	garlic cloves, finely chopped	2
1 tsp	chopped fresh ginger	5 mL
½	hot green pepper, chopped, *or* ½ tsp (2 mL) dried hot pepper flakes	½
1 tsp	tomato paste	5 mL
	pepper	

• Thread shrimp onto wooden skewers which have been soaked in water.

• In a food processor, combine 2 tbsp (30 mL) oil and all remaining ingredients.

• Baste onion mixture over shrimp, cover, and let marinate in refrigerator at least 1 hour.

• Cook on preheated barbecue grill about 3 minutes, turning once, and basting with remaining oil.

• Serve with rice, lemon wedges and sprigs of fresh mint.

SUGGESTION

When you remove fish from the pan, stir in a few spoonfuls of dry white vermouth to boost the flavor.

SOLE FILLETS WITH CAPERS AND LEMON

4 SERVINGS

4	sole fillets, about 4 oz (120 g) each	4
3 tbsp	all-purpose flour	45 mL
1 tbsp	peanut oil	15 mL
1 tbsp	butter *or* margarine	15 mL
½ cup	chicken stock	125 mL
1	lemon, rind and pith peeled, thinly sliced	1
2 tbsp	capers, drained	30 mL
	pepper	

• Coat sole fillets lightly with flour.

• Heat oil and butter in a non-stick skillet, and cook fillets 3 to 4 minutes on each side.

• Arrange fillets on serving plate and keep warm.

• Pour chicken stock into same skillet. Bring to a boil and add lemon slices and capers. Pepper to taste, and pour over sole. Serve at once.

Fish is a good source of protein, and high in minerals such as phosphorous, iron and zinc.

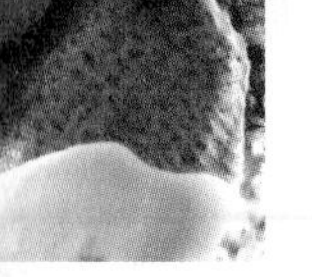

STUFFED SOLE FILLETS

4 SERVINGS

1½ lbs	sole fillets	675 g
½ cup	dry white wine	125 mL
2 tsp	lemon juice	10 mL

STUFFING

½ lb	salmon *or* haddock, deboned	225 g
2	egg whites	2
¼ cup	whipping cream	50 mL
½ cup	breadcrumbs	125 mL
1 tsp	chopped fresh parsley *or* dill	5 mL
	pepper	

(Continued on next page)

ZUCCHINI SAUCE

½ cup	dry white wine	125 mL
2 cups	grated zucchini	500 mL
¼ cup	butter *or* margarine	50 mL
¼ cup	all-purpose flour	50 mL
2 cups	milk	500 mL
2 tsp	dried tarragon	10 mL

- Wipe fillets with paper towel, then trim into even rectangles. Reserve trimmings for stuffing.
- In food processor, purée sole trimmings, salmon and egg whites. Gradually blend in cream, then breadcrumbs, parsley and pepper. Refrigerate 20 minutes.
- Preheat oven to 350°F (180°C).
- Spread puréed mixture over fillets, fold in half and arrange on buttered baking pan. Pour on ½ cup (125 mL) white wine and the lemon juice. Cover with foil and bake 20 minutes.
- To make sauce, in a saucepan, combine ½ cup (125 mL) wine with zucchini. Simmer uncovered over medium heat 5 minutes or until liquid has almost entirely evaporated.
- In a second saucepan, melt butter and stir in flour. Gradually stir in milk and bring to a boil, stirring constantly. Cook 3 minutes, or until sauce is thick and creamy.
- Strain ¼ cup (50 mL) of sole cooking juices and stir into sauce. Stir in tarragon and zucchini mixture. Arrange fillets on serving dish with sauce.

1

Trim fillets into even rectangles.

2

Prepare stuffing in food processor and refrigerate.

3

Spread stuffing over fillets, and fold over. Bake.

4

Prepare the sauce.

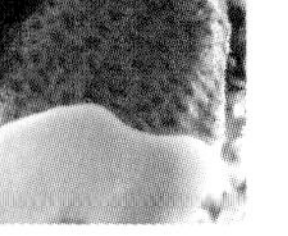

STEAMED SALMON WITH BLACK BEAN SAUCE

2 SERVINGS

3 tbsp	canned black beans	45 mL
2 tbsp	vegetable oil	30 mL
1 tsp	finely chopped garlic	5 mL
½ tsp	salt	2 mL
½ tsp	sugar	2 mL
2 tbsp	oyster sauce	30 mL
1 tbsp	dark soy sauce	15 mL
1	fresh salmon fillet, about 1 lb (450 g)	1
	finely chopped green onions	

Fish is perfectly cooked when a toothpick easily penetrates the flesh.

- Crush black beans well in a bowl.
- Heat oil in a skillet and cook black beans and garlic 2 minutes over medium heat.
- Pour bean mixture into a bowl, and stir in salt, sugar, oyster sauce and soy sauce.
- Rinse fish, pat dry with paper towels, and place flesh side down in a baking dish.
- Spread bean sauce evenly over skin of fish. Steam on a rack over boiling water at high heat about 10 minutes; or bake in preheated oven set at 400°F (200°C) on a rack set in a pan of water until fish flakes.
- Garnish with green onions to serve.

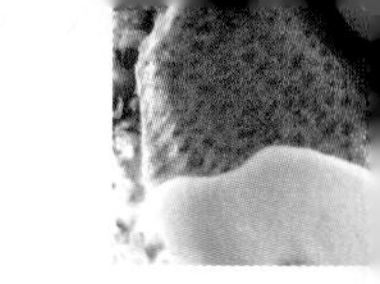

DORADO NIÇOISE

4 SERVINGS

3 tbsp	**corn oil**	**45 mL**
2 to 3 tbsp	**lemon juice**	**30 to 45 mL**
2	**garlic cloves, finely chopped**	**2**
2 lbs	**whole dorado, cleaned and scaled**	**900 g**
6	**sprigs thyme**	**6**

- In a bowl, combine oil, lemon juice and garlic.
- Score fish on both sides.
- Baste fish with oil mixture.
- Place thyme sprigs in fish cavity.
- Bake on oiled, preheated barbecue grill over high heat 15 minutes on each side.

You can judge a fresh fish by its shiny, bright skin, firmly attached to the flesh. The flesh should feel firm and elastic, and not swollen or flabby. There should be no "fishy" odor.

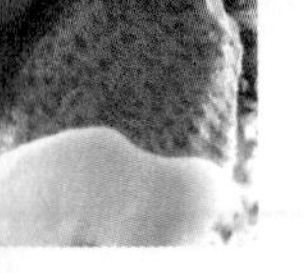

SOLE FILLETS IN BEER

4 SERVINGS

1 tbsp	butter *or* margarine	15 mL
1	onion, chopped	1
4	sole fillets, 3½ oz (100 g) each	4
1 cup	beer	250 mL
1	egg yolk, beaten	1
	pepper	

- Melt butter in a skillet and brown onion 2 minutes, stirring. Turn into a baking dish.
- Arrange sole fillets on top of onion. Pour beer over and let marinate 30 minutes.
- Preheat oven to 350°F (180°C).
- Bake fish in oven 10 minutes. Remove from oven, drain off liquid into the skillet, and set aside.
- Cook fish cooking juices over high heat until reduced by ½. Remove from heat.
- Stir in egg yolk, and heat, without allowing to boil. Pepper the fillets and cover with egg yolk sauce to serve.

(Step-by-step on next page)

1

Melt butter and cook onions, stirring.

2

Arrange fillets over onion in baking dish. Cover with beer and let marinate.

3

Cook fillets, then pour off cooking juice and cook to reduce.

4

Stir in egg yolk and pepper.

LOW-FAT BÉCHAMEL SAUCE

MAKES ¾ CUP (175 ML)

1 tbsp	**oil (*or* butter, if desired)**	**15 mL**
1 tbsp	**all-purpose flour**	**15 mL**
1 cup	**milk, heated**	**250 mL**
¼ tsp	**salt**	**1 mL**
1 tsp	**chopped fresh parsley**	**5 mL**

• Heat oil in a saucepan over low heat. Stir in flour.

• Pour in ½ the heated milk and stir with a whisk. Bring to a boil, whisking constantly.

• Gradually whisk in remaining milk, stirring constantly to avoid lumps.

• Add salt and let simmer 2 minutes over very low heat.

• If the sauce is lumpy, strain before serving (even a smooth sauce can benefit from straining). Stir in parsley.

When made with oil, this béchamel sauce contains ⅓ the fat and ⅛ the cholesterol of a traditional béchamel. You can reduce the fat and cholesterol even further by making it with skim milk; it will still have the same calcium content.

SALMON FILLETS WITH LEEK AND CORIANDER SAUCE

2 SERVINGS

2	fresh salmon fillets, about 5 oz (150 g) each	2
	butter	
	juice of ½ lemon	
	parsley sprigs	
	dill *or* tarragon sprigs	
	SAUCE	
1 tbsp	butter *or* margarine	15 mL
2	dry French shallots, chopped *or* green onions, sliced	2
⅓ cup	dry white vermouth *or* dry white wine	75 mL
½ cup	beef stock *or* chicken stock	125 mL
½ cup	whipping cream	125 mL
1	leek, white part only, cut in julienne	1
2 tbsp	chopped fresh coriander	30 mL
1	pinch cayenne pepper	1

• Preheat oven to 350°F (180°C). Butter 2 baking dishes. Set aside.

• Cut each fillet in half so as to make fillets half as thick; use a very sharp knife so you don't perforate the flesh. Place each thin fillet between 2 sheets of plastic wrap and flatten slightly with the flat edge of a large knife.

• Arrange fish in the buttered baking dishes and sprinkle with lemon juice.

• To make the sauce, melt butter in a skillet. Cook shallots 2 to 3 minutes over medium-high heat. Add vermouth and cook until only about 1 tbsp (15 mL) liquid remains.

• Stir in beef stock; cook to reduce by ⅓. Add cream and cook 1 to 2 minutes. Stir in leek, coriander and cayenne. Let simmer over low heat 3 to 4 minutes.

• Meanwhile, bake salmon in oven 8 to 10 minutes. Pour leek sauce on plates, and arrange salmon on top. Garnish with dill and parsley.

FISH FILLETS WITH TOMATO

4 SERVINGS

1 lb	fish fillets (sole, trout *or* cod)	450 g
2 tbsp	lemon juice	30 mL
1	onion, cut in rings	1
½ cup	vegetable stock	125 mL
1	pinch dried tarragon	1
1 cup	canned tomatoes, chopped	250 mL
¼ cup	grated Emmenthal cheese	50 mL
	pepper	

- Preheat oven to 400°F (200°C).
- Sprinkle fillets with lemon juice and set aside.
- Spread onion rings in bottom of a baking dish; arrange fish on top. Set aside.
- Combine all remaining ingredients, except cheese, in a bowl.
- Pour mixture over fillets. Cover with foil and bake 15 to 20 minutes. A few minutes before end of cooking time, remove foil and sprinkle cheese over fish to brown.

SUGGESTION

Cover the onion layer with a layer of thinly sliced potatoes.

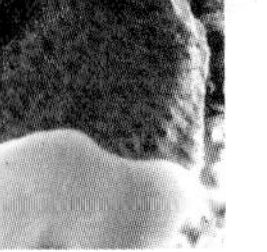

CAJUN CRAB AND SHRIMP STEW

4 SERVINGS

⅓ cup	corn oil	75 mL
¼ cup	all-purpose flour	50 mL
1	onion, finely chopped	1
1 to 2	garlic cloves, finely chopped	1 to 2
1	celery stalk, finely chopped	1
½	green pepper, diced	½
½	red pepper, diced	½
1 cup	finely chopped fresh tomato	250 mL
1 cup	tomato purée	250 mL
1 cup	dry white wine	250 mL
1 cup	fish stock *or* chicken stock	250 mL
3 tbsp	chopped fresh parsley	45 mL
2	bay leaves	2
½ tsp	dried basil	2 mL
½ tsp	dried thyme	2 mL
¼ tsp	fresh grated *or* ground nutmeg	1 mL
½ tsp	Cajun seasoning	2 mL
2 tsp	dark brown sugar	10 mL
2 tbsp	grated lemon zest	30 mL
1 to 2 tsp	cayenne pepper	5 to 10 mL
1 lb	raw medium *or* small shrimp, peeled except tails, and deveined	450 g
1 lb	crabmeat *or* imitation crabmeat	450 g
	salt and pepper	

• In a heavy-bottomed skillet, heat oil over medium-high heat. Add flour, and stir until flour browns slightly.

• Stir in onion, garlic, celery, and peppers. Cook until onion is clear. Add remaining ingredients except shrimp and crabmeat.

• Bring to a boil, stir well and let simmer over low heat 45 to 50 minutes or until a thick sauce-like consistency. Season to taste.

• Add shrimp and crab. Cover and continue cooking 8 to 10 minutes. Stir very gently so that crab does not disintegrate.

• Arrange in a large serving dish. Serve with rice.

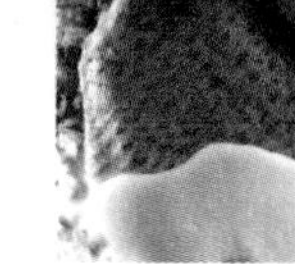

OCEAN PERCH KEBABS WITH MUSTARD

4 SERVINGS

4 or 5	ocean perch fillets	4 or 5
2 tsp	hot mustard	10 mL
1 tbsp	finely chopped fresh tarragon *or* dill	15 mL
2 tbsp	sesame seeds	30 mL
3 tbsp	olive oil	45 mL
	lemon wedges	

• Preheat oven to 375°F (190°C).

• Rinse and pat dry fillets. Baste with mustard and cut into cubes.

• Thread cubes on wooden skewers that have been soaked in water.

• Combine tarragon and sesame seeds in a shallow dish. Baste kebabs with oil, then roll in tarragon mixture.

• Arrange kebabs in a baking dish, and place in oven about 4 inches (10 cm) from the top element. Cook 3 to 4 minutes on each side, turning only once.

• Serve with lemon wedges and a vegetable.

SUGGESTION

Prepare vegetable kebabs with red onions, peppers, zucchini, etc. to serve with the fish.

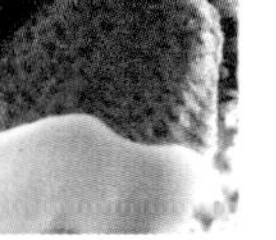

PAELLA NOVA SCOTIA-STYLE

4 TO 6 SERVINGS

8	mussels, cleaned	8
8	clams, cleaned	8
2 lbs	chicken, cut in serving pieces, fat trimmed	900 g
¼ cup	corn oil	50 mL
2	garlic cloves, coarsely chopped	2
1	onion, coarsely chopped	1
1	red pepper, cut in strips	1
2	squid, cleaned, washed, cut in pieces (optional)	2
2 tsp	paprika	10 mL
1 cup	fresh *or* frozen peas	250 mL
2 cups	raw long grain rice	500 mL
4 cups	chicken stock	1 liter
¼ tsp	saffron threads soaked in a little water	1 mL
¼ lb	large cooked shrimp	110 g
	meat of 1 cooked lobster, cut in pieces	
	pepper	

• Cook mussels and clams in a little boiling water until shells open. Drain and set aside, discarding any unopened shells.

• Sprinkle chicken pieces with pepper.

• Heat oil in a large casserole or baking dish and brown chicken in it on all sides. Add garlic, onion, red pepper and squid. Stir well and cook until onion is tender.

• Sprinkle in paprika. Add peas and then slowly pour in rice, stirring. Cook, stirring constantly, until rice is golden.

• In a saucepan, bring chicken stock to a boil. Pour over rice mixture. Add saffron, stir well

(Continued on next page)

and cook over very high heat about 5 minutes.

• Add mussels, clams, shrimp and lobster. Lower heat, cover and cook another 10 minutes, without stirring. The rice should be done when it has absorbed all the liquid.

• Let stand 5 minutes before serving.

1

Cook mussels and clams in a little boiling water until shells open.

2

Add garlic, onion, red pepper and squid to browned chicken.

3

Pour chicken stock over browned rice mixture. Add saffron and cook 5 minutes.

4

Add shellfish. Cover and cook 10 minutes.

SOLE WITH ALMONDS AND SHRIMP SAUCE

4 SERVINGS

4	sole fillets, 4 oz (120 g) each	4
2	eggs	2
1 tsp	water	5 mL
½ cup	all-purpose flour	125 mL
18	soda crackers, crumbled	18
¾ cup	chopped peeled almonds	175 mL
½ tsp	salt	2 mL
1	pinch white pepper	1
2 tbsp	vegetable oil	30 mL
2 tbsp	butter *or* margarine	30 mL
	SAUCE	
2 tbsp	soft butter *or* margarine	30 mL
1	small garlic clove, cut in 3	1
5 oz	raw peeled and deveined shrimp	150 g
¾ cup	water	175 mL
¼ cup	dry white wine	50 mL
2 tbsp	all-purpose flour	30 mL
1 tbsp	chopped fresh dill	15 mL
1 tbsp	lemon juice	15 mL
	pepper	

• To make the sauce, melt 1 tbsp (15 mL) butter in a saucepan. Add garlic and cook 1 minute over high heat. Add shrimp and toss over medium-high heat until pink. Add water and wine.

• Combine remaining butter and flour in a small bowl. Stir into shrimp mixture. Bring to a boil and cook to thicken to sauce consistency. Stir in dill, lemon juice and pepper. Keep warm.

• Pat fillets dry and set aside.

• Beat eggs together with water in a shallow dish. Put flour on a plate. In another dish, combine cracker crumbs, almonds, and salt and pepper.

• Dip fillets on both sides in flour, then in egg, and finally in crumb mixture.

• Heat oil and 2 tbsp (30 mL) butter in a skillet. Brown fillets 3 to 4 minutes on each side over medium-high heat. Arrange on plates with shrimp sauce poured over.

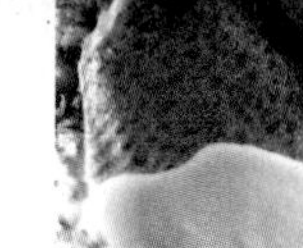

TROUT WITH SORREL AND MUSHROOMS

4 SERVINGS

1 tbsp	butter *or* margarine	15 mL
1	dry French shallot, finely chopped	1
4 cups	chopped mushrooms	1 liter
10	sorrel leaves, blanched, stems removed, chopped	10
½ cup	dry red wine	125 mL
1 cup	sliced green cabbage *or* onions	250 mL
4	medium trout, cleaned and bones removed	4
1 cup	fish stock *or* chicken stock	250 mL
1 cup	heated béchamel sauce (optional, see page 273)	250 mL
	pepper	

- Preheat oven to 375°F (190°C).
- Melt butter in a saucepan. Add shallot and cook over low heat until limp. Add mushrooms, sorrel and red wine. Cook over medium heat until liquid has evaporated. Add pepper, stir well and let cool.
- Arrange cabbage in bottom of a baking dish. Sprinkle fish with pepper and stuff them with mushroom mixture. Arrange on top of cabbage.
- Pour fish stock over. Cover with a sheet of waxed paper. Bake in oven about 15 minutes.
- Arrange braised cabbage on each plate, with a fish on top, garnished with béchamel if desired.

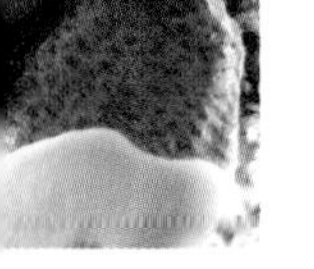

SUGGESTION

You can replace the turbot with any white-fleshed fish, cut in slices about ½ inch (1 cm) wide.

SESAME-BREADED FISH

4 SERVINGS

½ cup	breadcrumbs	125 mL
¼ cup	sesame seeds	50 mL
¼ cup	grated Parmesan cheese	50 mL
1 tbsp	paprika	15 mL
1 lb	turbot, cut in sticks	450 g
1	egg, beaten	1
1 tbsp	corn oil	15 mL
	salt and pepper	

- Preheat oven to 350°F (180°C).
- In a plate, combine breadcrumbs, sesame seeds, Parmesan, paprika, salt and pepper.
- Dip fish pieces in beaten egg, then in crumb mixture.
- Arrange fish on oiled baking sheet. Bake about 5 minutes.
- Turn fish pieces and cook another 5 minutes. Serve hot from oven.

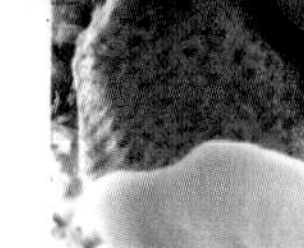

POPEYE SCALLOPS

4 SERVINGS

¾ lb	scallops, cut in half	350 g
1 cup	milk	250 mL
4 tsp	butter *or* margarine	20 mL
1	garlic clove, finely chopped	1
1	green onion, chopped	1
4 tsp	all-purpose flour	20 mL
¼ tsp	salt	1 mL
1	pinch pepper	1
1 tsp	lemon juice	5 mL
10 oz	package fresh spinach, washed and drained	300 g
1 tbsp	corn oil	15 mL
1 tsp	grated lemon zest	5 mL
	chopped green onion	

• Place scallops in a bowl and cover with milk. Cover and refrigerate 8 hours. Drain, reserving the milk.

• Melt butter in a saucepan. Add garlic and green onion and cook 4 minutes over low heat.

• Stir in flour, salt and pepper. Let simmer 2 minutes. Stir in reserved milk. Cook until mixture thickens to sauce consistency. Stir in lemon juice. Set aside.

• Steam spinach 5 minutes. Set aside.

• Heat oil in a skillet and cook scallops over medium-high heat until flesh is white through.

• Arrange spinach on serving plate, with scallops on top. Cover with sauce, and sprinkle with lemon zest and chopped green onion before serving.

Scallops are a good source of calcium, iron and potassium. Fresh scallops should be firm and odorless. They need only a few minutes cooking; overcooked, they become rubbery, dry and flavorless.

SUGGESTION

Steam the salmon in a steamer tray just until the flesh flakes easily with a fork.

SALMON WITH SPINACH

2 SERVINGS

1 tbsp	**butter *or* margarine**	15 mL
4	**boneless salmon slices, about 2 oz (60 g) each**	4
1	**package fresh spinach, washed and dried**	1
1 tbsp	**chopped dry French shallots**	15 mL
2 tbsp	**dry cider *or* dry white vermouth**	30 mL
1 tbsp	**raspberry vinegar**	15 mL
3 tbsp	**cream cheese**	45 mL
2	**lemon wedges**	2
	pepper	

• Heat butter in a non-stick skillet. Add salmon and cook quickly on both sides over medium-high heat. Set aside.

• Meanwhile, steam spinach, drain well and chop. Add pepper and set aside.

• Put shallot, cider and vinegar in the salmon skillet. Bring to a boil. Immediately stir in cream cheese, a little at a time, until consistency of thick sauce.

• Arrange spinach on heated plates, with salmon arranged on top. Cover with sauce, and serve with lemon.

FISH FILLETS WITH ORANGE SAUCE

4 SERVINGS

1 lb	fish fillets (ocean perch, sole *or* haddock)	450 g
1 tsp	julienned orange zest	5 mL
½ cup	unsweetened orange juice	125 mL
1 tbsp	finely chopped onion	15 mL
½	garlic clove, finely chopped	½
1 tbsp	light soy sauce	15 mL
1 tsp	grated fresh ginger	5 mL
1 tsp	cornstarch	5 mL
	chopped fresh parsley	

• Arrange fish fillets in a non-stick skillet.

• In a bowl, combine orange zest and juice, onion, garlic, soy sauce, ginger and parsley. Pour mixture over fish.

• Bring to a boil, lower heat, and let simmer, partially covered, 4 to 5 minutes or until the flesh flakes easily with a fork.

• Lift out the fish with a slotted spatula and arrange on a serving plate. Keep warm.

• Dissolve cornstarch in 1 tbsp (15 mL) water and add to skillet. Heat over low heat, stirring, until sauce-like consistency. Pour sauce on plates, and arrange fillets on top. Garnish with orange zest, if desired.

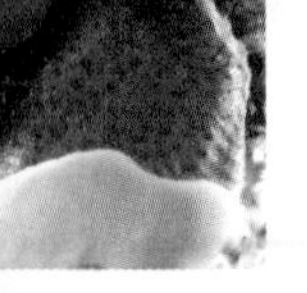

CATHAY FISH KEBABS

4 SERVINGS

1 lb	ocean perch, cod *or* turbot	450 g
1	lime	1
½ cup	dry white wine	125 mL
1 tsp	grated fresh ginger	5 mL
2	garlic cloves, chopped	2
½ tsp	hot red pepper flakes	2 mL
2 tbsp	packed brown sugar	30 mL
1 tbsp	light soy sauce	15 mL
1 tsp	cornstarch	5 mL

• Cut fish in long strips ½ inch (1 cm) wide. Grate the lime zest, then squeeze 3 tbsp (45 mL) lime juice.

• Combine wine, ginger, garlic and red pepper in a deep dish. Add fish and turn to coat. Let marinate 30 minutes at room temperature, or 8 hours covered and refrigerated. Turn fish from time to time.

• Preheat oven to 350°F (180°C).

• Drain fish, reserving marinade.

• Thread fish strips on wooden skewers that have been soaked in water. Arrange on a lightly greased roasting pan. Broil 7 to 8 minutes, about 3 or 4 inches (8 to 10 cm) from the upper element. The fish is cooked when the flesh is opaque through.

• In a saucepan, combine reserved marinade with brown sugar, soy sauce and cornstarch. Stir constantly over medium heat until it comes to a boil. Lower heat and continue cooking until sauce thickens. Serve with fish kebabs.

BARBECUED WHOLE SALMON WITH LIME SAUCE

6 SERVINGS

1	whole salmon, about 3 lbs (1.3 kg)	1
3 tbsp	liquid chicken stock concentrate	45 mL

STUFFING

1	onion, diced	1
2 cups	diced white bread	500 mL
1 cup	diced celery	250 mL
¼ cup	raisins	50 mL
1 tbsp	chopped fresh chives	15 mL
2 tbsp	chopped celery leaves	30 mL
¼ cup	milk	50 mL
	grated zest of 1 lime	

LIME SAUCE

¼ cup	mayonnaise	50 mL
2 tbsp	all-purpose flour	30 mL
1 cup	milk	250 mL
1 tbsp	lime juice	15 mL
1 tbsp	grated lime zest	15 mL
1 tbsp	chopped fresh chives	15 mL
¼ tsp	white pepper	1 mL
1 tbsp	liquid vegetable stock concentrate	15 mL

- Rinse salmon with cold water, pat dry, and set aside.
- Combine all stuffing ingredients in a bowl.
- Stuff salmon with stuffing mixture.
- Arrange salmon on sheet of foil, baste with chicken stock concentrate and seal the package carefully.
- Cook salmon on preheated barbecue grill about 20 minutes, turning once.
- To make the sauce, combine mayonnaise and flour in a saucepan. Heat slowly to boiling, and stir in milk gradually. Cook until smooth sauce consistency.
- Stir in remaining ingredients. Pour sauce on a serving platter and arrange salmon on it.

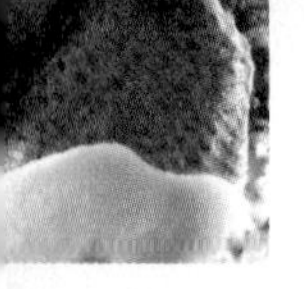

SHRIMP WITH COCONUT MILK

4 SERVINGS

24 to 32	raw medium shrimp	24 to 32
2 tbsp	vegetable oil	30 mL
1	onion, diced	1
1	green pepper, diced	1
4	garlic cloves, sliced	4
2	tomatoes, diced	2
2 tbsp	vegetable oil	30 mL
7 fl oz	coconut milk	200 mL
	freshly ground black and white pepper	
	fresh coriander leaves	
	chopped fresh parsley	
	salt	

- Peel shrimp, and remove the heads.
- Heat vegetable oil in a skillet. Cook onion, green pepper, garlic and tomatoes over medium heat until tender-crisp.
- Add oil, shrimp and coconut milk; let simmer until shrimp are pink.
- Stir in pepper, coriander leaves, parsley and salt. Serve with rice.

MEDITERRANEAN FISH AND TOMATO STEW

2 SERVINGS

2 tsp	olive oil *or* vegetable oil	10 mL
1	onion *or* white part of leek, chopped	1
1 tsp	chopped garlic	5 mL
1	celery stalk, thinly sliced	1
¼ tsp	fennel seed *or* 1 tbsp (15 mL) chopped fresh fennel leaves	1 mL
1	pinch dried hot red pepper flakes	1
14 oz	can tomatoes, chopped, with juice	398 mL
¼ cup	dry white wine *or* chicken stock	50 mL
¾ lb	fresh *or* frozen fish fillets (sole, cod, etc)	350 g
¼ cup	chopped fresh parsley *or* coriander	50 mL
1 tbsp	fresh grated Parmesan cheese	15 mL
	pepper	

SUGGESTION

Serve this dish topped with buttered crumbs and cheese, browned under the broiler. Or serve over couscous, rice or pasta.

- Heat oil over medium heat in a non-stick skillet. Cook onion and garlic 5 minutes or until tender.
- Add celery, fennel, hot pepper, tomatoes and white wine. Bring to a boil.
- Lower heat and let simmer 5 minutes. Add fish and cook until fish is opaque, about 5 minutes if fish is fresh and 10 if frozen.
- Serve in deep plates, garnished with parsley, Parmesan and pepper.

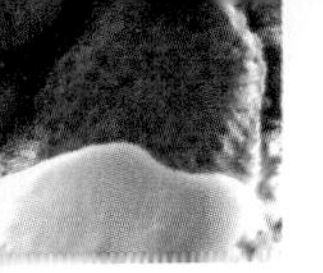

FISH NEWBURG

4 SERVINGS

3 tbsp	butter *or* margarine	45 mL
1 tbsp	canola oil	15 mL
1 lb	fish fillets (sole, cod *or* haddock)	450 g
1	carrot, diced	1
1	onion, chopped	1
1	garlic clove, finely chopped	1
½ cup	dry white wine	125 mL
1	tomato, peeled and diced	1
2 tbsp	tomato paste	30 mL
½ cup	chicken stock	125 mL
1 tbsp	all-purpose flour	15 mL
1 tbsp	lemon juice	15 mL
1 tbsp	chopped fresh parsley	15 mL
	pepper	

• Melt 1 tbsp (15 mL) butter in a skillet. Add oil and heat. Add fish and cook 3 minutes each side over medium-high heat. Set fish aside.

• Melt another tbsp (15 mL) butter in the skillet and add carrot, onion and garlic. Cook until tender.

• Add fish and white wine. Cover and let simmer 5 minutes over low heat.

• Push fish to one side of pan. Stir in tomato, tomato paste and chicken stock. Heat just to a boil. Combine remaining butter with flour. Stir into tomato mixture to thicken. Add lemon juice, parsley, and pepper. Serve with rice.

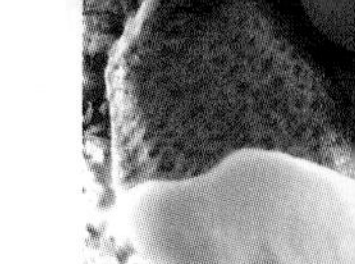

BARBECUED SCALLOPS

2 SERVINGS

10	large fresh scallops	10
1 tbsp	corn oil	15 mL
2 tbsp	lemon juice	30 mL
2 tsp	chopped fresh chives	10 mL
1 tsp	salt	5 mL
1	pinch pepper	1
5	bacon slices	5
½ cup	3-pepper sauce, from packaged envelope, prepared	125 mL
	paprika	

- Place scallops in a bowl.
- Combine oil, lemon juice, chives, salt and pepper in a small bowl. Pour over scallops and let marinate 30 minutes, stirring from time to time.
- Cut bacon slices in half crosswise. Cook in skillet until cooked, but not crisp. Drain on paper towels.
- Heat barbecue grill.
- Remove scallops from marinade. Wrap each in a bacon piece, and fasten with toothpicks.
- Sprinkle scallops with paprika and place on preheated barbecue 4 inches (10 cm) from coals. Cook 3 minutes, baste with reserved marinade, turn, and cook another 4 minutes, or until cooked through.
- Serve with rice and 3-pepper sauce.

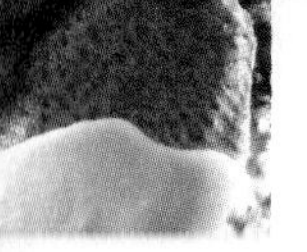

CHEESY FISH FILLETS

4 SERVINGS

4	**fish fillets (sole, cod *or* haddock)**	**4**
4 tsp	**butter *or* margarine**	**20 mL**
1 tsp	**Worcestershire sauce**	**5 mL**
¼ cup	**finely chopped onion**	**50 mL**
3 tbsp	**all-purpose flour**	**45 mL**
1 cup	**milk**	**250 mL**
3 oz	**grated cheddar cheese**	**90 g**
	juice of 1 lemon	

• Preheat oven to 425°F (220°C).

• Pat fillets dry and arrange in a lightly buttered baking dish.

• Combine Worcestershire sauce and lemon juice in a small bowl. Pour over fish and set aside.

• Melt remaining butter in a saucepan. Add onion and cook over medium-high heat until tender. Add flour and cook 1 to 2 minutes, stirring constantly.

• Stir in milk bit by bit and cook over medium heat, stirring, until sauce thickens.

• Remove saucepan from heat. Stir in cheese until sauce is smooth.

• Pour sauce over fish. Bake 10 to 15 minutes or until flesh flakes easily with a fork. Serve with julienned steamed vegetables, if desired.

SUGGESTION

Serve with a crisp green salad dressed with a plain vinaigrette dressing.

FISH AND MUSSEL RAGOUT

4 SERVINGS

1 tbsp	butter *or* margarine	15 mL
2	green onions, chopped	2
1	onion, thinly sliced	1
1	leek, white part only, thinly sliced	1
1 cup	dry white vermouth	250 mL
1	pinch saffron (optional)	1
1	pinch dried thyme	1
2 tsp	coarsely chopped fresh parsley	10 mL
1	bay leaf	1
1	garlic clove, crushed	1
2	potatoes with skin, washed and diced	2
1 cup	chopped tomatoes	250 mL
2 lbs	mussels, cleaned and debearded	900 g
½ lb	small raw shrimp, peeled and deveined	225 g
½ lb	fish fillet, diced	225 g
2 tbsp	whipping cream	30 mL
	pepper	
	juice of ½ lemon	

• Melt butter in a large saucepan. Add onions and leek. Cook over medium heat 2 to 4 minutes.

• Add ¾ of the vermouth. Stir in saffron, thyme, parsley, bay leaf, garlic, potatoes, tomatoes, pepper and lemon juice. Simmer 15 minutes over medium heat.

• Pour remaining vermouth in a saucepan. Add mussels, cover and cook until mussels open. Remove mussels from shells, and reserve their juice. Set aside a few mussels in shells for garnish. Discard any unopened mussels.

• Add mussels with their juice, shrimp and fish to the vegetable mixture. Let simmer 5 minutes over low heat. Stir in cream just before serving. Garnish with whole mussels.

SWORDFISH KEBABS

6 SERVINGS

2 lbs	swordfish, deboned, skin removed, cut in chunks	900 g
2	onions, in chunks	2
18	cherry tomatoes	18
½ cup	olive oil	125 mL
2	garlic cloves, halved	2
½ tsp	freshly ground pepper	2 mL
½ cup	dry white wine	125 mL
1	onion, finely chopped	1
½	envelope chicken à la king seasoning, prepared	½
1 tbsp	paprika	15 mL
½ cup	chopped fresh chives	125 mL
½ cup	chopped fresh parsley	125 mL
	juice of 2 lemons	

• Place fish in a shallow dish and sprinkle with juice of 1 lemon. Cover and refrigerate about 1 hour, turning fish once.

• Preheat the barbecue grill.

• Thread presoaked wooden skewers with swordfish chunks, alternating with onion and tomato. Set aside.

• Combine remaining lemon juice with olive oil, garlic and pepper. Brush kebabs with this mixture.

• Cook on barbecue 10 to 15 minutes, turning often and basting generously with lemon mixture throughout.

• Meanwhile, heat white wine in a saucepan. Add chopped onion, cover, and cook until liquid has evaporated.

• Stir in prepared sauce made according to envelope directions. Add paprika. Mix well and keep hot.

• In a bowl, stir together chives and parsley. Dip brochettes in herb mixture, then pour sauce over. This dish goes well with baked potatoes.

TROUT FILLETS WITH CORIANDER SAUCE

2 SERVINGS

2	trout fillets, bones removed	2
1 tbsp	corn oil	15 mL
	pepper	
	SAUCE	
¼ cup	dry white vermouth	50 mL
1	green onion, chopped	1
½ cup	fish stock *or* chicken stock	125 mL
½ cup	béchamel sauce (see page 273) *or* whipping cream	125 mL
1 tbsp	chopped fresh coriander	15 mL
1 tsp	green peppercorns	5 mL

- Arrange each trout fillet between 2 sheets of plastic wrap. Flatten lightly with flat edge of a large knife.
- Baste fillets with oil and pepper. Set aside.
- Preheat oven to 400°F (200°C).
- To make sauce, in a saucepan, heat vermouth and green onion over medium heat until 1 tbsp (15 mL) liquid remains.
- Add fish stock and cook until liquid is reduced by ½.
- Stir in béchamel, coriander and green peppercorns. Continue cooking until sauce consistency. Keep warm.
- Lightly oil a non-stick baking pan and arrange trout in it. Bake in oven 8 to 10 minutes.
- Pour sauce on heated plates, and arrange fillets on top.

HALIBUT STEAKS WITH DILL

4 TO 6 SERVINGS

4 to 6	dill sprigs, finely chopped	4 to 6
½ cup	mayonnaise	125 mL
3 to 4	halibut steaks	3 to 4
⅓ cup	fine cornmeal	75 mL
	salt and pepper	

• Preheat the barbecue grill.

• In a shallow bowl, combine dill with mayonnaise. Season to taste.

• Spread mayonnaise mixture on both sides of halibut steaks, then dip in cornmeal.

• Cook on oiled grill 10 to 15 minutes, turning only once. Serve garnished with fresh dill.

SAUTÉED SCALLOPS WITH VERMOUTH

2 SERVINGS

¾ lb	scallops	350 g
¼ cup	lemon juice	50 mL
1 tbsp	butter *or* margarine	15 mL
¾ cup	thinly sliced carrots	175 mL
2	garlic cloves, chopped	2
1 cup	sliced mushrooms	250 mL
¾ tsp	chopped fresh thyme	4 mL
2 tsp	cornstarch	10 mL
¼ cup	chopped green onions	50 mL
1 cup	snow peas, blanched	250 mL
¼ cup	dry white vermouth	50 mL

• Arrange scallops in a shallow dish, sprinkle with lemon juice, and let marinate 30 minutes.

• Heat butter in a non-stick skillet. Add carrots and garlic and cook over high heat, turning from time to time, about 3 minutes, or until tender-crisp.

• Add mushrooms and thyme. Cook over medium-high heat, stirring constantly, about 5 minutes. Sprinkle cornstarch over scallops, stir to blend, and pour scallops into the skillet.

• Continue cooking and stirring until scallops are opaque through, about 3 to 5 minutes. Add green onions, snow peas and vermouth. Mix well, remove from heat and serve hot.

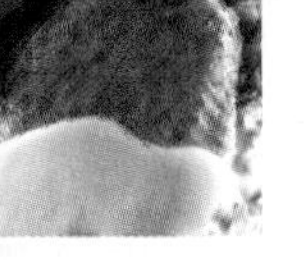

JOHN DORY WITH RED AND YELLOW PEPPER SAUCES

4 SERVINGS

4	John Dory steaks, 5 oz (150 g) each	4
2 tbsp	olive oil	30 mL
	RED SAUCE	
1 tbsp	butter *or* margarine	15 mL
½	red onion, sliced	½
1	fennel stalk, sliced	1
1	red pepper, peeled, seeded, coarsely chopped	1
2 tbsp	rice vinegar	30 mL
½ cup	dry white wine	125 mL
	YELLOW SAUCE	
1 tbsp	butter *or* margarine	15 mL
½	celery stalk, sliced	½
1	yellow pepper, peeled, seeded, coarsely chopped	1
½	mango, coarsely chopped	½
1 cup	pineapple juice	250 mL

• To make the red pepper sauce, melt the butter in a saucepan. Add onion, fennel, and red pepper. Cook over low heat 10 minutes, until limp. Add vinegar and wine. Cook 10 more minutes. Purée in food processor until smooth. Keep warm.

• To make the yellow pepper sauce, melt butter in a saucepan. Add celery, yellow pepper and mango. Cook 10 minutes over low heat. Add pineapple juice. Cook 10 more minutes. Purée in food processor. Keep warm.

• Heat olive oil in a skillet and cook steaks until fish flesh is opaque, about 2 to 3 minutes each side.

• Decorate plates with 2 pepper sauces, and arrange fish on top.

1

Prepare red pepper sauce.

2

Prepare yellow pepper sauce.

3

Heat olive oil and cook fish steaks.

4

Pour sauces on plates side by side, with fish on top.

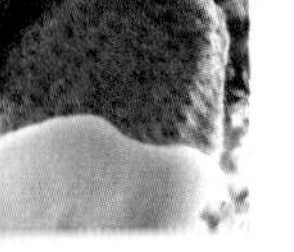

GRILLED MARINATED SALMON

4 SERVINGS

4	salmon steaks, 7 oz (200 g) each, wiped dry	4
	MARINADE	
1	lime, thinly sliced	1
1 tbsp	lime juice	15 mL
2 tbsp	corn oil	30 mL
2	garlic cloves, crushed	2
4	green onions, thinly sliced	4
1	dash tabasco sauce	1
1	bay leaf	1
1	small bunch fresh thyme, chopped	1
	pepper	

• Combine marinade ingredients. Pour over salmon steaks in a shallow dish. Cover and let marinate 2 to 3 hours refrigerated.

• Drain salmon, reserving marinade and lime slices for garnish. Grill steaks in a heavy skillet over medium-high heat a few minutes on each side.

• Baste fish throughout cooking with marinade. Cook just until flesh is barely opaque through; flesh should be soft rather than firm.

• Serve garnished with reserved lime slices.

SUGGESTION

Replace the lime with lemon or orange for a completely different flavor.

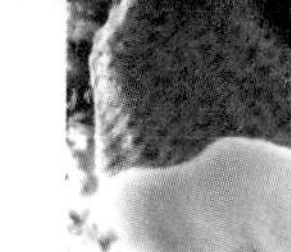

MEDITERRANEAN SHRIMP KEBABS

4 SERVINGS

2 tbsp	**canola oil**	**30 mL**
4 tbsp	**lemon juice**	**60 mL**
½ cup	**fine breadcrumbs**	**125 mL**
1 lb	**raw medium shrimp, peeled and deveined**	**450 g**
2	**garlic cloves, finely chopped**	**2**
2 tsp	**finely chopped fresh parsley**	**10 mL**
	pepper	

• In a bowl, combine oil, lemon juice and breadcrumbs to make a paste. Place shrimp in this mixture.

• Add garlic, parsley and pepper. Mix well. Let marinate 20 minutes refrigerated.

• Preheat barbecue grill.

• Thread shrimp lengthwise on skewers. Cook over high heat 3 minutes. Turn and cook 2 more minutes. Serve with rice and grilled peppers, if desired.

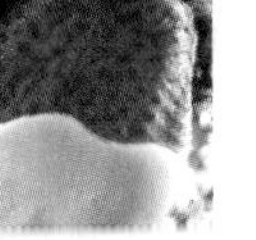

SEAFOOD PROVENÇALE

4 SERVINGS

1	medium onion, in rings	1
1	green pepper, in strips	1
1	garlic clove, finely chopped	1
1	bay leaf	1
2	fresh ripe tomatoes, chopped	2
4	pieces fish, your choice	4
1	cooked lobster, shelled and in pieces	1
10	clams, cleaned (see suggestion)	10
10	mussels	10
6	medium squid, cleaned and cut in pieces	6
¾ cup	dry white wine	175 mL
	olive *or* vegetable oil	
	salt and pepper	

• Preheat oven to 400°F (200°C).

• Pour a little oil in a skillet and cook onion, pepper and garlic over medium-high heat until soft. Add bay leaf and tomatoes. Let simmer a few minutes.

• Add fish and seafood. Cook over medium heat 2 to 3 minutes. Stir in wine, salt and pepper and cook 1 to 2 minutes.

• Pour mixture into baking dish, cover and bake 30 minutes.

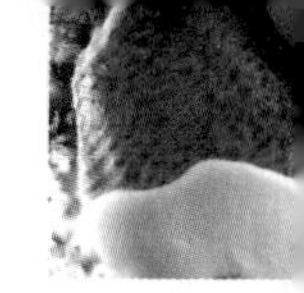

SUGGESTION

Soak the clams a few minutes in warm water so that they open and any sand inside is rinsed out.

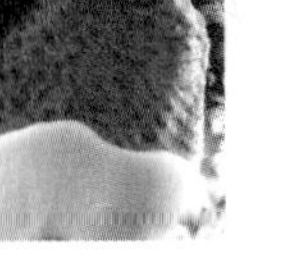

OLD-FASHIONED SALMON LOAF

4 SERVINGS

1	egg	1
½ cup	milk	125 mL
1 cup	fresh whole-wheat breadcrumbs	250 mL
15 oz	can salmon, drained and flaked	425 g
1 tbsp	melted butter *or* margarine	15 mL
¼ cup	finely chopped onion	50 mL
	pepper	
	SAUCE	
2 tbsp	butter *or* margarine	30 mL
2 tbsp	all-purpose flour	30 mL
¼ tsp	dry mustard	1 mL
1¼ cups	milk	300 mL
1 tsp	Worcestershire sauce	5 mL

• Preheat oven to 350°F (180°C).

• In a bowl, lightly beat egg with milk. Stir in breadcrumbs. Set aside.

• In a second bowl, combine salmon, melted butter, onion and pepper. Stir in egg mixture.

• Pour salmon mixture in a lightly greased loaf pan. Place pan in center of oven and bake 35 to 40 minutes.

• Meanwhile, make the sauce. Melt butter in a saucepan over medium heat. Stir in flour bit by bit, then mustard.

• Add milk and Worcestershire. Cook over medium heat, stirring constantly, until thickened and smooth.

• To serve, unmold salmon loaf onto a serving plate and pour sauce over.

SUGGESTION

If you wish, add to the salmon mixture some finely chopped shrimp and/or chopped stuffed olives.

SMOKED TROUT FILLETS WITH HORSERADISH SAUCE

2 SERVINGS

2	smoked trout fillets, 3½ oz (100 g) each	2
1 tbsp	plain yogurt	15 mL
1	pinch mixed dried herbs	1
1 to 2 tsp	prepared horseradish	5 to 10 mL
1	medium tomato, halved	1
6	onion rings	6
2	lemon slices	2
1 tbsp	capers	15 mL
2	slices toasted whole-wheat bread	2

• Cut the trout fillets in strips and arrange on plates.

• In a bowl, combine yogurt with herbs and horseradish.

• Decorate tomato halves with horseradish mixture and arrange alongside trout. Serve with onion rings, lemon, capers and toast.

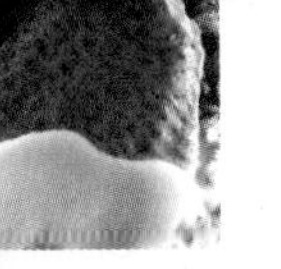

INDIAN-STYLE FISH

4 SERVINGS

4 tbsp	**all-purpose flour, sifted**	**60 mL**
2 tsp	**curry powder**	**10 mL**
4	**fish fillets**	**4**
2 tbsp	**vegetable oil**	**30 mL**
3 tbsp	**butter *or* margarine**	**45 mL**
⅓ cup	**slivered almonds**	**75 mL**
2 tbsp	**sultana raisins**	**30 mL**
2 tbsp	**grated unsweetened coconut**	**30 mL**
1 tbsp	**finely chopped fresh chives**	**15 mL**
	pepper	

• In a bowl, combine flour, pepper and curry powder; lightly coat fish in flour mixture.

• Heat oil and 2 tbsp (30 mL) butter in a non-stick skillet. Cook fish fillets over medium heat 4 to 5 minutes each side.

• Remove fish from pan and keep warm on a serving plate.

• Melt remaining butter in the skillet and cook almonds, raisins and coconut 2 to 3 minutes, stirring constantly with a wooden spoon.

• Garnish fish with coconut mixture and chopped chives.

SCALLOP STIR-FRY

4 SERVINGS

SAUCE

¼ cup	dry white wine	50 mL
¼ cup	cold water	50 mL
2 tbsp	light soy sauce	30 mL
1 tbsp	cornstarch	15 mL

STIR-FRY

1 tsp	grated fresh ginger	5 mL
¾ lb	fresh asparagus, cut diagonally	350 g
1 to 2 tsp	corn oil	5 to 10 mL
1 cup	finely chopped mushrooms	250 mL
1 lb	coarsely chopped scallops	450 g

• Combine sauce ingredients in a bowl. Set aside.

• Lightly oil a non-stick skillet and heat over medium heat. Stir-fry ginger 15 seconds. Add asparagus and cook 4 minutes.

• Stir in corn oil 1 spoonful at a time, then add mushrooms. Cook 1 to 2 minutes or until asparagus is tender-crisp. Remove vegetables from pan and set aside.

• Cook ½ the scallops in the hot pan 3 minutes. Remove and keep warm. Cook remaining scallops and keep warm.

• Pour reserved sauce into pan and cook, stirring, until thickened. Continue cooking 1 minute over medium-low heat.

• Return vegetables and scallops to skillet and cook 1 minute, stirring. Serve with rice if desired.

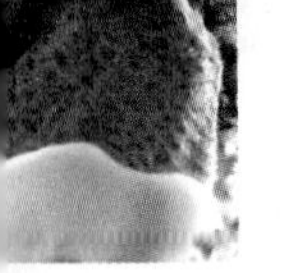

SUGGESTION

You can replace the fish with boneless chicken breast, if desired.

HALIBUT CHINESE-STYLE

4 SERVINGS

2 to 3	halibut fillets, in strips 3 inches (7.5 cm) long	2 to 3
¼ cup	all-purpose flour	50 mL
	BREADING	
2	eggs	2
¼ tsp	cayenne pepper	1 mL
1 tsp	soy sauce	5 mL
½ cup	breadcrumbs	125 mL
⅓ cup	sesame seeds	75 mL
½ cup	corn oil	125 mL
	pepper	
	VEGETABLES	
2 tbsp	corn oil	30 mL
1	large onion, cut in rings	1
1	garlic clove, finely chopped	1
½	red *or* green pepper, in strips	½
½	broccoli, in florets	½
12	mushrooms, sliced	12
2 cups	bean sprouts	500 mL
½ tsp	finely chopped fresh ginger	2 mL
2	tomatoes, fresh *or* canned, peeled, coarsely chopped	2
½ tsp	cornstarch, dissolved in a little water *or* stock	2 mL
2 tbsp	dry sherry (optional)	30 mL
1 tbsp	soy sauce	15 mL
2 tbsp	sesame oil	30 mL
½ cup	chicken stock	125 mL
1	pinch sugar	1
	pepper	

(Continued on next page)

• Coat fish strips with flour.

• In a bowl, beat eggs together with pepper, cayenne and 1 tsp (5 mL) soy sauce.

• Dip fish in egg mixture and drain.

• Combine breadcrumbs and sesame seeds on a plate. Coat fish on both sides in crumb mixture. Shake off excess.

• Heat ½ cup (125 mL) oil in a non-stick skillet over medium-high heat. Brown fish on both sides. Arrange fish on a baking sheet covered with waxed paper and keep warm in oven, with oven door ajar.

• Heat remaining 2 tbsp (30 mL) oil in clean non-stick skillet and stir-fry onion, garlic and pepper, stirring constantly.

• Add broccoli, mushrooms, bean sprouts and ginger. Stir-fry 3 to 4 minutes. Stir in tomatoes.

• Combine remaining ingredients in a bowl. Add to vegetables and cook over low heat until sauce thickens slightly.

• Arrange vegetable mixture on plates, topped with fish.

DORADO IN SALT

2 SERVINGS

1	**dorado, about 2 lbs (900 g)**	**1**
4 lbs	**coarse salt**	**1.8 kg**

• Preheat oven to 400°F (200°C).

• Gut and clean the fish, but leave scales on.

• Cover the bottom of a baking dish with a layer of salt. Place dorado on salt. Cover fish completely with salt. Moisten top of salt with a little water.

• Bake 40 minutes. Remove pan from oven and break open salt crust to serve.

GRILLED SALMON WITH PINK GRAPEFRUIT DRESSING

4 SERVINGS

¼ cup	**raspberry vinegary *or* other vinegar**	50 mL
2 tbsp	**light soy sauce**	30 mL
2 tbsp	**olive oil**	30 mL
1 tbsp	**grated fresh ginger**	15 mL
1 tsp	**ground cinnamon**	5 mL
¼ tsp	**tabasco sauce**	1 mL
1 tsp	**pink peppercorns**	5 mL
2 tbsp	**chopped fresh coriander**	30 mL
1	**pink grapefruit, segmented**	1
1	**orange, segmented**	1
2	**lemons, segmented**	2
4	**salmon fillets, 3½ oz (100 g) each**	4
4	**lettuce leaves**	4
	black pepper	

• Combine vinegar and soy sauce in a bowl. Stir in oil, ginger, cinnamon, tabasco, pink peppercorns, coriander and pepper.

• Put fruit segments and salmon in this marinade. Coat well. Cover and let marinate 1 to 2 hours, refrigerated.

• Remove fruit segments and salmon from marinade. Grill salmon on preheated barbecue grill until done to taste.

• Arrange on lettuce leaves, and garnish with fruit segments.

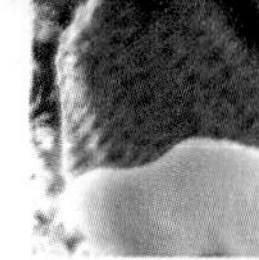

SCALLOP TIAN

4 SERVINGS

1 lb	fresh scallops	450 g
2 tbsp	butter	30 mL
1 lb	fresh spinach, washed and drained	450 g
½ lb	mushrooms, sliced	225 g
1 tbsp	olive oil	15 mL
1	onion, finely chopped	1
1 lb	tomatoes, peeled, coarsely chopped	450 g
1	garlic clove, finely chopped	1
	salt and pepper	
	lemon juice	

• Trim the scallops and slice in half widthwise. Season with salt, pepper and lemon juice. Set aside.

• Melt 1 tbsp (15 mL) butter in a saucepan. Add spinach and cook, stirring occasionally, until wilted. Season to taste and keep warm.

• Melt remaining butter in the saucepan. Cook mushrooms until their juices evaporate. Set aside.

• Heat oil in a non-stick skillet. Add onion and cook over low heat 2 minutes.

• Stir in tomatoes and garlic. Season to taste and cook uncovered 30 minutes. Keep warm.

• Steam scallops in a steamer about 1 minute.

• To serve, layer the spinach, tomatoes, and mushrooms. Top with scallops, and sprinkle with a little lemon juice.

Vegetables

ROMAN BROCCOLI

4 SERVINGS

2 lbs	**broccoli, broken into florets**	**900 g**
1	**hard-boiled egg**	**1**
¼ cup	**olive oil**	**50 mL**
2 tbsp	**lemon juice**	**30 mL**
2 tbsp	**chopped fresh chives**	**30 mL**
1 tbsp	**chopped fresh parsley**	**15 mL**
1 tbsp	**chopped fresh tarragon**	**15 mL**

Broccoli is a good source of fiber and calcium.

• Cook broccoli 10 minutes in a saucepan full of boiling salted water. Drain.

• Cut egg in half and spoon out yolk.

• In food processor, mix yolk with olive oil, lemon juice and herbs until smooth. Pour over warm broccoli and serve.

STIR-FRIED VEGETABLES

6 SERVINGS

1 tbsp	sesame seeds	15 mL
1 tbsp	vegetable oil	15 mL
1	onion, sliced	1
1	broccoli, in small florets	1
1	red *or* green pepper, sliced	1
1 cup	quartered mushrooms	250 mL
1 tsp	sesame oil (optional)	5 mL
2	garlic cloves, finely chopped	2
1 tsp	finely chopped fresh ginger	5 mL
½ cup	chicken stock	125 mL
2 tsp	cornstarch	10 mL
1 tsp	light soy sauce	5 mL

• Spread sesame seeds in a baking pan and toast in oven at 350°F (180°C) a few minutes, stirring from time to time, until golden. Set aside.

• Heat vegetable oil in a wok or large skillet. Add onion, broccoli, pepper and mushrooms and stir-fry over high heat 1 to 2 minutes.

• Sprinkle in sesame oil, garlic and ginger. Stir in chicken stock, cover and let cook until broccoli is tender-crisp.

• Dissolve cornstarch in a little chicken stock or water, and add soy sauce.

• Stir mixture into vegetables when they are tender-crisp. Remove vegetables from pan as soon as they are glossy.

• Serve sprinkled with toasted sesame seeds.

SUGGESTION

You can toast the sesame seeds in the wok, stirring without added oil, before you begin the recipe.

SPINACH-STUFFED POTATOES

4 SERVINGS

1	**10 oz (280 g) package fresh spinach, washed and stemmed**	1
¼ cup	**butter *or* margarine**	50 mL
1	**medium onion, finely chopped**	1
½ cup	**finely chopped mushrooms**	125 mL
1	**pinch nutmeg**	1
¼ tsp	**pepper**	1 mL
4	**large baking potatoes, with skin, baked**	4
⅓ cup	**plain yogurt**	75 mL
⅓ cup	**light mayonnaise**	75 mL
2 tbsp	**diced ham *or* crumbled bacon**	30 mL
2 tbsp	**melted butter *or* margarine**	30 mL
½ cup	**breadcrumbs**	125 mL
¼ cup	**slivered almonds**	50 mL

• Preheat oven to 400°F (200°C).

• Steam spinach just until soft. Drain, squeeze dry and chop finely. Set aside.

• Melt butter in a large skillet. Cook onion over medium heat 2 minutes. Add mushrooms, nutmeg and pepper. Cook over low heat 3 to 4 minutes. Stir in spinach and set aside.

• Cut a slice off the top of each potato. Spoon out potato flesh, leaving a shell about ¼ inch (0.5 cm) thick.

• Mash potato flesh. Stir in spinach mixture, yogurt, mayonnaise and ham. Add salt and pepper to taste.

• With a spoon, stuff spinach mixture into potato shells. Arrange on a baking sheet.

• In a bowl, combine melted butter, breadcrumbs and almonds. Sprinkle evenly over tops of potatoes. Bake 15 to 20 minutes or until topping is crisp.

VEGETABLE COUSCOUS

4 SERVINGS

8	**cups chicken stock, heated**	**2 L**
5 cups	**quick-cooking couscous**	**1.25 liters**
⅓ cup	**butter**	**75 mL**
2	**large onions, finely chopped**	**2**
2	**garlic cloves, finely chopped**	**2**
3	**carrots, diced**	**3**
½ cup	**water**	**125 mL**
19 oz	**can chickpeas, rinsed and drained**	**540 mL**
19 oz	**can red kidney beans, rinsed and drained**	**540 mL**
½ cup	**chopped pistachios *or* almonds**	**125 mL**
¼ cup	**coarsely chopped fresh parsley**	**50 mL**
	pepper	

• In a large bowl, combine heated chicken stock and couscous. Cover and let stand 10 minutes.

• Stir gently with a fork to prevent lumping. Set aside.

• Melt butter in a large saucepan. Add onions and garlic, and cook over medium heat 5 to 6 minutes.

• Add carrots and water. Cover and cook 5 to 6 minutes. Stir in chickpeas and beans. Lower heat and let simmer 5 minutes.

• Add reserved couscous, pistachios, parsley and pepper to taste. Serve with hot pepper sauce, if desired.

Most dried beans need to be soaked 12 hours in double their volume of cold water before cooking.

SUGGESTION

Arrange couscous on a bed of Romaine lettuce.

Garnish with lemon wedges.

ZUCCHINI WITH CORIANDER

4 SERVINGS

⅔ cup	chicken stock	150 mL
2	garlic cloves, crushed	2
3 tbsp	corn oil	45 mL
2 tbsp	tomato paste	30 mL
2 tbsp	chopped fresh coriander	30 mL
½ tsp	ground cumin	2 mL
2 lbs	zucchini, washed and cut up	900 g
1	lemon	1
	pepper	

• In a saucepan, combine chicken stock, garlic, oil, tomato paste, coriander, cumin and pepper. Boil for 15 minutes.

• Add zucchini and cook about 35 minutes. Drain, reserving cooking liquid.

• Put zucchini in heated serving dish. Pour a little of the cooking liquid over. Sprinkle with lemon juice. Serve hot, garnished with coriander leaves.

HUNTER-STYLE POTATO ROESTI

4 SERVINGS

2 lbs	potatoes, peeled	900 g
2 tbsp	butter *or* margarine	30 mL
2 tbsp	corn oil	30 mL
1	onion, finely chopped	1
2 cups	sliced mushrooms	500 mL
3 oz	ham cut in small strips	90 g
1	pinch dried thyme	1
	salt and pepper	

• Parboil the potatoes. Drain well, grate coarsely, and drain again if necessary.

• Heat butter and oil in a non-stick skillet. Cook onion, mushrooms and ham over medium-high heat until onion is transluscent.

• Add potatoes, thyme, salt and pepper. Cook to brown potatoes on all sides, stirring often with a metal spatula.

• When nearly done, flatten into a cake and cook until bottom is crisp and brown.

• Hold a plate firmly over skillet, then turn potatoes upside-down onto plate. Slide back into skillet to brown other side.

• Serve from a heated serving plate.

SUGGESTION

This recipe is marvelous for breakfast served with eggs.

TOFU AND SESAME VEGETABLES

4 SERVINGS

8 oz	**tofu**	**225 g**
¼ cup	**light soy sauce**	**50 mL**
2 tbsp	**dry sherry *or* marsala**	**30 mL**
1	**garlic clove, chopped**	**1**
6	**green onions**	**6**
1 tbsp	**butter *or* margarine**	**15 mL**
1 tbsp	**sesame oil**	**15 mL**
1½ cups	**broccoli florets**	**375 mL**
1 cup	**thinly sliced carrots**	**250 mL**
10	**mushrooms, thickly sliced**	**10**
1 tbsp	**shredded fresh ginger**	**15 mL**
2 cups	**cooked vermicelli noodles**	**500 mL**
2 tbsp	**sesame seeds**	**30 mL**

• Slice tofu ¾ inch (2 cm) thick and drain well.

• In a bowl, combine soy sauce, sherry and garlic. Pour over tofu. Let marinate 10 minutes. Drain, reserving 2 tbsp (30 ml) of the marinade.

• Line a baking pan with paper towels and arrange tofu on it. Cover with 2 thicknesses of paper towel, then a second baking pan. Press down to squeeze out liquid. Cut slices into strips ½ inch (1 cm) wide. Place in a bowl.

• Thinly slice white part of green onions.

• Heat butter and sesame oil in a wok or large skillet. Cook white part of onions until limp. Add broccoli and carrots. Stir-fry 2 to 3 minutes. Add mushrooms and ginger. Stir-fry another minute or 2.

(Continued on next page)

1 Prepare marinade, pour over tofu and let marinate.

2 Press the tofu.

3 Cook whites of green onion in butter and oil. Add vegetables.

4 Cook onion greens and tofu. Stir in vermicelli, marinade and sesame seeds.

• Slice green part of onions on the diagonal. Add to vegetables along with tofu. Stir-fry 2 minutes. Add cooked vermicelli, reserved marinade and sesame seeds. Stir gently and heat through before serving.

MUSHROOM FRICASSEE

4 SERVINGS

2 lbs	**mushrooms, sliced**	**900 g**
2 tbsp	**butter *or* margarine**	**30 mL**
3	**dry French shallots, chopped**	**3**
1 tbsp	**chopped fresh chives**	**15 mL**
	pepper	

• Cook mushrooms 4 minutes over medium heat in a non-stick skillet without butter. Drain cooking liquid into a bowl. Set aside mushrooms in a second bowl.

• Melt butter in the same skillet. Cook mushrooms in butter 10 minutes over medium heat.

• Add shallots and pepper. Cook 3 more minutes.

• Add mushroom juices, sprinkle with chives, and serve with a baked filo square, if desired.

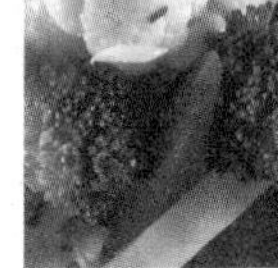

SPINACH AU GRATIN

4 SERVINGS

⅓ cup	grated gruyère cheese	75 mL
2	eggs	2
½ cup	milk	125 mL
½ cup	whipping cream *or* buttermilk	125 mL
4	packages fresh spinach, washed and drained	4
	nutmeg	
	pepper	

- Preheat oven to 400°F (200°C).
- In food processor, combine ½ the cheese with the eggs, milk, cream, a little nutmeg, and pepper until smooth.
- Turn to slow speed and add spinach. Process until spinach is coarsely chopped.
- Butter a gratin dish. Pour in spinach mixture, smoothing surface. Sprinkle with remaining cheese. Bake 25 to 30 minutes. Serve very hot.

Look for spinach that is a good dark green. Remove any yellowed, blotchy, mushy or soft leaves. Spinach should not be left to soak in water, and should be washed only just before using to preserve its color.

SUGGESTION

Stir some diced cooked ham into the chopped spinach mixture before baking.

POTATOES FLORENTINE

4 SERVINGS

8	potatoes, scrubbed	8
1½ tbsp	butter *or* margarine	25 mL
2 cups	sliced fresh mushrooms	500 mL
¾ cup	finely chopped onion	175 mL
1	garlic clove, finely chopped	1
2 cups	chopped fresh spinach, washed and drained	500 mL
4	egg whites, lightly beaten	4
2	pinches ground nutmeg	2
½ cup	Italian *or* plain breadcrumbs	125 mL
	pepper	
	paprika	

• Preheat oven to 400°F (200°C).

• Bake potatoes in oven about 45 minutes.

• Melt butter in a non-stick skillet. Cook mushrooms, onion and garlic over medium-high heat until limp.

• Add spinach and cook another 3 to 4 minutes. Set aside.

• Cut potatoes in half, and spoon out flesh, leaving a thin shell. Set aside.

• Mash potato flesh and stir in mushroom mixture, beaten egg whites, pepper and nutmeg.

• Fill potato shells with spinach mixture. Sprinkle with breadcrumbs and paprika. Return to oven for 15 to 20 minutes to brown before serving.

BEAN SALAD BURRITOS

4 TO 6 SERVINGS

¼ cup	canola oil	50 mL
⅔ cup	white vinegar *or* dry white wine	150 mL
½ cup	sugar	125 mL
¼ tsp	pepper	1 mL
2 tbsp	chopped fresh parsley	30 mL
1 tbsp	Worcestershire sauce	15 mL
2 cups	cooked drained chickpeas	500 mL
2 cups	cooked drained red kidney beans	500 mL
1 cup	thinly sliced celery	250 mL
¼ cup	finely chopped onion	50 mL
4 to 6	flour tortillas	4 to 6

- In a large bowl, combine oil, vinegar, sugar, pepper, parsley amd Worcestershire sauce.
- Add chickpeas, beans, celery and onion. Let marinate overnight in refrigerator, covered.
- Serve wrapped in tortillas.

Use canned chickpeas and beans, if you wish. They are just as high in fiber and low in fat. To reduce salt content, rinse in cold water before adding to salad.

GREEK VEGETABLE POCKETS

4 SERVINGS

2	pita breads	2
1 tbsp	olive oil	15 mL
½ lb	feta cheese	225 g
1	tomato, sliced	1
1	cucumber, sliced	1
1	onion, sliced	1
½ cup	plain yogurt	125 mL
8	Greek olives, pitted and sliced	8
1 tbsp	chopped fresh mint	15 mL

• Cut pitas in halves or wedges. Brush interiors with olive oil.

• Divide feta between pita pockets. Add tomato, cucumber and onion slices.

• Top with yogurt, black olives and mint to serve.

1

Cut pita breads in half. Brush insides with olive oil.

2

Divide feta between pockets.

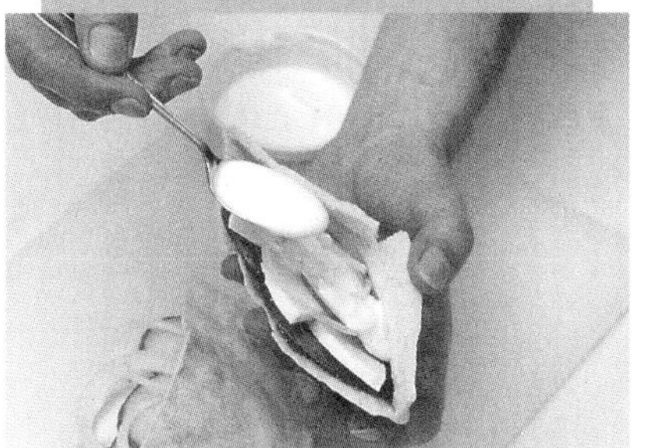

3

Add tomato, cucumber and onion slices.

4

Top with yogurt, black olives and mint.

SEASONED POTATO PACKAGES

4 SERVINGS

1 tbsp	corn oil	15 mL
2	garlic cloves, chopped	2
4	potatoes, scrubbed	4
1 tsp	paprika	5 mL
½ tsp	cayenne pepper	2 mL
	pepper	

- Combine oil and garlic. Set aside 30 minutes.
- Preheat oven to 400°F (200°C).
- Cut potatoes in half. Baste with garlicky oil. Sprinkle with paprika, cayenne and pepper.
- Wrap each half potato in foil. Bake 30 minutes.
- Unwrap potatoes and cook under broiler 5 to 10 minutes until nicely browned.

SUGGESTION

If you wish, replace the garlic with chopped herbs or spices chosen to enhance the flavoring of the main dish you serve with the potatoes.

ZUCCHINI WITH TOMATO AND CHEESE

6 SERVINGS

3 tbsp	**olive oil**	**45 mL**
1	**garlic clove, crushed**	**1**
1	**onion, finely chopped**	**1**
4 to 6	**medium zucchini, diced**	**4 to 6**
2	**tomatoes, peeled, seeded and coarsely chopped**	**2**
1	**small hot pepper, seeded and chopped *or* 1 pinch cayenne pepper**	**1**
3½ oz	**grated cheese**	**100 g**
½ cup	**fresh breadcrumbs**	**125 mL**

• Grease a baking dish and set aside. Heat oil in a non-stick skillet. Cook garlic and onion over medium heat until transluscent.

• Stir in zucchini, tomatoes and hot pepper. Cover and cook over low heat about 10 minutes, stirring from time to time to prevent sticking.

• Pour zucchini mixture into baking dish.

• In a bowl, combine cheese and breadcrumbs. Spread over zucchini.

• Brown 3 to 5 minutes under the broiler, or until top is nicely golden and crisp. Serve immediately.

SWISS ONION PIE

6 TO 8 SERVINGS

¼ lb	**bacon, cut in strips**	**110 g**
4	**large onions, sliced**	**4**
½ cup	**milk**	**125 mL**
¾ cup	**cream (whipping *or* light)**	**175 mL**
2	**eggs**	**2**
2 tbsp	**all-purpose flour**	**30 mL**
1 lb	**shortcrust pastry**	**450 g**
	grated fresh nutmeg	
	ground cumin	
	pepper	

• Preheat oven to 375°F (190°C).

• Cook bacon and onions in a non-stick skillet 2 minutes over medium-high heat, or until onions are golden. Let cool.

• In a bowl, combine milk, cream, eggs, flour, nutmeg, cumin and pepper. Set aside.

• Line quiche or pie pan with pastry.

• Spread bacon mixture over bottom of pastry. Pour milk mixture over bacon. Bake 30 minutes in oven, or until set. Serve pie very hot.

SUGGESTION

Add very thinly sliced tomatoes to the topping.

Serve with a green salad for a complete meal.

RED ONION, OLIVE AND GOAT'S CHEESE PIZZA

10 SERVINGS

CRUST

1 tsp	sugar *or* honey	5 mL
1¼ cups	warm water	300 mL
1	envelope dry yeast	1
3 cups	all-purpose flour	750 mL
1 tsp	salt	5 mL
2 tbsp	olive oil	30 mL

TOPPING

3 tbsp	olive oil	45 mL
3	red onions, thinly sliced into rings	3
1	garlic clove, chopped	1
¼ tsp	pepper	1 mL
½ cup	grated Parmesan cheese	125 mL
¾ cup	black olives, pitted and halved	175 mL
½ lb	goat's cheese, creamy type	225 g
2 tbsp	chopped fresh oregano *or* basil	30 mL
	chopped fresh parsley	

• In a small bowl, dissolve sugar in ¼ cup (50 mL) warm water. Sprinkle in yeast and let stand 10 minutes, or until mixture foams well.

• Combine 2½ cups (625 mL) flour and salt in a large bowl. Set aside.

• In another bowl, combining remaining warm water and oil. Stir yeast mixture, then stir yeast into liquid mixture.

• Add liquid mixture to flour and stir until dough is smooth. Add just enough remaining flour to make a dough that can be handled without sticking.

• Sprinkle a little flour on a clean work surface. Put dough on surface and knead about 8 minutes or until smooth and elastic. Shape into a ball, place in a lightly oiled bowl, and turn once to coat with oil on all sides. Cover with a clean cloth and let stand in warm place about 1 hour or until doubled in volume.

• To make the topping, heat oil in a skillet. Cook onions and garlic over medium-low heat 5 minutes or until tender but not browned. Add pepper.

• Preheat oven to 400°F (200°C).

• Punch down dough and spread it on a lightly greased pizza pan or large cookie sheet. Brush with olive oil and sprinkle with Parmesan.

• Top dough with onion mixture, then with black olives, crumbled goat's cheese, oregano and parsley, in that order.

• Bake 25 to 30 minutes, until crust is golden-brown. Serve hot or cold.

BRAISED LEEKS IN TOMATO SAUCE

4 SERVINGS

2 tsp	**corn oil**	**10 mL**
1	**onion, chopped**	**1**
1	**tomato, chopped**	**1**
1 tbsp	**tomato paste**	**15 mL**
½ cup	**chopped fresh parsley**	**125 mL**
1	**garlic clove, chopped**	**1**
¾ cup	**chicken stock**	**175 mL**
4	**fresh leeks, split in half, washed and drained**	**4**
3	**slices bread, toasted**	**3**
3 tbsp	**grated gruyère cheese**	**45 mL**
	pepper	
	lemon juice	

• Heat oil in a large saucepan or skillet. Cook onion over medium heat until transluscent. Add tomato and continue cooking until soft.

• Stir in tomato paste, ½ the parsley, garlic and chicken stock. Bring to a boil, cover and let simmer 7 to 8 minutes.

• Add leek halves, cover, and cook over low heat until leeks are tender. Add pepper, lemon juice, and remaining parsley.

• Sprinkle toast with grated cheese and brown under broiler, then cut in triangles.

• To serve, cut leeks in half again and arrange on a serving plate. Garnish with cheesy toast points.

JULIENNE VEGETABLES WITH FRESH MINT

6 SERVINGS

1	red *or* green pepper, cut in thin strips	1
2	carrots, cut in julienne	2
2	leeks, white part only, cut in julienne	2
1 to 2	pinches nutmeg	1 to 2
2 tbsp	melted butter *or* margarine	30 mL
1 tsp	chopped fresh mint leaves	5 mL
	juice of 1 lemon *or* 1 orange	
	pepper	

• Cook vegetables in boiling salted water or steam them until barely tender. Drain and add pepper.

• Toss with nutmeg and lemon juice.

• Toss gently with melted butter and chopped mint just before serving.

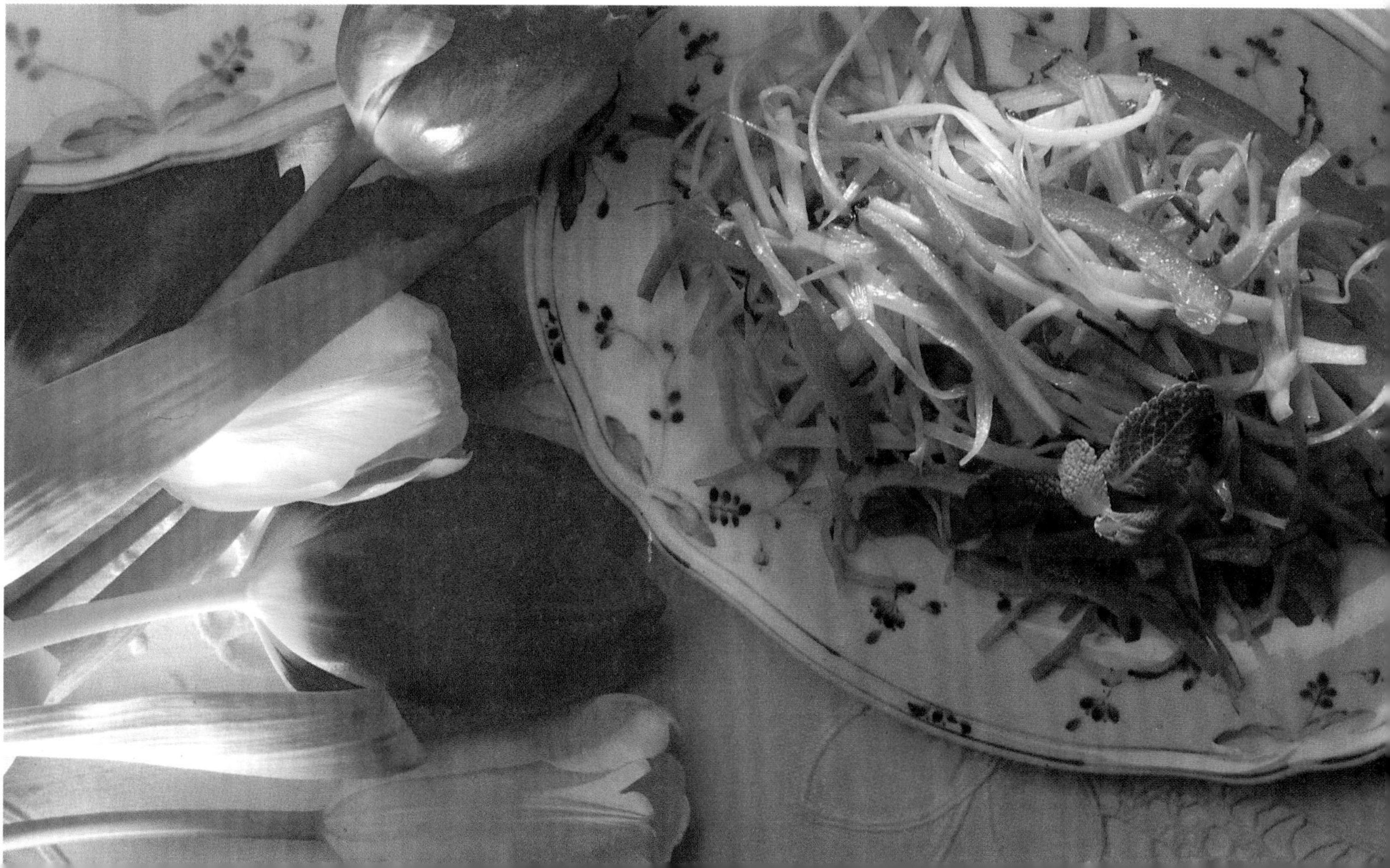

TEX-MEX STUFFED PEPPERS

4 SERVINGS

4	**large green and/*or* red peppers**	4
1 lb	**cooked diced chicken breast**	450 g
1	**carrot, thinly sliced**	1
½ cup	**grated gruyère cheese**	125 mL
1	**jalepeno pepper (optional)**	1
8	**black California olives, chopped**	8

DRESSING

½ cup	**plain yogurt**	125 mL
1 tbsp	**mayonnaise**	15 mL
1	**dash tabasco sauce**	1
2	**garlic cloves, chopped**	2
1	**green onion, chopped**	1
	juice of 1 lime	
	pepper	

• Cut the tops off the peppers. Clean out pith and seeds carefully. Steam peppers 5 minutes. (They should still be somewhat crisp.) Chill in refrigerator.

• In a bowl, combine chicken, carrot, cheese, jalepeno and black olives. Set aside.

• Combine all dressing ingredients in a bowl. Pour over chicken mixture. Mix well.

• Stuff peppers with chicken mixture and keep refrigerated until ready to serve.

VEGETABLE CHOP SUEY

4 SERVINGS

2 tbsp	corn oil	30 mL
2	carrots, cut in julienne strips	2
1	leek, cut in julienne strips	1
1	green pepper, cut in julienne strips	1
½ lb	bean sprouts	225 g
1	tomato, peeled and diced	1
1	garlic clove, finely chopped	1
½ cup	chicken stock	125 mL
2 tbsp	light soy sauce	30 mL
1½ tsp	cornstarch dissolved in a little cold water	7 mL
	pepper	

• Heat oil in a large skillet. Add carrots, leek, and green pepper. Cover and cook over low heat 5 minutes.

• Add bean sprouts and cook 2 more minutes, covered.

• Stir in tomato, garlic, chicken stock and soy sauce. Let simmer 5 minutes.

• Stir in cornstarch mixture to thicken, and pepper to taste. Serve hot.

SUGGESTION

You can add other vegetables of your choice, such as mushrooms or snow peas.

Bean sprouts, which are sprouted mung beans, should be cooked whole and just until tender-crisp, in order to have the highest nutritive value.

FELAFEL

4 SERVINGS

	FELAFEL	
2 cups	canned chickpeas, drained	500 mL
4	garlic cloves, sliced	4
3 tbsp	peanut butter	45 mL
1	green onion	1
1	onion, cut in 8ths	1
1	egg	1
¼ tsp	ground coriander	1 mL
¼ tsp	ground cumin	1 mL
¼ tsp	cayenne pepper	1 mL
1 tbsp	light soy sauce	15 mL
1 tbsp	corn oil	15 mL
4	pita breads, cut in ½	4
	GARNISH	
2	tomatoes, sliced	2
2	cucumbers, sliced	2
1 cup	plain yogurt	250 mL

When you use canned chickpeas, it is a good idea to rinse them to remove excess salt, and drain well. If you decide to cook your own, 1 cup (250 mL) dried chickpeas will make 2 to 2 ½ cups (500 to 625 mL) when cooked.

- Purée chickpeas in the food processor.
- Add all remaining felafel ingredients except oil and pita breads. Process until well mixed. Shape into balls, using about 1 tbsp (15 mL) for each.
- Heat oil in a non-stick skillet. Brown felafel balls on all sides over medium-high heat.
- Stuff felafel into pita pockets. Garnish with tomato, cucumber and yogurt to serve.

ZUCCHINI AU GRATIN

4 SERVINGS

¼ cup	all-purpose *or* whole-wheat flour	50 mL
1 tsp	dried oregano *or* basil	5 mL
4 to 5	medium zucchini, sliced ¼ inch (.5 cm) thick	4 to 5
¼ cup	olive *or* vegetable oil	50 mL
2	medium tomatoes, sliced	2
1 cup	plain yogurt *or* sour cream	250 mL
1	garlic clove, finely chopped	1
½ cup	grated Sbrinz *or* Parmesan cheese	125 mL
	pepper	
	lemon juice	

Zucchini are high in Vitamins A and C, calcium and potassium.

• Preheat oven to 350°F (180°C). Lightly grease a baking dish.

• In a bowl, combine flour, oregano, and pepper. Coat zucchini slices in flour mixture.

• Heat oil in a non-stick skillet. Brown zucchini over medium-high heat about 4 minutes on each side. Drain on paper towels.

• Arrange zucchini in baking dish, sprinkle with a little lemon juice and cover with tomato slices.

• In a smal bowl, combine yogurt and garlic. Pour over tomatoes. Sprinkle with grated cheese.

• Bake in oven about 30 minutes or until cheese forms a golden crust.

SUGGESTION

If you flour the zucchini before frying, they absorb far less oil.

POTATO AND LEEK PIE

4 SERVINGS

2	**sheets puff pastry rolled ⅛ inch (2 mm) thick**	2
¼ lb	**bacon, cut in strips**	110 g
2	**leeks, thinly sliced**	2
½ cup	**dry white wine**	125 mL
4	**potatoes, with skin, thinly sliced**	4
6	**chicken sausages, in rings**	6
5 oz	**grated gruyère *or* Sbrinz cheese**	150 g
1	**egg, beaten**	1
	pepper	

• Preheat oven to 400°F (200°C).

• Line a pie plate with puff pastry. Set aside.

• Cook bacon in a skillet over medium-high heat until golden, then add leeks. Cook until barely limp. Add white wine and pepper. Simmer until leeks are just tender. Drain and let cool.

• Layer in the pie shell ⅓ of the leeks, potato, sausage and cheese, in that order.

• Repeat layers twice. Fold in edges of pastry shell. Baste with beaten egg.

• Cover top with second pastry layer. Trim and seal edges. Baste top with remaining egg.

• Bake in oven about 40 minutes, until nicely golden.

RAGOUT OF AUTUMN VEGETABLES

4 SERVINGS

⅓ cup	olive oil	75 mL
1	medium carrot, cut in chunks	1
2	small turnips, in chunks	2
1	potato, peeled, cut in chunks	1
1	medium onion, in chunks	1
1	leek, in chunks	1
3	garlic cloves, finely chopped	3
1	pinch dried thyme	1
1	pinch ground rosemary	1
1	bay leaf	1
1 cup	dry white wine	250 mL
1½ cups	chicken stock *or* water	375 mL
2 tbsp	butter	30 mL
½ lb	mushrooms, halved *or* quartered	225 g
1	large tomato, peeled and chopped	1
3 tbsp	chopped fresh parsley	45 mL
	salt and pepper	

- Heat olive oil in a large, heavy saucepan. Add carrot, turnips, potato, onion and leek. Cook over medium heat, stirring, about 5 minutes.
- Add garlic, thyme, rosemary, bay leaf, white wine, salt, pepper, and chicken stock. Cover and cook another 15 to 20 minutes.
- Melt butter in a large skillet. Brown mushrooms over high heat. Stir mushrooms and tomato into vegetable mixture. Cook another 5 minutes. Vegetables should be tender but firm.
- Place in a serving dish, and sprinkle with parsley to serve.

MEDITERRANEAN PIZZA

4 SERVINGS

1	ready-made pizza crust	1
1 tsp	olive oil	5 mL
½ cup	tomato sauce	125 mL
2	tomatoes, sliced	2
4	artichoke hearts, quartered	4
10	Greek olives, pitted and finely chopped	10
½	6.5 oz (184 g) can flaked tuna, drained	½
½ cup	crumbled feta cheese	125 mL
1 tsp	oregano	5 mL

• Preheat oven to 350°F (180°C).

• Brush pizza crust lightly with olive oil.

• Cover with thin layer of tomato sauce. Garnish with tomatoes, artichokes, olives and tuna.

• Sprinkle feta and oregano over top.

• Bake 10 to 15 minutes, or until cheese has melted. Serve hot.

SUGGESTION

If you slice the potatoes ahead of time, keep them in cold water so they do not darken. Drain well and pat dry before using.

POTATOES AU GRATIN

2 SERVINGS

½	**garlic clove**	½
1 tbsp	**butter *or* margarine**	**15 mL**
2	**large potatoes, peeled, thinly sliced**	2
1½ cups	**grated gruyère cheese**	**375 mL**
1	**egg**	1
½ cup	**plain yogurt *or* buttermilk**	**125 mL**
½ cup	**milk**	**125 mL**
¼ tsp	**ground nutmeg**	**1 mL**
	salt and pepper	

• Preheat oven to 325°F (160°C).

• Rub a baking dish with garlic, then grease with the butter.

• Arrange ⅓ potato slices in dish so that they overlap. Season with salt and pepper. Sprinkle with ⅓ cup (75 mL) cheese.

• Repeat layering, ending with a layer of potatoes.

• Beat together the egg, yogurt, milk and nutmeg. Pour over potatoes. Top with remaining cheese. Bake in oven until potatoes are tender and top is nicely browned.

HERB-MARINATED VEGETABLES

4 SERVINGS

2	dry French shallots, halved	2
2	green onions, cut up	2
½ cup	small broccoli florets	125 mL
½ cup	small cauliflower florets	125 mL
½ cup	quartered mushrooms	125 mL
2	carrots, cut in sticks	2
½ cup	cubed red pepper	125 mL
½ cup	cubed yellow pepper	125 mL
6	whole green beans	6
6	whole yellow beans	6
	MARINADE	
2 cups	white vinegar	500 mL
1 tsp	crushed dried hot pepper	5 mL
1	garlic clove	1
¼ tsp	white pepper	1 mL
2 tbsp	chopped fresh oregano	30 mL
1 tbsp	chopped fresh thyme	15 mL
1 tsp	honey	5 mL
1 cup	water	250 mL

• Combine all marinade ingredients in a saucepan. Bring to a boil.

• Place all vegetables in a large bowl. Pour hot marinade over.

• Place vegetables with marinade in a jar with a tight-fitting lid. Keep in refrigerator several weeks before serving.

TUSCAN-STYLE LENTILS

4 SERVINGS

Lentils are an excellent source of iron. They also contain vegetable protein, but to get its full benefit, serve lentils with a grain such as rice, or with nuts. To make a vegetarian version, simply omit the bologna.

2 cups	dried green lentils	500 mL
1 tbsp	olive oil	15 mL
1	large onion, chopped	1
2	garlic cloves, chopped	2
2	celery stalks, diced	2
½ lb	bologna, in slivers	225 g
1 tbsp	dried oregano	15 mL
	salt and pepper	

• Rinse and pick over lentils. Soak 1 hour in cold water.

• Heat olive oil in a large saucepan. Cook onion, garlic and celery over medium heat until onion is golden. Add bologna and cook 2 minutes.

• Add lentils, and cover with water. Season with salt and pepper. Bring to a boil. Lower heat and let simmer, covered, about 1 hour.

• Add oregano. Continue cooking until lentils are cooked but retain their shape. Add water when necessary. Finished dish should not have much liquid.

SUGGESTION

Traditionally, Tuscan-style lentils are serving with a dollop of olive oil flavored with herbs.

POTATO CAKES

3 SERVINGS

1 tbsp	chopped onion	15 mL
1 tbsp	butter *or* margarine	15 mL
1 lb	potatoes, peeled, cooked and mashed	450 g
3 tbsp	grated mozzarella *or* gruyère	45 mL
½ tsp	pepper	2 mL
½ tsp	salt	2 mL
2 tbsp	butter *or* corn oil	30 mL

• In a non-stick skillet, cook onion in 1 tbsp (15 mL) butter until limp. Let cook.

• In a bowl, combine potatoes, cooked onion, cheese, pepper and salt.

• Shape potato mixture into patties ¾ inch (2 cm) thick and 2 inches (5 cm) in diameter.

• Heat 2 tbsp (30 mL) butter in the same skillet. Brown patties on both sides over high heat.

Cabbage is rich in vitamins. It has twice as much Vitamin A as broccoli, and twice the Vitamin C of almost every other vegetable with the exception of peppers.

HOW TO STUFF CABBAGE ROLLS

Blanch the cabbage leaves.

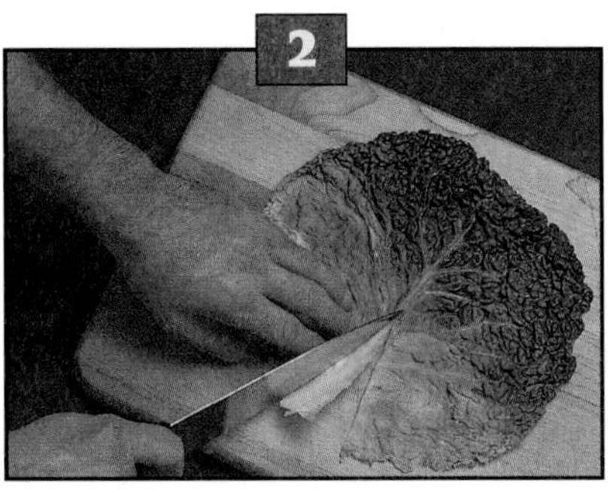

Cut out the central ridge with scissors, so leaves are easier to roll.

Top with filling.

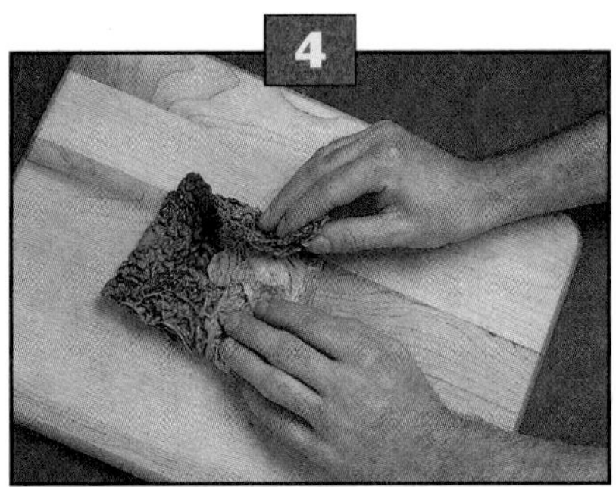

Fold in base of leaf, then sides.

Roll up the stuffed leaves.

STUFFED CABBAGE ROLLS

4 TO 6 SERVINGS

1 tbsp	butter *or* margarine	15 mL
1 cup	sliced mushrooms	250 mL
2	onions, finely chopped	2
1	garlic clove, finely chopped	1
3 tbsp	chopped fresh parsley	45 mL
1 lb	lean ground veal	450 g
1 cup	cooked long grain *or* brown rice	250 mL
¼ cup	crumbled cooked bacon	50 mL
1	envelope beef stew seasoning, divided in ½	1
10 to 12	large cabbage leaves, blanched	10 to 12
1 cup	water	250 mL
14 oz	can tomato juice	540 mL
	dried savory	
	lemon juice	

• Preheat oven to 350°F (180°C).

• Melt butter in a saucepan. Brown mushrooms over medium heat. Add onions, garlic, parsley, savory and meat. Cook to brown meat. Stir in rice, bacon and ½ envelope beef seasoning. Remove from heat.

• Arrange cabbage leaves on work surface. With a spoon, divide meat mixture between them.

• Fold in bottom and slides of leaves, then roll. Arrange in baking dish.

• Combine remaining stew seasoning with water in a bowl. Add tomato juice. Pour mixture over cabbage rolls. Sprinkle with lemon juice. Cover with foil.

• Bake in oven 1 to 1½ hours, or until rolls are tender.

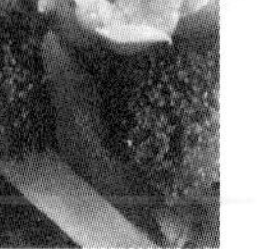

POTATO AND DILL CRABCAKES

4 SERVINGS

2	potatoes, peeled and cooked	2
1	egg	1
¼ cup	all-purpose flour	50 mL
½ tsp	baking powder	2 mL
1	pinch salt	1
½ tsp	pepper	2 mL
2 tbsp	melted butter *or* margarine	30 mL
1⅓ cups	buttermilk *or* 10% cream	325 mL
1 cup	chopped imitation crabmeat	250 mL
½ cup	diced cheddar	125 mL
3 tbsp	chopped fresh dill *or* parsley	45 mL

• Mash potatoes and let cool.

• In a bowl, beat egg and stir in flour, baking powder, salt and pepper. Whisk in 1 tbsp (15 mL) melted butter and the buttermilk.

• Gradually beat egg mixture into potatoes. Fold in imitation crabmeat, cheese and dill.

• Heat remaining butter in a large skillet. Drop large spoonfuls of potato mixture into pan about 4 inches (10 cm) apart. Cook 3 to 4 minutes over medium-high heat, turning once, to brown both sides.

• Keep cooked crabcakes warm in 150°F (65°C) oven while you cook the rest.

SUGGESTION

Serve these pancakes with a yogurt sauce and a green salad as a main course.

BAKED HERBED ZUCCHINI

6 TO 8 SERVINGS

6	small zucchini	6
3	eggs	3
2 tsp	chopped fresh chives	10 mL
2 tbsp	chopped fresh dill	30 mL
2 tbsp	chopped fresh mint	30 mL
2 tbsp	chopped fresh parsley	30 mL
½ cup	grated gruyère cheese	125 mL
2 tbsp	diced feta	30 mL
1½ cups	all-purpose flour	375 mL
10	black olives, pitted (optional)	10
	pepper	
	cayenne pepper	

• Preheat oven to 350°F (180°C).

• Coarsely grate zucchini. Place in a large bowl and stir in well the eggs, herbs and cheeses.

• Gradually stir in flour. Season with pepper and cayenne.

• Grease a 9-inch (23 cm) square baking pan.

• Spread mixture in pan. Garnish with olives.

• Bake 45 to 55 minutes, or until top is nicely browned.

• Remove from oven, cut in squares, and serve cold or hot.

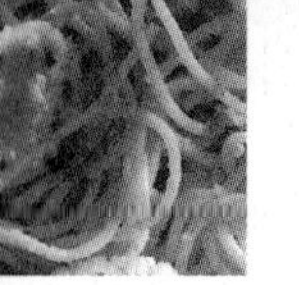

Pasta

SUGGESTION

Chopped fresh oregano or basil will give an added flavor boost.

FUSILLI WITH BLACK OLIVES

2 SERVINGS

1 tsp	**olive oil**	**5 mL**
1 tsp	**butter *or* margarine**	**5 mL**
1¾ cups	**canned tomatoes, drained, finely chopped**	**425 mL**
½	**garlic clove, chopped**	**½**
½ cup	**chopped Greek-style black olives**	**125 mL**
¼ cup	**cream cheese**	**50 mL**
3 tbsp	**grated Sbrinz *or* gruyère cheese**	**45 mL**
7 oz	**fusilli pasta, cooked**	**200 g**
	chopped fresh parsley	
	pepper	

- Heat oil and butter in a skillet.
- Add tomatoes, garlic and olives. Let simmer 5 to 6 minutes. Pepper to taste.
- Add cream cheese and stir until well blended.
- Stir in grated cheese and parsley.
- Gently stir in cooked pasta to coat evenly. Serve hot.

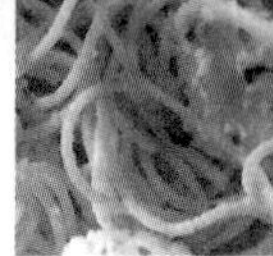

PASTA WITH PESTO

2 SERVINGS

2	garlic cloves	2
¾ cup	packed fresh basil leaves	175 mL
½ cup	pine nuts	125 mL
⅓ cup	olive oil	75 mL
1½ oz	grated Sbrinz *or* Parmesan	45 g
7 oz	pasta (spaghetti, linguini etc.), cooked	200 g
	pepper	

• In a food processor, chop garlic, basil and pine nuts.

• Add oil bit by bit with motor running, until mixture is creamy. Season with pepper.

• Blend in grated cheese.

• Heat pasta in a non-stick skillet coated with a little olive oil or butter.

• Use 1 tbsp (15 mL) pesto sauce per serving, stirring it well into pasta. Serve at once.

Basil goes well with garlic, chives and black olives. It is one of the richest in Vitamin A of all the herbs, and a good source of calcium.

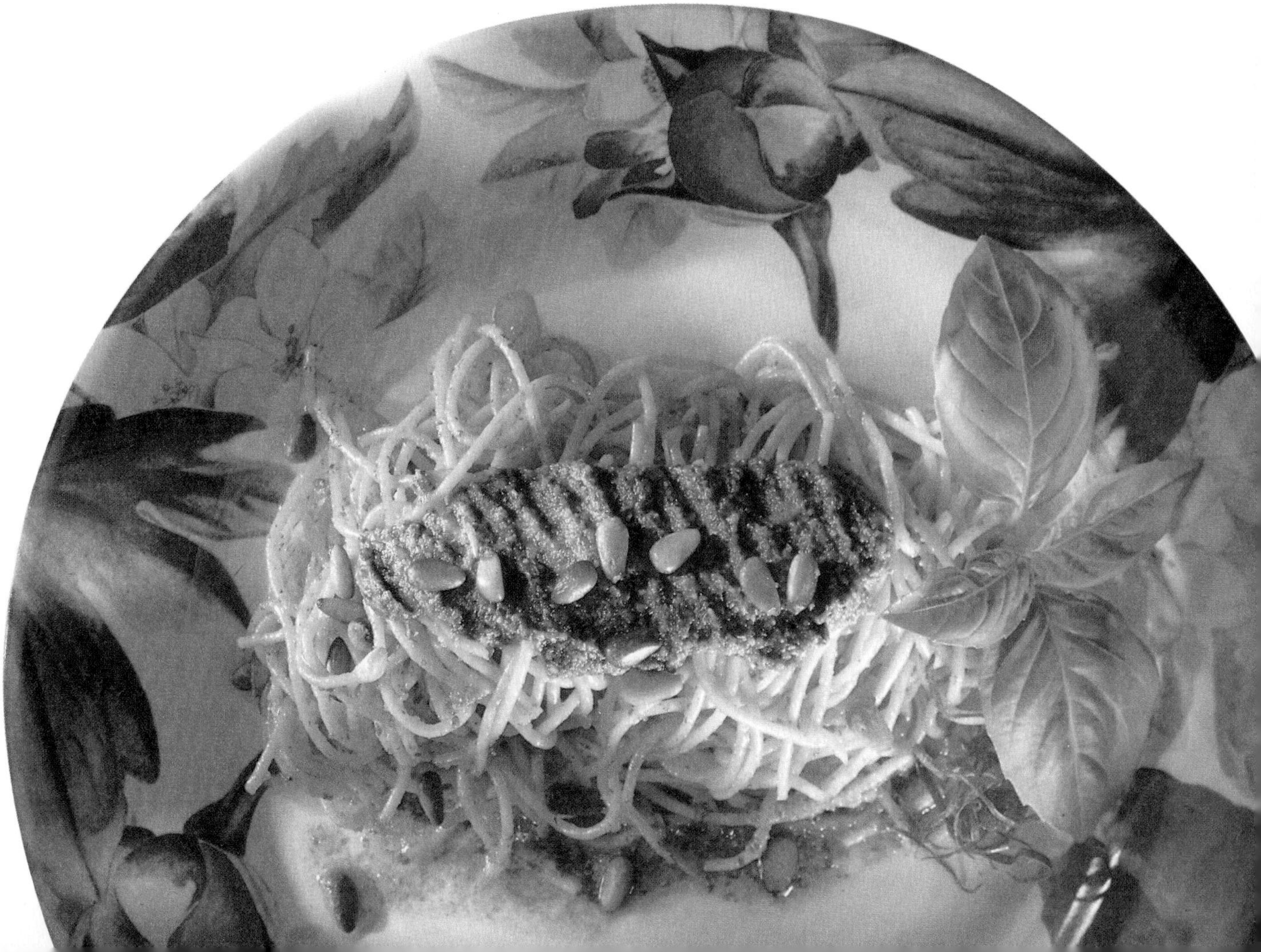

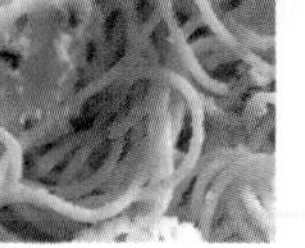

PASTA WITH VEAL LIVER RAGOUT

2 SERVINGS

2 tbsp	butter *or* margarine	30 mL
2 tsp	olive oil *or* vegetable oil	10 mL
1	dry French shallot, finely chopped	1
½	onion, chopped	½
1	garlic clove, finely chopped	1
2	medium-thin slices veal liver, cut in strips	2
2 tbsp	raspberry vinegar	30 mL
2 cups	fresh *or* canned tomato sauce	500 mL
7 oz	spaghettini *or* other thin pasta, cooked	200 g
5 to 6	black olives, pitted and chopped	5 to 6
3 tbsp	grated Parmesan cheese	45 mL
	chopped fresh basil and oregano	
	chopped fresh parsley	
	pepper	

• Heat butter and oil in a skillet. Add shallot, onion, garlic and liver, and cook, turning, 5 to 6 minutes over high heat.

• Add raspberry vinegar, and basil, parsley and pepper to taste.

• Stir in tomato sauce and cook a few more minutes over high heat.

• Pour sauce over hot pasta. Garnish with olives and serve with Parmesan.

SUGGESTION

Veal liver should be cooked just until slightly pink inside.

Stir some finely chopped garlic and parsley into the hot pasta before topping it with the sauce.

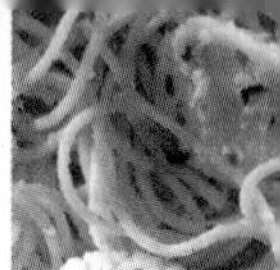

MUSHROOM LASAGNE

6 SERVINGS

2 tbsp	canola oil	30 mL
1	small onion, chopped	1
1	garlic clove, finely chopped	1
1	celery stalk, chopped	1
1 cup	sliced mushrooms	250 mL
½	red pepper, diced	½
½ tsp	dried thyme	2 mL
½ tsp	dried oregano	2 mL
½ tsp	dried basil	2 mL
2 cups	canned plum tomatoes	500 mL
9	lasagne noodles	9
1½ cups	cottage cheese	375 mL
1½ cups	grated gruyère cheese	375 mL
¼ cup	grated Sbrinz *or* Parmesan cheese	50 mL
	pepper	

• Preheat oven to 350°F (180°C).

• Heat oil in a saucepan, add onion, garlic, celery, mushrooms and red pepper, and cook 3 minutes over medium-high heat, stirring.

• Add herbs and tomatoes. Bring to a boil. Lower heat and let simmer 15 minutes uncovered. Stir in pepper to taste and set aside.

• Cook lasagne in boiling salted water until *al dente*. Drain and rinse under cold water. Spread out on a clean damp cloth.

• Put some of tomato mixture into bottom of a baking dish. Cover with a layer of lasagne noodles, ½ the cottage cheese, then ½ the gruyère. Cover with a second layer of sauce, then repeat layers, ending with sauce. Sprinkle Sbrinz or Parmesan over top. Bake about 35 minutes.

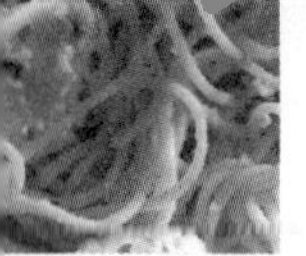

SPAGHETTINI WITH SCALLOPS

2 SERVINGS

12	large raw scallops	12
1 tbsp	corn oil	15 mL
2	garlic cloves, finely chopped	2
1 tbsp	finely chopped flat-leaf *or* curly parsley	15 mL
7 oz	spaghettini, cooked and hot	200 g
½ cup	Italian *or* plain fine breadcrumbs	125 mL
	crushed hot red pepper flakes	

- Rinse scallops in cold water and pat dry. Cut in ½ widthwise and set aside.
- Heat oil in a non-stick skillet and brown garlic lightly.
- Add parsley and crushed hot pepper to taste. Stir well. Add scallops and cook over high heat until scallop flesh is opaque through.
- Stir in hot spaghettini. Stir in breadcrumbs. Serve immediately.

PASTA SHELLS WITH ARTICHOKE HEARTS

2 SERVINGS

7 oz	**pasta shells**	**200 g**
2 tbsp	**corn oil**	**30 mL**
2	**garlic cloves, finely chopped**	**2**
6 to 8	**mushrooms, sliced**	**6 to 8**
4 to 5	**canned artichoke hearts, quartered**	**4 to 5**
¼ cup	**tomato sauce**	**50 mL**
2 tbsp	**chopped fresh parsley**	**30 mL**
4 to 6	**black olives, pitted and chopped**	**4 to 6**
	pepper	

• Cook pasta shells in boiling salted water until *al dente*. Drain and set aside.

• Heat oil in a saucepan. Cook garlic very quickly over medium-high heat. Stir in mushrooms. Stir in artichokes and cook 3 to 4 minutes.

• Add tomato sauce, parsley and pepper to taste.

• Stir in pasta shells and olives and serve immediately.

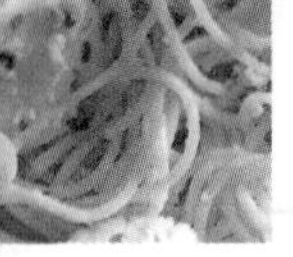

VEGETABLE MACARONI

2 SERVINGS

1	egg	1
2	egg whites	2
¼ cup	milk	50 mL
½ cup	grated mozzarella *or* Emmenthal cheese	125 mL
2 tbsp	grated Sbrinz *or* Parmesan cheese	30 mL
1	pinch dried oregano *or* ½ tsp (2 ml) chopped fresh coriander	1
1 tbsp	butter *or* margarine	15 mL
1	green onion, sliced	1
1	garlic clove, finely chopped	1
2 cups	macaroni, cooked and drained	500 mL
2 cups	diced mixed vegetables, cooked	500 mL
	pepper	

- In a bowl, beat the egg and egg whites well.
- Stir in milk, cheeses, oregano and pepper. Set aside.
- Melt butter in a saucepan. Cook green onion and garlic over medium heat until limp. Add cooked macaroni, mix well, then stir in egg mixture.
- Cook over low heat, stirring constantly, 2 to 3 minutes or until sauce becomes thick and creamy.
- Stir in hot vegetables and serve at once.

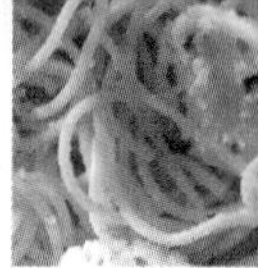

GRILLED TOMATO LASAGNE

4 SERVINGS

6	tomatoes, peeled, seeded and cut in wedges	6
1 tbsp	corn oil	15 mL
2 tbsp	finely chopped garlic	30 mL
4	pork and beef sausages, sliced in rounds	4
½ cup	mushroom sauce	125 mL
1 tsp	red wine vinegar	5 mL
¼ cup	finely chopped fresh basil	50 mL
12	lasagne noodles, broken in 3, cooked and drained	12
	grated Parmesan cheese	
	pepper	

• Cook tomatoes a few minutes in a non-stick skillet. Set aside in a bowl.

• Heat oil in a saucepan. Add garlic and sausages. Cook over low heat until meat is cooked. Add tomatoes and mushroom sauce. Cook over low heat a few more minutes until well blended and smooth.

• Add vinegar, basil and pepper to taste.

• Stir sauce gently into hot noodles. Sprinkle with cheese to serve.

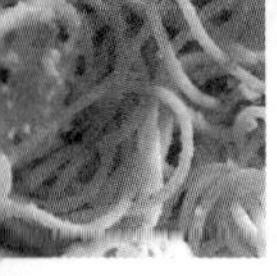

VENETIAN FETTUCINE

6 SERVINGS

1½ lbs	Italian turkey sausage	675 g
2 tbsp	butter *or* margarine	30 mL
1 tbsp	corn oil	15 mL
1	onion, chopped	1
1	garlic clove, chopped	1
2 tbsp	chopped fresh parsley	30 mL
1 tsp	dried basil	5 mL
1 tsp	dried tarragon	5 mL
1 tsp	dried thyme	5 mL
1 lb	mushrooms, sliced	450 g
2 cups	canned plum tomato purée	500 mL
1 lb	fettucine	450 g
½ cup	grated Parmesan cheese	125 mL
	pepper	

• Peel skin from sausages and set sausage meat aside.

• Heat 1 tbsp (15 mL) butter and the oil in a large skillet. Cook onion and garlic over high heat until golden.

• Add sausage meat and herbs. Cook over medium heat 10 minutes, stirring from time to time.

• Stir in mushrooms, tomato purée and pepper. Bring to a boil, lower heat and let simmer 10 minutes.

• Cook fettucine in boiling salted water until *al dente*. Drain and set aside.

• Melt remaining butter in a saucepan and add pasta. Stir to coat with melted butter. Add ½ sausage mixture, stirring well.

• Arrange fettucine on a serving plate, and top with remaining sausage mixture. Sprinkle with Parmesan to serve.

1 Peel skin from sausages and set sausage meat aside.

2 Add sausage meat and herbs to cooked onion. Cook.

3 Stir in mushrooms, tomato purée and pepper. Bring to a boil.

4 Cook fettucine in boiling salted water. Toss with melted butter. Stir in ½ sausage mixture.

PASTA WITH CHEESE

4 SERVINGS

You can use almost any kind of cheese you wish to make this recipe, with the exception of soft rind cheeses such as camembert and brie. Blue cheese makes an especially tasty dish.

2 tbsp	butter *or* margarine	30 mL
1 tbsp	all-purpose flour	15 mL
1 cup	milk	250 mL
¼ cup	diced mozzarella	50 mL
1 cup	diced gruyère cheese	250 mL
½ cup	ricotta	125 mL
1 lb	short pasta lengths	450 g
	pepper	

• Melt butter in a saucepan over medium heat. Stir in flour until smooth.

• Gradually stir in milk and cheeses. Cook over low heat until cheese melts.

• Meanwhile, cook pasta in boiling salted water until *al dente*. Drain.

• Stir pasta and pepper to taste into cheese sauce, mixing well. Serve hot.

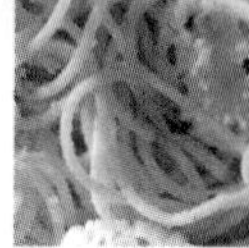

CHEESY MUSHROOM SPAGHETTINI

2 SERVINGS

2 tsp	butter *or* margarine	10 mL
1	dry French shallot, chopped	1
10 to 12	mushrooms, sliced	10 to 12
3 tbsp	dry white wine	45 mL
3 tbsp	chopped mixed frozen vegetables	45 mL
1 cup	homemade *or* commercial cheese sauce	250 mL
¼ cup	cream cheese	50 mL
7 oz	spaghettini, cooked and hot	200 g
2 tbsp	chopped fresh parsley	30 mL
	pepper	

• Melt butter in a skillet. Cook shallot 1 minute over medium heat.

• Add mushrooms and white wine. Cook until liquid evaporates.

• Stir in vegetables, cheese sauce, and cream cheese. Cook to thicken slightly.

• Add pepper and pasta, and toss gently.

• Serve garnished with parsley.

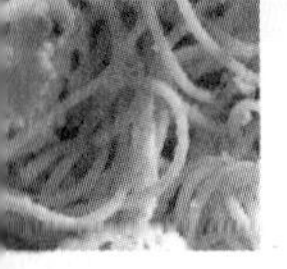

TAGLIATELLE WITH ROSY SAUCE

2 SERVINGS

1 tbsp	butter *or* margarine	15 mL
½	onion, finely chopped	½
½ cup	tomato sauce *or* crushed tomatoes	125 mL
¾ cup	béchamel sauce (see page 273)	175 mL
½	garlic clove, finely chopped	½
1	pinch chopped fresh oregano *or* dried basil	1
¼ cup	commercial cheese spread *or* cream cheese	50 mL
7 oz	imitation crabmeat	200 g
7 oz	tagliatelle, cooked and hot	200 g
	chopped fresh parsley	
	pepper	

• Melt butter in a saucepan. Cook onion over medium-high heat until translucent.

• Add tomato sauce, béchamel, garlic and oregano. Stir well.

• Stir in cheese, and heat until cheese melts. Remove from heat, pepper to taste and gently stir in crabmeat.

• Arrange pasta on heated plates, pour sauce over, and garnish with parsley.

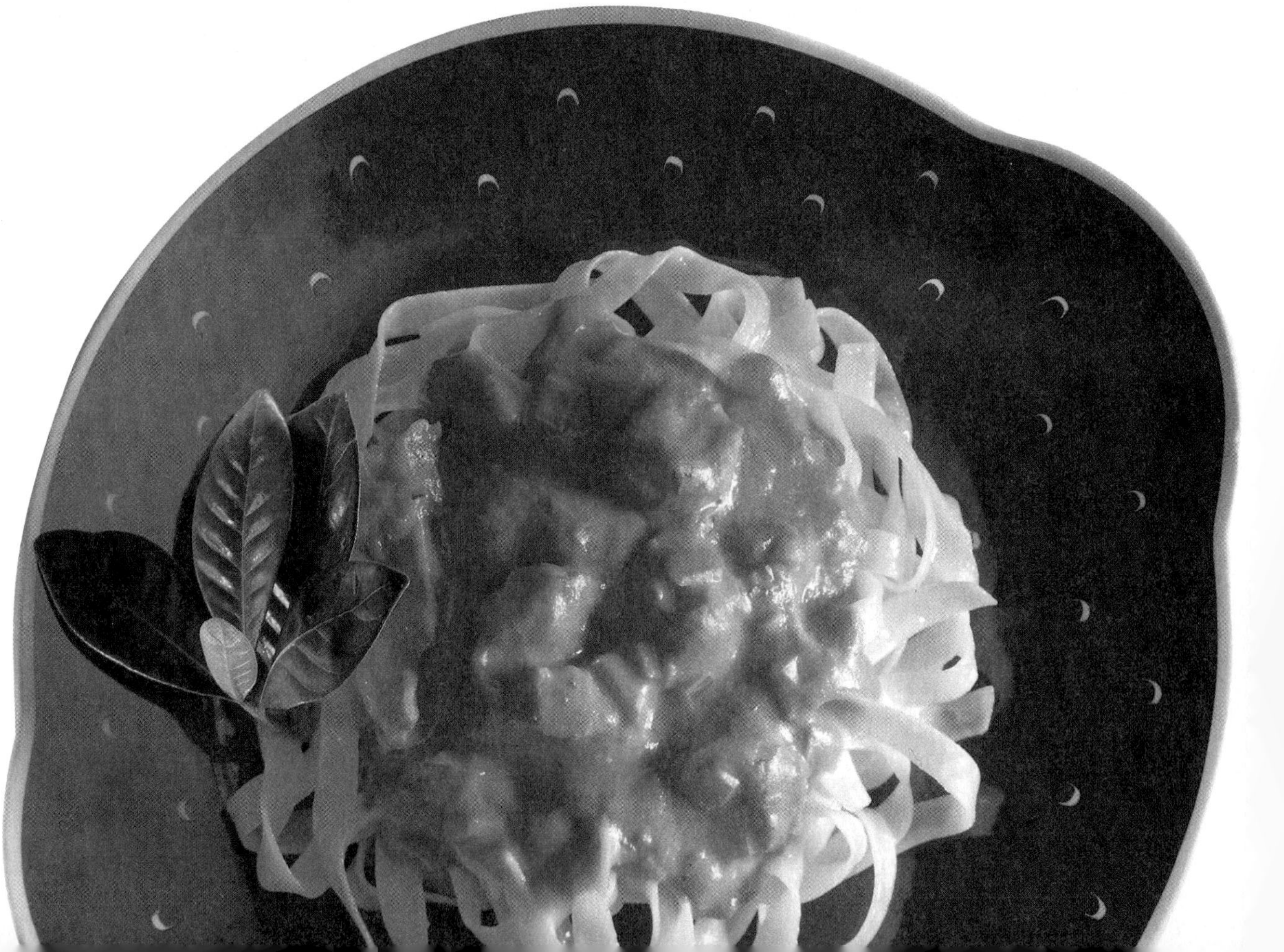

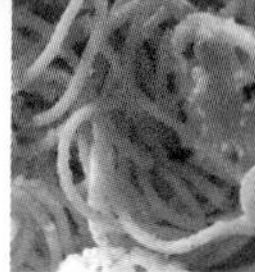

FUSILLI WITH BEEF

4 SERVINGS

1 tbsp	butter *or* margarine	15 mL
1	dry French shallot, chopped	1
1 lb	thinly sliced lean beef	450 g
½	green pepper, sliced	½
½ cup	sliced mushrooms	125 mL
1 tbsp	raspberry vinegar *or* dry white wine	15 mL
1	envelope brown sauce mix, prepared	1
10 oz	fusilli, cooked	300 g
¼ cup	sliced black olives	50 mL
	grated nutmeg	

• Heat butter in a non-stick skillet. Cook shallot until soft.

• Add beef and cook, stirring, 2 to 3 minutes over medium heat. Stir in green pepper and mushrooms.

• Add vinegar and brown sauce made according to package directions.

• Gently stir in cooked pasta.

• Sprinkle with nutmeg and chopped olives.

PASTA WITH FRESH GINGER

2 SERVINGS

½ cup	15% cream	125 mL
½ cup	plain yogurt	125 mL
1 tsp	finely chopped garlic	5 mL
1 tsp	finely chopped fresh ginger	5 mL
1 tsp	cornstarch dissolved in a little cold water	5 mL
⅓ cup	zucchini cut in julienne	75 mL
3 cups	cooked pasta shells	750 mL
1 tbsp	coarsely chopped fresh parsley	15 mL
	pepper	

• Combine cream, yogurt, garlic and ginger in a large skillet. Bring to a boil and cook over medium heat, stirring often, about 5 minutes to reduce by ½.

• Stir in dissolved cornstarch, then zucchini. Cook 1 to 2 minutes. Stir in cooked pasta and let simmer 30 seconds. Pepper to taste and stir well.

• Serve on heated plates garnished with parsley.

SUGGESTION

You will find that a little grated cheese (gruyère, Sbrinz or Parmesan) makes a nice addition.

COLD PASTA AND AVOCADO SALAD

4 SERVINGS

¾ lb	tagliatelle	375 g
2	tomatoes, peeled, seeded and coarsely chopped	2
2	avocados, pitted and peeled	2
1	white onion	1
4 tsp	olive oil	20 mL
	pepper	
	tabasco sauce	
	chopped fresh chives *or* coriander	
	juice of 1 lemon	

• Cook pasta in boiling salted water until *al dente*.

• Meanwhile, purée all remaining ingredients, except chives or coriander, in food processor.

• Drain pasta and toss well with avocado mixture.

Sprinkle with chopped chives, let cool, and serve.

SUGGESTION

Sbrinz is a hard, strongly-flavored Swiss cheese that can easily replace Parmesan.

GARLIC SPAGHETTI

4 SERVINGS

¼ cup	olive oil *or* vegetable oil	50 mL
2	large garlic cloves, chopped	2
3 tbsp	chopped fresh parsley	45 mL
1 lb	spaghetti *or* spaghettini, cooked	450 g
	grated Sbrinz *or* Parmesan cheese	
	pepper	

• Heat oil in a skillet, and cook garlic about 5 minutes over medium heat.

• Add parsley and pepper.

• Place spaghetti in skillet with garlic to reheat. Toss delicately with 2 forks.

• Serve in deep plates, and sprinkle with cheese.

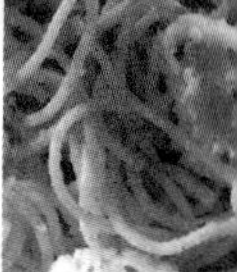

RIGATONI WITH SAUSAGE

4 SERVINGS

10 oz	chicken sausages	300 g
1 cup	diced eggplant, with skin	250 mL
1	red pepper, diced	1
1	green pepper, diced	1
1	garlic clove, chopped	1
19 oz	can tomatoes, with their juice	540 mL
½ tsp	dried basil	2 mL
½ tsp	dried oregano	2 mL
½ tsp	dried thyme	2 mL
10 oz	rigatoni	300 g
	pepper	

• Cut sausages in 1 inch (2.5 cm) pieces. Put pieces in a skillet with ¼ cup (50 mL) water and cook uncovered over medium-high heat. When water has evaporated, continue cooking to brown sausage lightly.

• Add eggplant and cook over medium heat 15 minutes, stirring from time to time. Stir in peppers and garlic. Cook 3 minutes.

• Stir in tomatoes, basil, oregano and thyme. Crush tomatoes with back of a spoon. Let simmer 5 minutes uncovered. Add pepper.

• Meanwhile, cook rigatoni in boiling salted water until *al dente*. Drain and toss with sausage mixture. Serve at once.

SUGGESTION

For a change, use zucchini instead of eggplant.

FUSILLI WITH BLUE CHEESE

2 SERVINGS

2 oz	blue cheese	60 g
1 cup	15% cream *or* béchamel sauce (see page 273)	250 mL
2 tbsp	dry red wine	30 mL
1 tsp	butter *or* margarine	5 mL
½ cup	sliced mushrooms	125 mL
7 oz	fusilli, cooked	200 g
2 tsp	coarsely chopped fresh parsley	10 mL
	whole green *or* black peppercorns	

- In a large bowl, mash together with a fork the blue cheese, cream and red wine. Stir in peppercorns and set aside.
- Heat butter in a non-stick skillet. Brown mushrooms over medium-high heat.
- Stir in cooked pasta and parsley. Pour pasta over blue cheese mixture and toss with a wooden spoon. Serve at once.

SUGGESTION

If you use whole green peppercorns, crush them with the blade of a large knife before adding.

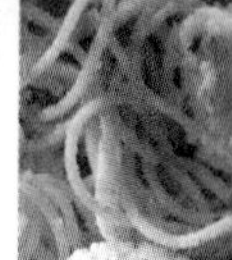

LEMON PASTA

4 SERVINGS

4	**green onions, chopped**	**4**
1 tbsp	**paprika**	**15 mL**
4 tbsp	**olive oil**	**60 mL**
10 oz	**fettucine**	**300 g**
3 tbsp	**chopped fresh parsley**	**45 mL**
	julienned zest and juice of 1 lemon	
	salt and pepper	

• Put green onions in a saucepan with paprika, olive oil, lemon zest and juice, salt and pepper. Heat to steaming, but do not allow to boil.

• Cook pasta in boiling salted water until *al dente*.

• Drain pasta and toss with lemon sauce. Garnish with parsley to serve.

SUGGESTION

If you wish, you can reheat the cooked spaetzle in a skillet with melted butter.

SPAETZLE

2 TO 4 SERVINGS

3 cups	**all-purpose flour**	**750 mL**
3	**eggs**	**3**
1¼ cups	**water**	**300 mL**
1 tsp	**salt**	**5 mL**
1 tsp	**powdered chicken stock concentrate**	**5 mL**
1 tbsp	**butter *or* margarine**	**15 mL**
	coarsely grated gruyère cheese	

• In a large bowl, stir together with a spoon all ingredients except cheese. Beat until dough is soft and smooth, with bubbles escaping. Cover dough with a clean cloth and let rest about 1 hour.

• Bring 3 to 4 quarts (3 to 4 liters) of water to a boil in a large pot.

• Place some of the dough on a wooden board and cut it into small pieces with a knife.

• Drop dough pieces in boiling water a few at a time. They are cooked as soon as they float to the surface.

• Drain spaetzle well and arrange in a serving dish. Stir in a little butter to prevent sticking.

• Sprinkle with grated cheese just before serving.

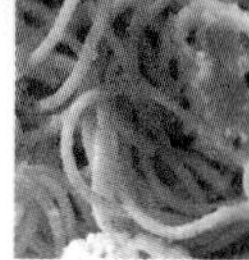

AUTUMN VEGETABLE PASTA

4 SERVINGS

1 tbsp	butter *or* margarine	15 mL
1	garlic clove, finely chopped	1
½ cup	carrots cut in julienne	125 mL
½ cup	sliced leeks	125 mL
½ cup	green beans, sliced lengthwise	125 mL
½ cup	chicken stock	125 mL
¼ cup	grated Parmesan cheese	50 mL
¼ cup	chopped fresh parsley	50 mL
2 tbsp	chopped fresh basil	30 mL
10 oz	penne	300 g
	salt and pepper	

- Melt butter in a saucepan. Cook garlic and vegetables 2 minutes over medium-high heat.
- Add chicken stock. Bring to a boil, lower heat and let simmer 7 minutes.
- Over medium heat, stir in cheese and herbs. Cook until cheese melts. Remove from heat.
- Meanwhile, cook pasta in boiling salted water 4 to 5 minutes or until *al dente*. Drain pasta and stir into sauce. Season to taste before serving.

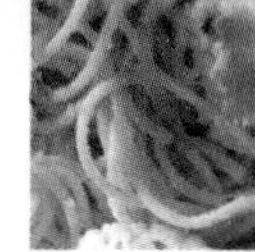

PENNE WITH OYSTER MUSHROOMS AND ASPARAGUS

4 SERVINGS

24	**asparagus spears**	**24**
2 tbsp	**butter *or* margarine**	**30 mL**
6 to 8	**medium oyster mushrooms, sliced**	**6 to 8**
10 oz	**penne, cooked**	**300 g**
1 tbsp	**balsamic vinegar**	**15 mL**
2 cups	**fresh *or* canned tomato sauce**	**500 mL**
3 tbsp	**grated Sbrinz *or* Parmesan cheese**	**45 mL**
	pepper	

• Break off woody tips of asparagus, then slice on the diagonal the same length as penne. Steam or cook in boiling salted water until tender-crisp. Drain and set aside.

• Melt butter in a saucepan. Brown mushrooms in butter. Stir in asparagus and cooked penne.

• Season with pepper and balsamic vinegar.

• Gently stir in tomato sauce and heat over medium-low until heated through.

• Serve in deep plates, sprinkled with cheese.

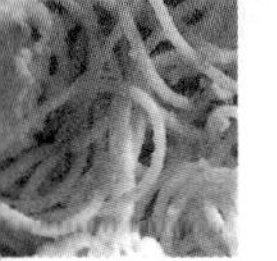

SPAGHETTINI WITH ZUCCHINI JULIENNE

4 SERVINGS

1	large zucchini, cut in julienne strips	1
10 oz	spaghettini, cooked	300 g
1 tsp	butter *or* margarine	5 mL
2	garlic cloves, finely chopped	2
2	eggs, lightly beaten	2
¾ cup	processed cheese spread	175 mL
	juice of ½ lemon	
	pepper	

• Steam the zucchini until tender-crisp. Set aside.

• Reheat pasta in a skillet with the butter and garlic.

• In a bowl, beat eggs together with cheese. Pour over pasta, mix well and heat several minutes over medium heat. Add pepper.

• Arrange pasta on plates and top with zucchini. Sprinkle with lemon juice before serving.

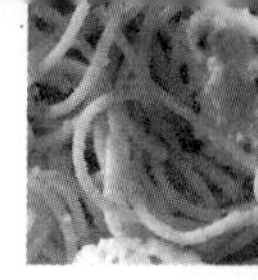

SUGGESTION

Brown the completed dish a minute or 2 under the broiler before serving.

Replace carrots with any leftover cooked vegetable.

SAUSAGE AND CHEESE MACARONI

2 SERVINGS

2 tbsp	butter *or* margarine	30 mL
2 tbsp	all-purpose flour	30 mL
1 tbsp	hot mustard	15 mL
2 cups	milk	500 mL
4	smoked chicken sausages *or* weiners, sliced	4
2 cups	elbow macaroni, cooked	500 mL
1½ cups	sliced carrots, cooked	375 mL
1 cup	processed cheese spread	250 mL
4	green onions, chopped	4
	pepper	

• Melt butter in a saucepan. Stir in flour until smooth. Stir in mustard, then gradually add milk.

• Cook over medium-high heat 2 to 3 minutes, whisking, until sauce is thick and creamy.

• Lower heat, stir in sausage pieces and cook 1 to 2 minutes.

• Stir in pasta and carrots. Heat 2 to 3 minutes, stirring. Add cheese and green onions. Cook 1 more minute until mixed. Add pepper to taste.

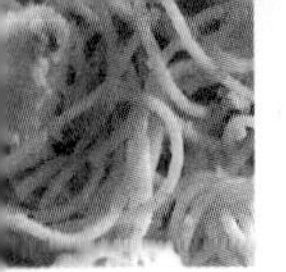

PENNE WITH SHRIMP

2 SERVINGS

7 oz	penne	200 g
2 tbsp	butter *or* margarine	30 mL
1	garlic clove, finely chopped	1
5 to 7 oz	small cooked peeled shrimp	150 to 200 g
2	lemon wedges	2
1 tsp	brandy, cognac *or* whisky	5 mL
1 cup	béchamel sauce (see page 273)	250 mL
1 tbsp	catsup *or* chili sauce	15 mL
2 tbsp	chopped fresh parsley	30 mL
	pepper *or* cayenne pepper	

• Cook pasta in boiling salted water until *al dente*. Keep warm.

• Heat butter and garlic in a saucepan.

• Toss shrimp in garlic and butter. Squeeze lemon juice over. Add brandy if desired.

• Combine béchamel and catsup; stir into shrimp.

• Season with pepper and let simmer 2 to 3 minutes.

• Arrange pasta on heated plates and top with shrimp sauce. Garnish with parsley to serve.

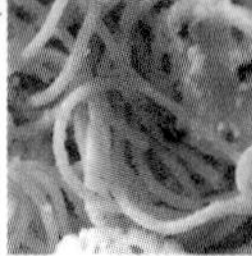

PASTA WITH BAYONNE HAM AND PISTACHIOS

2 SERVINGS

3 tbsp	**dry white wine *or* dry white vermouth**	**45 mL**
3 tbsp	**finely chopped pistachios**	**45 mL**
1 cup	**garlic-herb flavored tomato sauce**	**250 mL**
2 tbsp	**chopped fresh parsley**	**30 mL**
2 tbsp	**15% cream *or* cream cheese**	**30 mL**
1	**pinch nutmeg**	**1**
7 oz	**linguini, spaghetti *or* other pasta, cooked**	**200 g**
4	**thin slices Bayonne ham**	**4**
	pepper	

• In a non-stick skillet, heat white wine and pistachios over medium-high heat. Cook until wine has almost completely evaporated.

• Add tomato sauce and parsley. Cook another 2 minutes over very low heat.

• Stir in cream, nutmeg and pepper.

• Arrange hot pasta on plates, garnish with ham, and top with sauce and serve at once.

Bayonne ham is raw ham which is dried, pickled in brine and sometimes smoked. Whether raw or cooked, Bayonne ham is always rather salty, and so should be eaten in moderation.

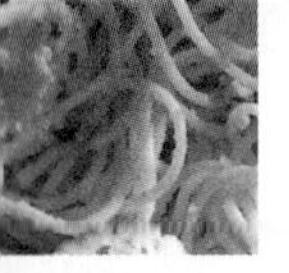

TORTELLINI PRIMAVERA

4 SERVINGS

1 tbsp	**butter *or* margarine**	**15 mL**
1 cup	**sliced mushrooms**	**250 ml**
½ cup	**chopped onion**	**125 mL**
1	**garlic clove, chopped**	**1**
½ lb	**fresh spinach**	**225 g**
1	**medium tomato, chopped**	**1**
¼ cup	**milk**	**50 mL**
¼ cup	**grated Sbrinz *or* Parmesan**	**50 mL**
½ tsp	**dried thyme**	**2 mL**
½ tsp	**dried oregano**	**2 mL**
10 oz	**tortellini, cooked and drained**	**300 g**
8 oz	**cream cheese**	**225 g**
	pepper	

• Melt butter in a saucepan, and cook mushrooms, onion and garlic over medium heat until limp. Add all remaining ingredients except tortellini and cream cheese. Mix well. Bring to a boil, stirring constantly.

• Add tortellini and cream cheese. Heat a few minutes over low heat, stirring gently. Serve hot.

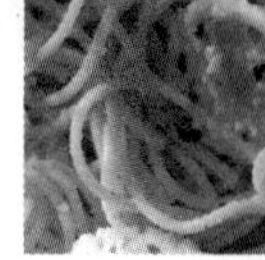

HAM AND NOODLE CASSEROLE

4 SERVINGS

2 tbsp	butter *or* margarine	30 mL
½ cup	chopped onion	125 mL
½ cup	diced green pepper	125 mL
10 oz	can cream of mushroom soup	284 mL
¾ cup	plain yogurt	175 mL
12 oz	package egg noodles, cooked	375 g
1½ cups	grated mozzarella	375 mL
2 cups	diced cooked ham	500 mL

- Preheat oven to 350°F (180°).
- Melt butter in a saucepan and cook onion and pepper until limp.
- Remove from heat and stir in undiluted soup and yogurt.
- Lightly oil a baking pan and layer noodles, cheese, ham, and mushroom sauce in that order, ending with a layer of cheese.
- Bake 30 to 45 minutes. Serve hot with a vegetable salad.

SUGGESTION

Add a chopped garlic clove with the onion, and some chopped parsley with the yogurt.

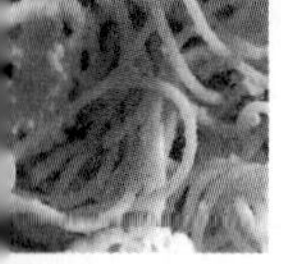

ONION SPAGHETTINI

4 SERVINGS

2 tbsp	butter *or* margarine	30 mL
4	onions, sliced	4
2 cups	garlic-herb flavored tomato sauce	500 mL
½ tsp	pepper	2 mL
10 oz	spaghettini, cooked and hot	300 g
¼ cup	crumbled crisp-cooked bacon	50 mL
1 cup	grated Parmesan cheese	250 mL
3 tbsp	chopped fresh parsley	45 mL

• Melt butter in a non-stick skillet, and cook onions over medium-high heat until tender.

• Add tomato sauce and pepper. Bring to a boil and let simmer 2 minutes.

• Arrange spaghettini on plates with sauce on top. Sprinkle with bacon, Parmesan and parsley to serve.

SCALLOPS RAVIOLI WITH SAFFRON

4 SERVINGS

	PASTA	
3 cups	all-purpose flour	750 mL
¾ cup	semolina flour	175 mL
5	eggs	5
½ tsp	salt	2 mL
	FILLING	
¾ lb	scallops	375 g
⅓ cup	whipping cream	75 mL
¼ cup	olive oil	50 mL
2 tbsp	chopped green onions	30 mL
3 tbsp	chopped black olives	45 mL
	pepper	
	SAUCE	
2 cups	chicken stock *or* fish stock	500 mL
1	pinch saffron	1
1 tsp	finely chopped garlic	5 mL
¼ cup	dry white wine (optional)	50 mL
1 tsp	curry powder	5 mL
¼ cup	sun-dried tomatoes, drained and chopped *or* 1 fresh tomato, peeled, seeded and chopped	50 mL

• Combine all pasta ingredients in a food processor until mixture forms a ball.

• Lightly flour the pasta ball, wrap in plastic wrap, and refrigerate at least 1 hour.

• To make the filling, purée scallops in a food processor. Mix in cream and oil. With a spatula, stir in pepper, green onions and olives.

• Roll out pasta very thinly. Cut into 3 inch (7.5 cm) circles. Place about 1 tbsp (15 mL) filling in middle of ½ the circles. Brush edges with water. Top each with a second pasta circle and press edges to seal.

• Cook in boiling salted water about 10 minutes. Drain and set aside.

• To make the sauce, combine all sauce ingredients in a saucepan and bring to a boil. Remove from heat and stir in ravioli. Serve in deep plates.

Add lobster meat or crabmeat to the filling. Instead of making the pasta, use a package of ready-made wonton skins.

Desserts

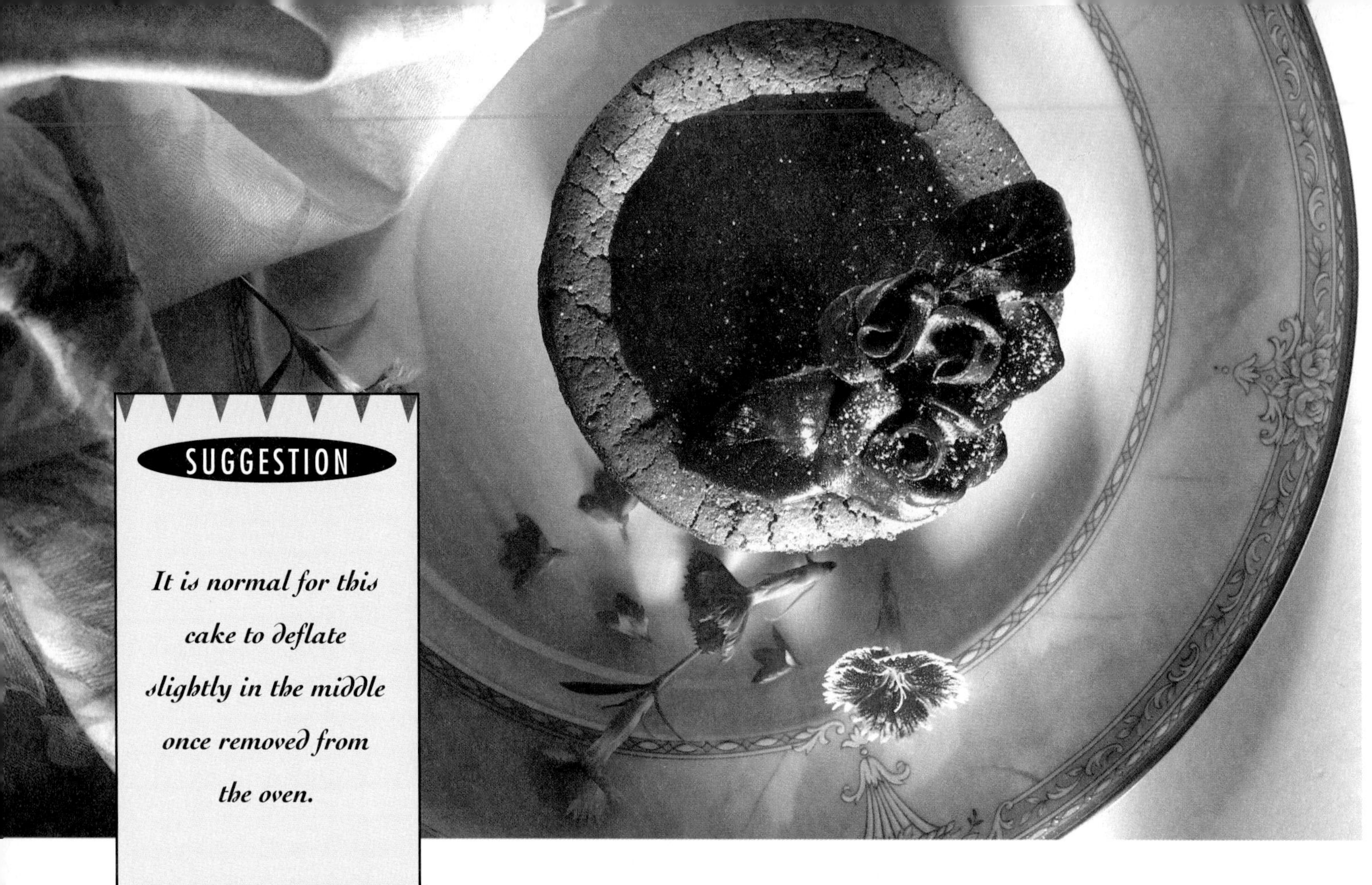

SUGGESTION

It is normal for this cake to deflate slightly in the middle once removed from the oven.

GLORIOUS CHOCOLATE CAKE

8 TO 10 SERVINGS

6	**squares semi-sweet chocolate**	**6**
¾ cup	**butter *or* margarine**	**175 mL**
4	**egg yolks**	**4**
¾ cup	**sugar**	**175 mL**
⅓ cup	**all-purpose flour**	**75 mL**
4	**egg whites**	**4**
	chocolate shavings for garnish	
	ICING	
4	**squares semi-sweet chocolate**	**4**
2 tbsp	**butter *or* margarine**	**30 mL**
2 tbsp	**water**	**30 mL**

- Preheat oven to 375°F (190°C).
- Melt chocolate and butter together in a saucepan over low heat.
- In a bowl, beat egg yolks with ½ cup (125 mL) sugar until lemon-colored and frothy. Stir in chocolate mixture and flour; blend well.
- In a second bowl, beat egg whites until stiff with remaining sugar. Stir gently into chocolate mixture.
- Pour batter into a greased and floured 9-inch (23 cm) springform pan. Bake 35 to 40 minutes.
- To make the icing, melt chocolate with butter and water in a double boiler. Stir well and spread over cake.
- Decorate with chocolate curls.

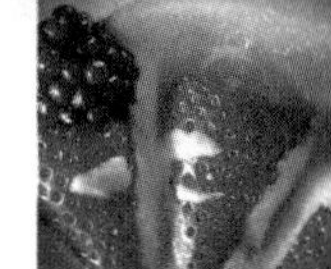

FRESH PEARS WITH COGNAC SAUCE

4 SERVINGS

2	ripe pears	2
⅓ cup	brown sugar	75 mL
2 tbsp	white sugar	30 mL
1 tbsp	commercial white sauce thickener	15 mL
½ cup	water	125 mL
1 tsp	butter *or* margarine	5 mL
1 tsp	cognac	5 mL
¼ cup	chopped walnuts	50 mL

• Peel pears, but leave stem in place. Cut in ½ lengthwise, and remove core. Arrange in 4 small dishes, round side up, or slice them thinly to within ½ inch (1.5 cm) of the stalk and arrange in a fan shape.

• In a saucepan, combine brown sugar, sugar and sauce thickener. Stir in water. Cook uncovered over medium heat 1½ minutes.

• Stir in butter and cognac.

• Pour syrup over pear halves. Sprinkle with nuts. Garnish with maraschino cherries if desired.

SUGGESTION

Instead of pears, use apples or even fresh pineapple slices.

SUGGESTION

This dessert freezes well.

Reheat gently in oven to serve.

LEMONY PEACH CLAFOUTIS

8 SERVINGS

4	**fresh *or* canned peaches, peeled and drained**	**4**
¾ cup	**sugar**	**175 mL**
4	**eggs**	**4**
½ cup	**milk**	**125 mL**
4 tbsp	**all-purpose flour**	**60 mL**
1	**pinch salt**	**1**
1 cup	**plain yogurt**	**250 mL**
1 tbsp	**melted butter *or* margarine**	**15 mL**
	grated zest of 1 lemon	

• Preheat oven to 375°F (190°C).

• Slice peaches thinly and spread over the bottom of a well-buttered 10-inch (25 cm) quiche or pie plate. Sprinkle with lemon zest and 2 tbsp (30 mL) sugar.

• In a food processor, mix eggs, milk, flour, remaining sugar and salt for 1 minute. Blend in yogurt and melted butter. Pour over peaches.

• Bake about 50 minutes, or until golden and puffy.

COOL MELON SHERBET

4 SERVINGS

½ cup	unsweetened white grape juice	125 mL
¼ cup	sugar	50 mL
½ tsp	grated lemon zest	2 mL
1 tbsp	lemon juice	15 mL
1 tbsp	slivered fresh ginger	15 mL
1 cup	peeled, seeded and diced honeydew melon	250 mL

GARNISH

green grape halves
fresh mint (optional)

• In a saucepan, combine grape juice, sugar, lemon zest and juice, and ginger. Bring to a boil, reduce heat and let simmer 5 minutes. Remove ginger. Set aside syrup.

• Process melon in food processor until smooth. Add reserved syrup and mix. Pour into a shallow dish and chill in freezer until firm.

• Break mixture up with a fork and process again in food processor until thick and smooth. Pour into a container with a tight-fitting lid, and freeze at least 4 hours.

• Serve in sherbet dishes garnished with grapes and small mint leaves.

Honeydew melon is a good source of potassium and Vitamin C, but unlike cantaloupe, has very little beta-carotene.

HOW TO MIX AND BAKE CAKES

Preheat oven to 350°F (180°C). Grease and lightly flour a tube pan.

In a large bowl, combine dry ingredients (flour, baking powder, baking soda and salt). Add any dried fruit or nuts called for in recipe to dry mixture.

Mix butter, eggs and sugar in food processor.

Mix in ⅓ the dry ingredients, then ½ the liquid. Repeat, ending with dry ingredients.

Pour into cake pan and bake about 30 minutes, or until a knife inserted in the center comes out clean.

ORANGE RING CAKE

12 SERVINGS

½ cup	butter *or* margarine	125 mL
½ cup	sugar	125 mL
1 tbsp	grated orange zest	15 mL
3	egg yolks	3
½ cup	plain yogurt	125 mL
1 tsp	vanilla extract	5 mL
1¾ cups	all-purpose flour	425 mL
2 tsp	baking powder	10 mL
2 tsp	baking soda	10 mL
¼ cup	unsweetened orange juice	50 mL
2 tbsp	lemon juice	30 mL
3	egg whites	3
1	pinch salt	1

• Preheat oven to 350°F (180°C).

• Grease and lightly flour a 12-cup (3 liter) tube pan.

• In food processor, mix butter, sugar, orange zest and egg yolks until mixture is light and fluffy. Mix in yogurt and vanilla.

• In a bowl, mix flour, baking powder and baking soda thoroughly.

• In a second bowl, combine orange juice and lemon juice.

• Alternately mix dry ingredients and juice into egg yolk mixture, beginning and ending with dry ingredients

• Beat egg whites until stiff and glossy. Fold gently into batter.

• Pour batter into tube pan and bake 35 to 40 minutes, or until a toothpick in the center comes out clean.

FRUIT TART

8 SERVINGS

BASE

puff pastry

CREAM FILLING

2 cups	milk	500 mL
½ cup	sugar	125 mL
1 tsp	vanilla extract	5 mL
3 tbsp	cornstarch	45 mL
3 tbsp	water	45 mL

TOPPING

3	kiwis, peeled and sliced	3
10 oz	can mandarin orange segments	284 mL
6	raspberries	6
	blueberries	

- To make the cream filling, heat milk together with sugar and vanilla in a saucepan.
- Dissolve cornstarch in the water, then stir into milk mixture. Heat, stirring constantly, until thickened. Let cool.
- To make the pastry shell, roll out pastry to make a circle 12 inches (30 cm) in diameter. Slash the surface only in a circle 2 inches (5 cm) from the outside edge (this will keep center from puffing up). Place pastry on cookie sheet and let rest in refrigerator at least 1 hour.
- Preheat oven to 350°F (180°C).
- Bake pastry in oven about 20 minutes, until golden.
- Let pastry cool, then fill center with cream filling. Decorate top with fruit.

1 Prepare cream filling.

2 Roll out pastry circle. Slash surface only to mark smaller circle.

3 Bake pastry and let cool.

4 Fill with cream filling and top with fruit.

EASY CHOCOLATE MOUSSE WITH ORANGE LIQUEUR

4 SERVINGS

4 oz	package instant chocolate pudding mix	113 g
1½ cups	cold milk	375 mL
2 tbsp	orange liqueur	30 mL
¼ cup	whipping cream	50 mL
¼ cup	slivered almonds	50 mL
	plain yogurt (garnish)	
	shredded unsweetened coconut (garnish)	

• Prepare chocolate pudding according to package instructions, using milk and orange liqueur. Refrigerate 5 minutes.

• Beat cream with electric beater until stiff. Gently fold in chocolate mixture with rubber spatula. Stir in almonds.

• Pour into individual serving dishes. Refrigerate until ready to serve. Garnish with a little yogurt and coconut if desired.

SUGGESTION

For a different presentation, use this mousse to fill small baked tart shells.

PEAR AND HAZELNUT UPSIDE-DOWN CAKE

4 SERVINGS

8	egg whites	8
½ cup	sugar	125 mL
1 tsp	vanilla extract	5 mL
1 cup	all-purpose flour	250 mL
¼ cup	unsweetened cocoa powder	50 mL
½ tsp	baking powder	2 mL
2 tbsp	heated milk	30 mL
6	canned pear halves, drained and sliced thin lengthwise	6
½ cup	chopped blanched hazelnuts	125 mL
¼ cup	brown sugar	50 mL

• Preheat oven to 400°F (200°C). Grease an 8-inch (20 cm) round cake pan. Line bottom with waxed paper.

• In a bowl, beat egg whites until foamy with an electric beater. Still beating, gradually add sugar and vanilla.

• Sift flour, cocoa powder and baking powder into a second bowl. Stir dry ingredients into egg mixture, alternating with milk.

• Arrange pear slices close together in bottom of lined pan. Combine hazelnuts and brown sugar, and sprinkle over pears. Cover with batter.

• Bake about 20 minutes, or until a knife inserted in cake comes out clean. Remove cake from oven and unmold while still warm.

SUGGESTION

Serve this cake with a fresh fruit coulis (a sauce of sieved, unsweetened fruit).

PINEAPPLE COCONUT CAKE

12 TO 14 SERVINGS

1 cup	**all-purpose flour**	**250 mL**
1 cup	**quick-cooking oatmeal, ground in food processor**	**250 mL**
1 tsp	**baking soda**	**5 mL**
1 tsp	**baking powder**	**5 mL**
¼ tsp	**salt**	**1 mL**
2 tsp	**ground cinnamon**	**10 mL**
1 tsp	**ground nutmeg**	**5 mL**
¾ cup	**corn oil**	**175 mL**
¾ cup	**packed light brown sugar**	**175 mL**
4	**eggs**	**4**
1 tbsp	**vanilla extract**	**15 mL**
1 cup	**grated raw carrots**	**250 mL**
⅓ cup	**shredded unsweetened coconut**	**75 mL**
2 cups	**crushed and drained fresh *or* canned pineapple**	**500 mL**
½ cup	**chopped nuts (optional)**	**125 mL**

• Preheat oven to 350°F (180°C). Grease and lightly flour a tube pan.

• In a large bowl, combine flour, oatmeal, baking soda, baking powder, salt, cinnamon and nutmeg. Set aside.

• In food processor, combine oil, brown sugar, eggs and vanilla. Stir dry ingredients little by little into egg mixture, then fold in carrots, coconut, pineapple and chopped nuts.

• Pour mixture into cake pan and bake about 55 to 60 minutes.

• Let cool 10 minutes before unmolding.

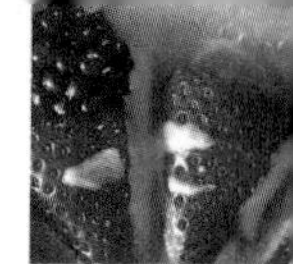

STEAMED WINTER FRUIT WITH GINGER

4 SERVINGS

2	dried prunes *or* apricots, sliced	2
2	pears, peeled, cored and diced *or* 4 pear halves canned in light syrup, diced	2
¼ cup	raisins *or* currants	50 mL
1 tbsp	finely chopped fresh ginger	15 mL
½ tsp	vanilla extract	2 mL
2 tbsp	icing sugar	30 mL
1 tbsp	cornstarch	15 mL
1 tsp	grated lemon zest *or* orange zest	5 mL
4	circles of waxed paper *or* foil	4
2	green apples, peeled, cored and halved	2
2 tbsp	lemon juice	30 mL
2 tbsp	liquid honey (optional)	30 mL

GARNISHES

vanilla yogurt

fresh mint leaves

• Preheat oven to 400°F (200°C).

• In a bowl, combine prunes, pears, raisins, ginger and vanilla. Add icing sugar and cornstarch and mix well. Stir in lemon zest.

• Divide fruit mixture between paper or foil circles. Top with ½ apple. Sprinkle a little lemon juice and honey over each apple. Seal packages well and bake about 15 to 20 minutes.

• Remove packages from oven, open, and top with a little vanilla yogurt and fresh mint.

APRICOT DELIGHT

6 SERVINGS

2 cups	**dried apricots, washed**	**500 mL**
⅓ cup	**chopped blanched almonds**	**75 mL**
1 cup	**plain yogurt**	**250 mL**
3 tbsp	**sugar**	**45 mL**
1 tbsp	**orange liqueur *or* Grand Marnier (optional)**	**15 mL**
2 tbsp	**chopped toasted almonds**	**30 mL**

• Place apricots in a saucepan and cover with water. Bring to a boil, lower heat and let simmer very gently 30 minutes. Drain and set aside.

• Purée apricots in a food processor until smooth.

• Add almonds and process to slightly crush them. Set aside.

• In a bowl, combine yogurt, sugar and liqueur.

• Spoon apricot mixture into a serving dish. Top with yogurt mixture and toasted almonds. Serve chilled.

ORANGE CHOCOLATE CAKE

8 TO 10 SERVINGS

3 oz	unsweetened chocolate	90 g
½ cup	milk	125 mL
½ cup	white sugar	125 mL
½ cup	butter *or* margarine	125 mL
½ cup	brown sugar	125 mL
3	eggs, beaten	3
¼ cup	unsweetened orange juice	50 mL
2 tbsp	grated orange zest	30 mL
1¾ cups	all-purpose flour	425 mL
½ tsp	salt	2 mL
2 tsp	baking powder	10 mL
¾ tsp	baking soda	3 mL

ORANGE CREAM

2 cups	milk	500 mL
¼ cup	orange juice	50 mL
2	egg yolks	2
½ cup	sugar	125 mL
2 tbsp	cornstarch, dissolved in a little water	30 mL
	grated zest of 1 orange	

• Preheat oven to 350°F (180°C). Grease and lightly flour an 8-inch (20 cm) square cake pan.

• In a saucepan, combine chocolate, milk and white sugar. Heat over low heat, stirring, until chocolate melts. Let cool.

• In a bowl, cream the butter until fluffy. Add brown sugar and mix well. Stir in egg yolks. Add orange juice and zest. Mix well.

• Sift together flour, salt, baking powder and baking soda. Add flour mixture bit by bit to chocolate mixture, alternating with egg mixture. Blend well. Pour into prepared pan and bake 45 to 50 minutes.

• To make orange cream, heat together milk, orange juice and zest in a saucepan until just steaming. Set aside.

• In a bowl, beat egg yolks and sugar until light. Gradually whisk in hot milk mixture. Return mixture to saucepan. Cook a few minutes over low heat. Stir in cornstarch mixture until thickened. Remove from heat and let cool.

• When cake is done, let it stand 15 minutes before unmolding. Cut in ½ to make 2 layers. Spread some orange cream between layers and use the rest as icing.

> **SUGGESTION**
>
> *You can make these squares out of season by substituting canned fruit, unsweetened or in light syrup.*

FRESH FRUIT SQUARES

10 TO 12 SERVINGS

1¼ cups	all-purpose flour	300 mL
1½ tsp	baking powder	7 mL
¼ cup	white sugar	50 mL
¼ cup	butter *or* margarine	50 mL
1	egg, beaten	1
¼ cup	milk	50 mL
1 tsp	vanilla extract	5 mL
3	fresh plums, peeled, pitted and sliced	3
2	fresh peaches *or* pears, peeled, cored and sliced	2
1	green apple, cored and thinly sliced	1
1 cup	seedless green *or* red grapes	250 mL
	GLAZE	
¼ cup	corn syrup	50 mL
1 tsp	ground cinnamon	5 mL
¼ cup	melted butter *or* margarine	50 mL
⅓ cup	raspberry, apricot *or* other jelly	75 mL

- Preheat oven to 400°F (200°C). Lightly grease a 13 x 9 x 2 inch (32 x 23 x 5 cm) baking pan.
- In food processor, combine flour, baking powder, sugar and butter. Add beaten egg, milk and vanilla. Process until mixture is smooth.
- Spread batter over bottom of baking pan. Arrange different fruit slices in slightly overlapping rows. Arrange grapes between rows.
- To make the glaze, combine corn syrup, cinnamon and melted butter. Spread over fruit. Bake about 35 minutes, or until fruit is tender.
- Combine raspberry jelly with 1 tbsp (15 mL) hot water and baste over top. Cut into rectangles and serve hot.

STRAWBERRY RHUBARB CHEESECAKE

4 SERVINGS

CRUST

1 cup	vanilla wafer crumbs	250 mL
2 tbsp	ground almonds *or* hazelnuts	30 mL
¼ cup	butter *or* margarine	50 mL
1 tbsp	brown sugar	15 mL

FILLING

1 cup	apple juice	250 mL
2	envelopes unflavored gelatin	2
3 cups	cottage cheese	750 mL
2	bananas	2
¼ cup	sugar	50 mL

SAUCE

2 cups	chopped rhubarb	500 mL
1 cup	sliced strawberries	250 mL
¾ cup	sugar	175 mL
2 tbsp	orange liqueur (optional)	30 mL
2 tbsp	cornstarch dissolved in a little water	30 mL

GARNISH

½ cup	toasted unsweetened shredded coconut	125 mL
	grated lemon *or* lime zest	
	sliced strawberries	

• Combine all crust ingredients in food processor. Pat mixture into a 9-inch (23 cm) springform pan.

• Pour ¼ cup (50 mL) apple juice into a bowl. Sprinkle in gelatin and let soak 5 minutes. Place bowl over a pan of hot water and heat gently until gelatin has completely dissolved. Remove from heat and set aside.

• In food processor, combine cottage cheese, bananas, sugar and remaining apple juice until smooth. Mix in gelatin mixture, then pour over crust. Refrigerate 3 to 4 hours, or until set.

• To make sauce, combine rhubarb, strawberries, sugar and liqueur in a saucepan. Bring to a boil over medium-high heat. Lower heat and let simmer about 5 minutes. Add cornstarch mixture. Mix well.

• Unmold cheesecake, cover with sauce, and sprinkle with toasted coconut. Decorate with lemon zest and strawberries, if desired.

CHILLED COFFEE RING

8 SERVINGS

1¾ cups	strong cold coffee	425 mL
½ cup	15% cream	125 mL
½ cup	sugar	125 mL
2	envelopes unflavored gelatin	2
3	egg yolks	3
½ tsp	vanilla extract	2 mL
¼ tsp	salt	1 mL
3	egg whites	3

- Chill a tube pan or ring mold in the freezer.
- In a bowl, combine coffee, cream, ½ the sugar, and gelatin. Heat over a pan of hot water over low heat until dissolved.
- In a second bowl, lightly beat egg yolks. Stir in remaining sugar, vanilla and salt.
- Pour coffee mixture over egg mixture. Place bowl over pan of hot water and heat 8 to 10 minutes, stirring constantly, until mixture coats the back of a metal spoon. Remove from heat and let cool.
- Beat egg whites until stiff. Fold into cooled coffee mixture with a rubber spatula. Pour into chilled mold. Refrigerate a few hours before serving.
- Unmold and slice to serve on chilled plates.

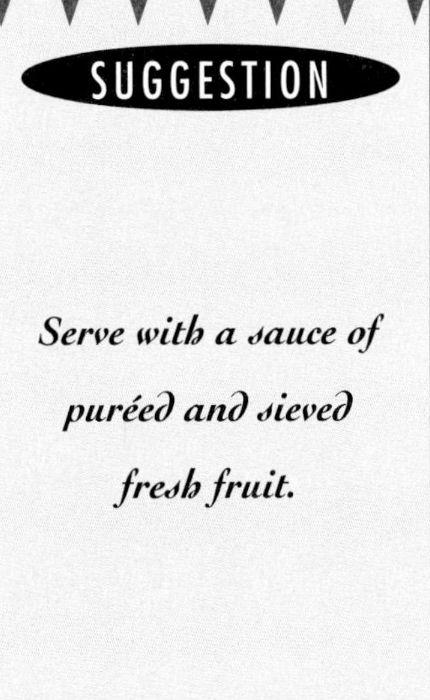

SUGGESTION

Serve with a sauce of puréed and sieved fresh fruit.

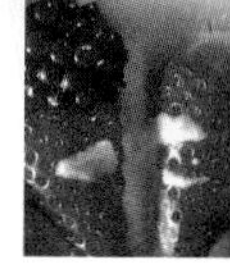

APPLES PROVENÇALE

4 SERVINGS

4	**firm apples**	4
1 cup	**sugar**	250 mL
2 cups	**water**	500 mL
1 tsp	**anise seeds**	5 mL
3 tbsp	**anise liqueur *or* syrup *or* 1 tsp (5 mL) anise extract (optional)**	45 mL
	cold water	
	lemon juice	

• Peel apples, cut in wedges and trim out core. Place wedges in cold water with a little lemon juice added to prevent browning.

• Combine sugar, water and anise seeds in a saucepan. Bring to a boil, stirring constantly until sugar dissolves. Lower heat and let simmer 5 minutes.

• Drain apples and place in the syrup. Raise heat until mixture bubbles, then lower heat, cover and let simmer 10 minutes. (Do not let boil or overcook.)

• Remove apples from liquid and divide between individual dishes. Bring liquid to a boil, and cook uncovered until thickened and syrupy. Skim off foam. Stir in anise flavoring and pour syrup over apples.

SUGGESTION

Bake in 2 square tins, then cut into smaller squares and decorate individual portions as shown.

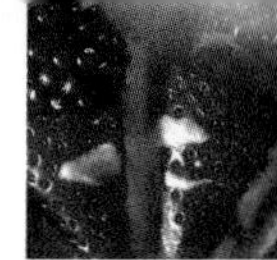

BLACK FOREST CAKE

8 TO 10 SERVINGS

CAKE

2 cups	all-purpose flour	500 mL
½ cup	unsweetened cocoa powder	125 mL
2 tsp	baking powder	10 mL
½ tsp	salt	2 mL
6	eggs	6
2 cups	sugar	500 mL
6 tbsp	water	90 mL
2 tsp	vanilla extract	10 mL

CREAM

2½ cups	whipping cream	625 mL
2 to 3 tbsp	kirsch	30 to 45 mL

GARNISH

2 cups	coarsely chopped maraschino *or* Bing cherries	500 mL
2 cups	chocolate shavings	500 mL
8 to 10	maraschino *or* candied cherries, with stems	8 to 10
1 tsp	icing sugar	5 mL

- To make the cake, preheat oven to 350°F (180°C).
- In a bowl, combine flour, cocoa powder, baking powder and salt. Set aside.
- Beat eggs well in a food processor. With motor running, gradually add sugar, then water and vanilla.
- Gradually add dry ingredients to egg mixture.
- Divide batter between 2 9-inch (23 cm) round cake pans. Bake 20 to 25 minutes, or until a toothpick inserted in center comes out clean. Let cool.
- Turn out cakes, trim tops of cakes flat, then slice each cake into 2 equal layers. Cover and set aside.
- Beat cream until stiff and beat in kirsh. Set aside.
- Place 1 cake layer on a plate or round of cardboard. Cover with cream and chopped cherries. Cover with another cake layer and repeat garnish until all layers are used.
- With a spatula, cover layers with whipped cream. Cover top and sides with chocolate shavings.
- Pipe 8 to 10 whipped cream rosettes on top of cake. Garnish with maraschino cherries. Sprinkle with icing sugar just before serving.

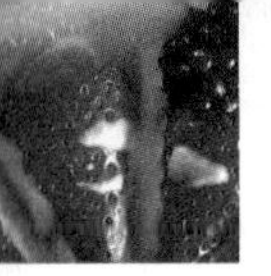

PERFECT PIE CRUST

2½ cups	all-purpose flour	625 mL
1	pinch salt	1
1 cup	butter *or* shortening	250 mL
1	egg	1
1 tsp	vinegar	5 mL
½ cup	very cold water	125 mL

Combine flour and salt in food processor.

With motor still running, add butter bit by bit.

In a measuring cup, combine egg, vinegar and water. With motor running, gradually pour into food processor.

As soon as dough pulls away from sides of processor bowl, turn off motor and remove dough.

Lightly flour pastry ball, wrap in plastic wrap, and refrigerate at least 1 hour before using.

APPLE OATMEAL PIE

8 SERVINGS

5 cups	thinly sliced peeled cooking apples	1.25 liters
2 tsp	lemon juice	10 mL
3 tbsp	sugar	45 mL
3 tbsp	all-purpose flour	45 mL
2 tsp	grated lemon zest	10 mL
1 tsp	ground cinnamon	5 mL
¼ tsp	ground nutmeg	1 mL
1	9-inch (23 cm) pie shell, unbaked	1
	TOPPING	
¼ cup	lightly packed light brown sugar	50 mL
3 tbsp	quick-cooking oatmeal	45 mL
3 tbsp	whole-wheat flour	45 mL
1 tsp	ground cinnamon	5 mL
1 tbsp	butter *or* margarine	15 mL
4 tbsp	plain yogurt	60 mL

- Preheat oven to 425°F (220°C).
- Place apple slices in a bowl and sprinkle with lemon juice.
- In a second bowl, combine sugar, all-purpose flour, lemon zest, cinnamon and nutmeg.
- Pour flour mixture over apples and toss well. Spread mixture in pie shell.
- To prepare the topping, combine brown sugar, oatmeal, whole-wheat flour and cinnamon in a food processor. Work in butter and yogurt to make a crumbly mixture. Spread over apples.
- Bake 15 minutes, then lower oven temperature to 350°F (180°C) and cook another 30 to 35 minutes or until topping is golden-brown.

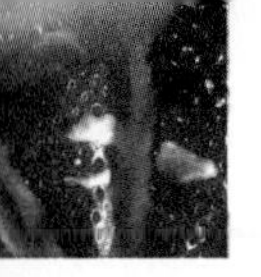

RASPBERRY YOGURT CAKE

8 TO 12 SERVINGS

1½ cups	all-purpose flour	375 mL
½ cup	sugar	125 mL
1½ tsp	baking powder	7 mL
2 tbsp	finely ground hazelnuts	30 mL
⅓ cup	butter *or* margarine	75 mL
2	egg whites	2
1 tsp	vanilla extract	5 mL
¼ cup	milk	50 mL
3 cups	fresh *or* frozen unsweetened, drained raspberries	750 mL

TOPPING

2 cups	plain yogurt	500 mL
2 tbsp	all-purpose flour	30 mL
1	egg, lightly beaten	1
¼ cup	honey	50 mL
2 tsp	grated lemon zest	10 mL
1 tsp	vanilla extract	5 mL

• Preheat oven to 350°F (180°C). Oil a baking pan about 8 inches (20 cm) in diameter.

• In a food processor, combine flour, sugar, baking powder, ground hazelnuts, butter, egg whites, vanilla and milk.

• Pour mixture into pan and top with raspberries.

• To prepare the topping, combine yogurt and flour in a bowl. Mix in beaten egg, honey, lemon zest and vanilla. Stir until mixture is smooth. Spread over raspberries.

• Bake 50 to 60 minutes, or until top of cake is golden-brown. Serve hot or cold.

SUGGESTION

Instead of raspberries, use any fruit you wish as the fruit layer.

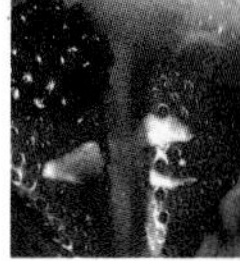

BLOOD ORANGE PARFAIT

4 SERVINGS

PARFAIT

2	egg yolks	2
¼ cup	sugar	50 mL
1 cup	whipping cream	250 mL
2	egg whites	2
1 tbsp	sugar	15 mL
	juice of 2 blood oranges	
	grated zest of 1 orange	

PASTRY SHELLS

3	sheets filo pastry	3
3 tbsp	melted butter *or* margarine	45 mL

SYRUP

3	blood oranges, segmented, membranes removed	3
½ tsp	orange flower water	2 mL
¼ cup	honey	50 mL
1 tbsp	cornstarch, dissolved in 2 tbsp (30 mL) water	15 mL
	juice of 3 oranges	
	fresh mint leaves	

• To prepare the parfait, beat egg yolks and sugar together in a bowl until foamy. Stir in orange juice and zest. Set aside.

• Whip cream until stiff. Stir into yolk mixture.

• Whip egg whites until stiff, whipping in 1 tbsp (15 mL) sugar. Gently fold into yolk mixture with rubber spatula.

• Turn into 4 ramekins and freeze at least 3 hours.

• Preheat oven to 350°F (180°C).

• Stack 3 filo sheets and cut out 4 circles 7 inches (17.5 cm) in diameter. Brush with melted butter. Arrange in muffin molds and bake 5 minutes.

• To make the syrup, heat juice of 3 oranges, orange flower water and honey in a saucepan. Stir in cornstarch mixture to thicken.

• Remove from heat and stir in orange segments. Let cool.

• Place a pastry shell on each plate. Unmold a parfait and place in shell. Pour syrup over, and garnish with fresh mint.

NEAPOLITAN PIE

6 SERVINGS

BASE

2 cups	sifted all-purpose flour	500 mL
1	pinch salt	1
3 tbsp	sugar	45 mL
4 tbsp	soft butter	60 mL
2	egg yolks	2
	finely grated zest of ½ lemon	

TOPPING

12 oz	ricotta *or* cottage cheese	350 g
2 tbsp	icing sugar	30 mL
3	eggs, beaten	3
2 oz	finely chopped almonds	60 g
3 oz	candied fruit, finely chopped	90 g
¼ tsp	vanilla extract	1 mL
	finely grated zest of ½ lemon	
	finely grated zest of ½ orange	

• To make the base, combine flour, salt, sugar and lemon zest in food processor. Gradually add butter, then egg yolks one by one. Process until well combined.

• Cover dough and refrigerate about 1 hour.

• To make the topping, combine cheese and icing sugar in food processor. With motor at low speed, add eggs one by one, then remaining ingredients. Set aside.

• Preheat oven to 350°F (180°C). Grease and lightly flour a quiche pan.

• Roll out dough and spread in pan.

• Spread topping evenly over dough.

• Bake about 45 minutes, until set. Let cool completely on a wire rack before serving.

KIWI MOUSSE

6 SERVINGS

½ cup	cold water	125 mL
2	envelopes unflavored gelatin	2
2 cups	puréed kiwi	500 mL
½ cup	sugar	125 mL
¾ cup	plain yogurt	175 mL
½ tsp	grated orange zest	2 mL
4	egg whites	4
	kiwi slices for garnish	

• Pour water in a small saucepan and sprinkle gelatin over; let soak 5 minutes. Heat over low heat until gelatin has dissolved. Set aside.

• In a second saucepan, heat kiwi purée with ½ the sugar over low heat 5 minutes.

• In a bowl, combine kiwi mixture with yogurt, orange zest and gelatin mixture.

• Refrigerate until slightly set.

• Beat egg whites in large bowl until foamy. Add remaining sugar gradually, still beating, until stiff peaks form.

• Beat about ¼ of the egg white mixture into kiwi mixture. Fold in remaining egg whites gently with a rubber spatula. Pour into individual ramekins or a large mold.

• Cover and refrigerate at least 1 hour. Serve garnished with kiwi slices.

Kiwis are high in Vitamin C. The thin velvety skin is edible.

APPLE CINNAMON STRUDEL

6 SERVINGS

PASTRY

2 cups	all-purpose flour	500 mL
1	egg, at room temperature	1
1 tbsp	powdered sugar	15 mL
1	pinch salt	1
2 tbsp	butter *or* margarine	30 mL
¼ cup	lukewarm water	50 mL
	melted butter *or* margarine	

FILLING

¼ cup	raisins	50 mL
1½ lbs	apples, peeled, cored, cut in wedges	675 g
3 tbsp	butter *or* margarine	45 mL
3 tbsp	breadcrumbs	45 mL
⅓ cup	sugar	75 mL
1 tbsp	ground cinnamon	15 mL
	juice of ½ lemon	
	icing sugar	

• To make the pastry, combine flour, egg, sugar, salt, 2 tbsp (30 mL) butter and ½ the water in food processor. Add more water as necessary to make a soft but workable dough.

• Shape dough into a ball, brush with melted butter, cover with a clean cloth and let stand at room temperature ½ hour.

• To make the filling, put raisins in a bowl and cover with water. Let soak 20 minutes. Drain well and set aside. Sprinkle apple wedges with lemon juice and set aside.

• Melt butter in a skillet. Add breadcrumbs and toast a few minutes over medium heat. Set aside.

• Roll out pastry using technique on the facing page. Brush with melted butter if dough seems dry.

• Preheat oven to 350°F (180°C).

(Continued on next page)

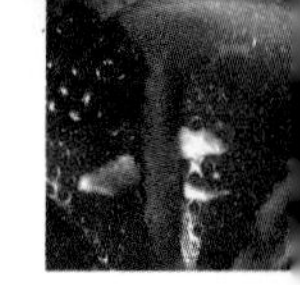

• Combine apples, soaked raisins, breadcrumbs, sugar and cinnamon. Arrange in a band along one edge of dough. Carefully roll dough to enclose filling. Press ends to seal.

• Slide strudel onto a greased cookie sheet. Brush with melted butter and bake about 50 to 60 minutes, until nicely golden.

• Arrange on a serving plate and sprinkle with icing sugar. Serve hot or cold.

MAKING STRUDEL PASTRY

Combine pastry ingredients in food processor, adding enough water to make soft dough.

Form into a ball and brush with melted butter.

Cover with a clean cloth and let rest.

Place the dough on top of a sheet of plastic wrap, cover with a second sheet of plastic wrap, and roll it out into a rectangle.

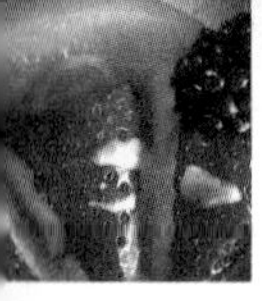

CANTALOUPE YOGURT

4 SERVINGS

2	**cantaloupes, halved and seeded**	**2**
¼ cup	**lemon juice *or* lime juice**	**50 mL**
2 cups	**plain *or* vanilla yogurt**	**500 mL**
2 to 3 tbsp	**sugar**	**30 to 45 mL**

- Spoon out cantaloupe flesh into food processor.
- Add lemon juice, yogurt and sugar.
- Process until mixture is smooth.
- Serve in individual bowls.

Cantaloupe is a good source of Vitamins A and C. Darker colored fruits and vegetables are higher in minerals and vitamins.

PEAR CAKE

10 SERVINGS

4 cups	all-purpose flour	1 liter
1 tbsp	baking powder	15 mL
¾ cup	sugar	175 mL
1 cup	creamed cottage cheese *or* plain yogurt	250 mL
⅓ cup	corn oil	75 mL
4	eggs, beaten	4
14 oz	can pears, with their juice, cut in wedges	398 mL
¼ cup	milk	50 mL
	grated zest of ½ lemon	

• Preheat oven to 350°F (180°C). Grease an 8-inch (20 cm) round cake pan.

• Sift together flour and baking powder.

• Place flour in a bowl, and make a well in the center. Add sugar, cheese, oil, beaten eggs, juice from pears, milk and lemon zest. Mix until smooth.

• Pour into cake pan and arrange pears on top.

• Bake in center of oven about 45 minutes.

• Unmold as soon as cooked. Serve warm or cold.

SPECIAL FRUIT SALAD

4 SERVINGS

2	large oranges, segmented, membranes removed	2
1	green apple, unpeeled, cored and diced	1
½	cantaloupe, diced *or* in balls	½
15	grapes, halved	15
1	kiwi, peeled and diced	1
6	strawberries, sliced	6
6	pitted dates, chopped (optional)	6
2 cups	unsweetened orange juice	500 mL
½ cup	unsweetened apple juice	125 mL
2 tbsp	brandy	30 mL

GARNISH
chopped walnuts
mint leaves

- Combine all ingredients except garnishes in a bowl.
- Refrigerate 2 to 3 hours, covered.
- Garnish with walnuts and mint just before serving.

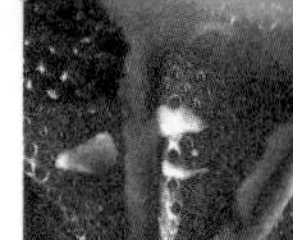

AMARETTO CHEESECAKE

10 TO 12 SERVINGS

CRUST

1 cup	**blanched almonds**	**250 mL**
1 cup	**crumbled vanilla wafers**	**250 mL**
⅓ cup	**melted butter *or* margarine**	**75 mL**

FILLING

¼ cup	**water**	**50 mL**
1½	**envelopes unflavored gelatin**	**1½**
3	**egg yolks**	**3**
¾ cup	**sugar**	**175 mL**
1 lb	**cream cheese**	**450 g**
¼ tsp	**almond extract**	**1 mL**
3 tbsp	**amaretto liqueur**	**45 mL**
1 cup	**milk, heated**	**250 mL**
2 cups	**whipping cream**	**500 mL**
3	**egg whites**	**3**
¼ cup	**toasted almonds**	**50 mL**

• To make the crust, coarsely chop almonds in food processor. Add crumbled wafers and process until finely ground. Add butter and mix.

• Pack crumb mixture into bottom of a 10-inch (25 cm) springform pan, pressing some partway up the sides. Refrigerate.

• To make the filling, put water in a bowl and sprinkle with gelatin. Let soak 5 minutes.

• In food processor, combine egg yolks, sugar, cream cheese, almond extract and amaretto. Add milk and gelatin mixture and process again.

• Heat mixture in top of a double boiler over low heat until it thickens. Chill about 10 minutes.

• Beat cream until stiff. Set aside.

• Beat egg whites until stiff. With a rubber spatula, gradually fold egg whites into ⅔ of the whipped cream. Fold mixture into egg yolk mixture. Pour into crust.

• Pipe or spoon remaining whipped cream on top of cake, and garnish with toasted almonds.

PEACH MELBA

4 SERVINGS

1 cup	**boiling water**	**250 mL**
¼ cup	**sugar**	**50 mL**
1 tbsp	**cognac**	**15 mL**
8	**peach halves, canned in light syrup, drained**	**8**
½ cup	**frozen unsweetened raspberries, drained**	**125 mL**
2 cups	**vanilla ice milk**	**500 mL**
3 tbsp	**toasted almonds**	**45 mL**

• Pour boiling water in a saucepan. Stir in 2 tbsp (30 mL) sugar until dissolved. Add cognac.

• Put peach halves in liquid and cook gently 3 minutes over low heat. Remove from heat. Let cool, then drain.

• Purée raspberries in food processor. Mix in remaining sugar. Pour into a saucepan and cook over low heat 3 minutes. Let cool.

• Divide ice milk between 4 bowls, top with 2 peach halves, and pour raspberry sauce over. Garnish with toasted almonds.

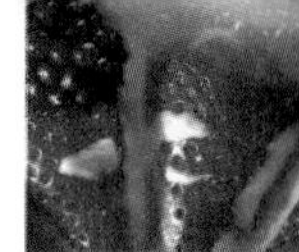

FRUIT MIRROR

8 SERVINGS

3½ cups	**cranberry juice**	**875 mL**
6 oz	**lemon jelly powder**	**180 g**
1 cup	**peeled sliced peaches *or* nectarines**	**250 mL**
½ cup	**blueberries *or* strawberries**	**125 mL**
½ cup	**seedless green grapes**	**125 mL**
¼ cup	**slivered almonds**	**50 mL**

- Lightly oil a 6-cup (1.5 liter) mold. Set aside.
- In a saucepan, bring 1½ cups (375 mL) cranberry juice to a boil.
- Dissolve jelly powder in hot juice.
- Add remaining cranberry juice. Refrigerate until partially set.
- Stir in fruit and almonds. Pour mixture into mold. Refrigerate 3 to 4 hours. Unmold on a serving dish.

SUGGESTION

Use thawed frozen fruit or canned fruit instead of fresh fruit. Drain them well before adding to jelly mixture. Chill the mixture in individual molds.

BUTTERSCOTCH PIE

6 SERVINGS

PASTRY CRUST

2 cups	all-purpose flour	500 mL
1	pinch salt	1
2 tbsp	ground hazelnuts (optional)	30 mL
½ lb	butter *or* shortening	225 g
1	egg	1
½ cup	ice water	125 mL
1 tsp	white vinegar	5 mL

BUTTERSCOTCH MIXTURE

¾ cup	lukewarm water	175 mL
½ cup	evaporated milk	125 mL
1⅔ cups	packed light brown sugar	400 mL
2	eggs	2
½ cup +1 tbsp	all-purpose flour	140 mL
3 tbsp	soft butter	45 mL
1 tsp	vanilla extract	5 mL

• To make the pastry, combine flour, salt and hazelnuts in food processor. Add butter cut in chunks, and process.

• Mix egg, water and vinegar in a bowl. Pour egg mixture into food processor. Process until mixture forms a ball.

• Place pastry ball on lightly floured surface. Pat into a ball, cover with plastic wrap and refrigerate at least 1 hour before using.

• Preheat oven to 375°F (190°C). Roll out pastry and line a pie plate.

• To prepare the filling, heat water and evaporated milk over low heat. Add brown sugar and stir until melted. Set aside.

• Beat eggs in food processor until foamy. Gradually add flour, then the soft butter. Mix in sugar mixture and vanilla until well combined. Pour into pie shell. Bake about 40 minutes, or until filling is set.

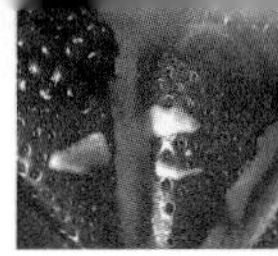

CRÈME CARAMEL

10 SERVINGS

	CARAMEL	
1 cup	sugar	250 mL
	CUSTARD	
2 cups	milk	500 mL
1	pinch salt	1
½ tsp	vanilla extract	2 mL
4	eggs	4
3 tbsp	sugar	45 mL

- To make the caramel, heat the sugar over low heat in a saucepan, stirring constantly, until it starts to turn golden.
- Remove pan from heat as soon as sugar is copper-colored.
- Pour sugar into 4 ramekins. Set aside.
- Preheat oven to 350°F (180°C).
- To make the custard, put milk, salt and vanilla in a saucepan. Bring to a boil. Set aside.
- Beat eggs and sugar together in a bowl until mixed but not foamy. Gradually add hot milk mixture, stirring constantly.
- Divide mixture between ramekins on top of caramel.
- Place a sheet of waxed paper or a cloth in the bottom of a baking pan. Arrange ramekins on top.
- Pour hot water in pan to halfway up ramekins.
- Bake 45 minutes, checking from time to time that water has not boiled away.
- The crème caramels are cooked when the custard mixture is firm. Let chill well before unmolding.

TIRAMISU

6 SERVINGS

6	**egg whites**	**6**
1 cup	**sugar**	**250 mL**
6	**egg yolks**	**6**
1 lb	**mascarpone cheese**	**450 g**
¼ cup	**whipping cream**	**50 mL**
3 tbsp	**kirsch, rum *or* cognac**	**45 mL**
1¼ cups	**cold strong coffee**	**300 mL**
25	**ladyfingers**	**25**
1 tbsp	**unsweetened cocoa powder**	**15 mL**

• Beat egg whites until stiff. Set aside.

• Beat together ⅓ cup (75 mL) sugar with egg yolks.

• With a wooden spoon, stir in mascarpone, beaten egg whites, cream and kirsch until mixture is smooth. Set aside.

• Dissolve remaining sugar in coffee. Dip ends of ladyfingers quickly in coffee mixture, then use them to line a rectangular glass baking dish.

• Cover with a layer of cheese mixture. Repeat layerings, ending with a layer of cheese mixture.

• Cover and refrigerate several hours. Sprinkle with chocolate just before serving.

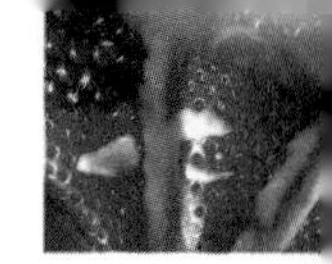

SUGGESTION

You can prepare tiramisu a day or two in advance. Keep refrigerated.

STUFFED PINEAPPLE

4 TO 6 SERVINGS

1	pineapple, cut in half	1
¾ cup	strawberries, hulled and halved	175 g
½ cup	green grapes	125 mL
2	kiwis, peeled and sliced	2
1	carambola, thinly sliced	1
¼ cup	water	50 mL
¼ cup	corn syrup	50 mL
1	1-inch (2.5 cm) piece fresh ginger, finely chopped	1
2	oranges, segmented, membranes removed	2
	juice and zest of 1 lime	

• With a sharp knife, cut out fibrous center of pineapple and discard. Cut out pineapple flesh carefully and dice.

• In a bowl, combine diced pineapple, strawberries, grapes, kiwis and carambola. Set aside.

• Combine water and corn syrup in a saucepan. Add ginger, lime juice and ½ the zest, grated.

• Bring slowly to a boil, stirring constantly. Let simmer 1 minute, or until syrupy.

• Cut remaining zest in julienne strips. Add to syrup and let simmer 1 minute. Remove from heat and set aside.

• Arrange fruit in pineapple shells and top with syrup. Garnish with orange segments and chill before serving.

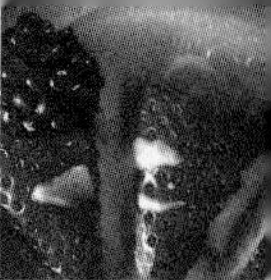

SPONGE CAKE WITH BERRIES

8 SERVINGS

6	**eggs**	**6**
¾ cup	**sugar**	**175 mL**
1½ cups	**all-purpose flour**	**375 mL**
1¼ cups	**whipping cream**	**300 mL**
1 tbsp	**kirsch *or* brandy (optional)**	**15 mL**
1 cup	**fresh raspberries**	**250 mL**
4 cups	**fresh strawberries, halved**	**1 liter**
	butter *or* margarine	
	grated zest of 1 lemon and 1 orange	
	sugar	
	icing sugar	

• Preheat oven to 350°F (180°C). Grease a 9-inch (23 cm) round cake pan. Sprinkle lightly with sugar and flour.

• In a bowl, beat eggs until foamy. Beat in sugar and grated lemon and orange zest until thick.

• Sift flour and stir into mixture gradually and gently. Pour into cake pan and bake 12 to 15 minutes, until top is golden. Let cool and unmold.

• In a bowl, whip cream until stiff. Mix in kirsch and sugar to taste. Stir in ½ the raspberries. Set aside.

• Combine remaining raspberries and strawberries in another bowl. Set aside.

• Cut a lid from the top of the cake. Hollow out the lower part. Fill hollow with some whipped cream mixture and bits of cake that were removed. Top with cake lid, more whipped cream and mixed berries. Sprinkle with icing sugar before serving.

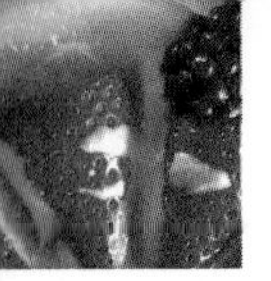

PEACH AND BERRY BROIL

2 SERVINGS

2	**egg yolks**	**2**
3 tbsp	**sugar**	**45 mL**
3 tbsp	**orange liqueur**	**45 mL**
2	**fresh *or* canned peaches, thinly sliced**	**2**
1 cup	**mixed berries of your choice (raspberries, strawberries, blueberries, gooseberries, cranberries)**	**250 mL**
1 tbsp	**icing sugar**	**15 mL**

• Preheat the broiler.

• In a bowl, combine egg yolks, sugar and liqueur. Cook in top of double boiler over low heat, whisking, about 3 minutes or until slightly thickened.

• Divide mixture between 2 deep ovenproof plates, and surround with a ring of peach slices.

• Top egg mixture with berries and peaches. Sprinkle with icing sugar.

• Place under broiler until surface is golden-brown. Serve immediately.

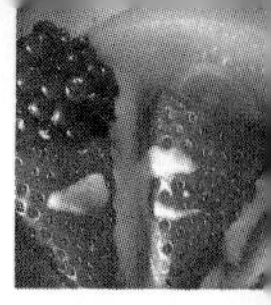

CANTALOUPE GRANITA

4 SERVINGS

4 cups	**diced cantaloupe**	**1 liter**
½ cup	**sugar**	**125 mL**
1 tbsp	**lemon juice**	**15 mL**
1½ tsp	**grated fresh ginger**	**7 mL**
	fresh mint leaves	

- Purée cantaloupe together with sugar until smooth.
- Stir in lemon juice and ginger.
- Pour mixture into a container with a tight-fitting lid and put in freezer until mixture is firm.
- Serve in bowls garnished with fresh mint.

APPLE CAKE

14 TO 16 SERVINGS

CAKE

2 cups	all-purpose flour	500 mL
2 tsp	baking powder	10 mL
¼ tsp	salt	1 mL
½ cup	soft butter *or* margarine	125 mL
⅔ cup	sugar	150 mL
2	eggs	2
2 tbsp	lemon juice	30 mL
4	apples, peeled, cored and thinly sliced	4

TOPPING

1 cup	crushed *or* ground almonds	250 mL
½ cup	plain yogurt	125 mL
2	eggs, beaten	2
2 tbsp	all-purpose flour	30 mL
1 tsp	grated lemon *or* orange zest	5 mL

GLAZE

¼ cup	raspberry jam	50 mL
1 to 2 tsp	lemon juice	5 to 10 mL

• Preheat oven to 350°F (180°C). Grease and lightly flour a 9-inch (23 cm) springform pan.

• In a bowl, combine flour, baking powder and salt. Set aside.

• In food processor, combine butter and sugar until light and creamy. With motor running at low speed, add eggs one by one, then lemon juice. With motor at low speed, gradually mix in flour mixture.

• Pour into prepared pan, and cover with apple slices, pressing them lightly into batter.

• Mix topping ingredients in a bowl, then spread over apples. Bake in oven 55 to 60 minutes, or until a toothpick inserted in center comes out clean.

• Combine raspberry jam and lemon juice. Pour over hot cake. Let stand 10 minutes before carefully unmolding.

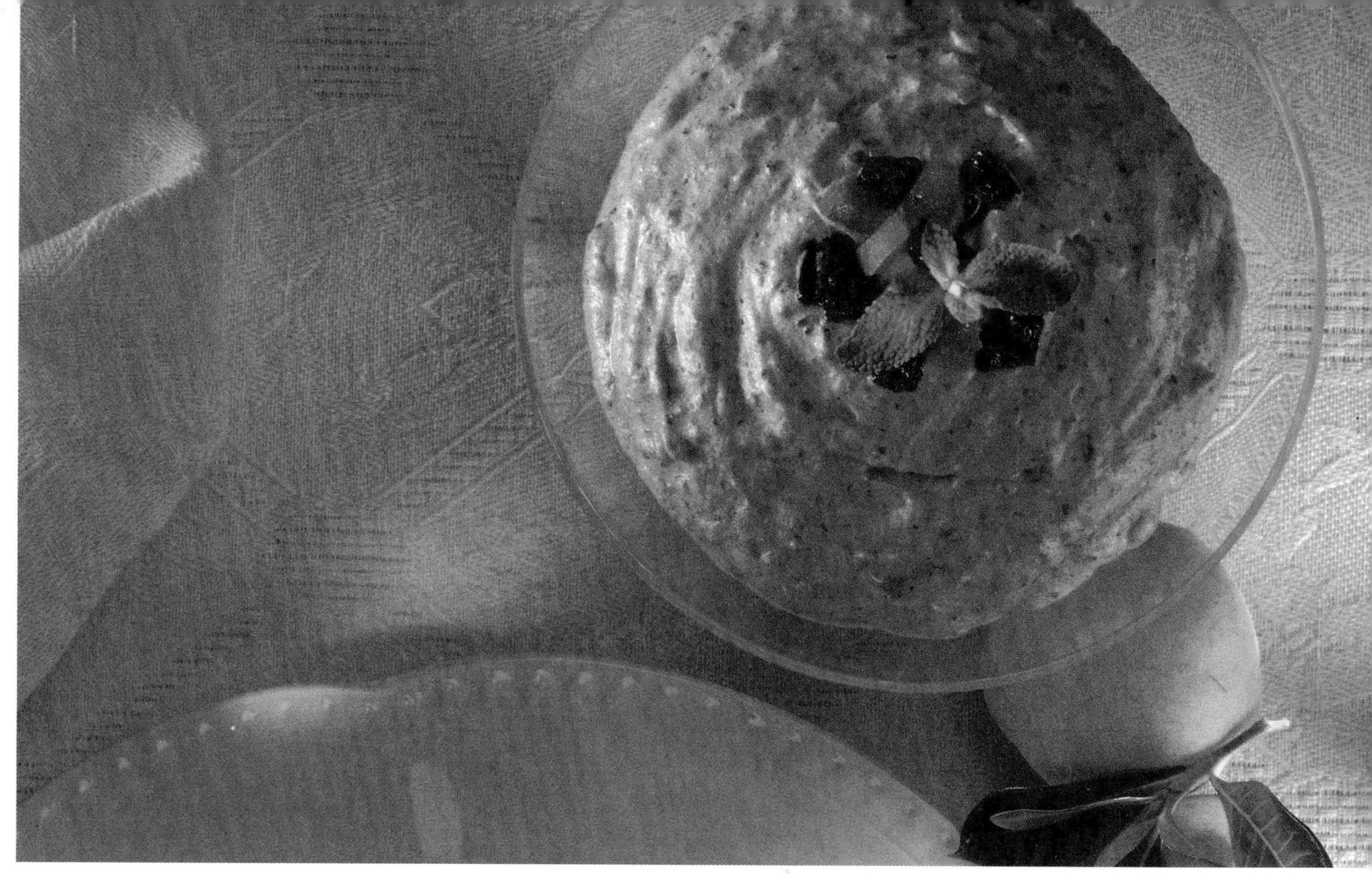

PRUNE MOUSSE

4 SERVINGS

6 oz	pitted prunes	180 g
6 oz	dried apricots	180 g
2 tsp	lemon juice	10 mL
2	egg whites	2
1	pinch salt	1
2 tbsp	sugar	30 mL
¼ cup	whipped cream	50 mL
	mint leaves	

• Put prunes and apricots in a saucepan and cover with water. Cook 5 minutes over medium heat to soften. Drain, reserving cooking liquid. Set aside ¼ of fruit.

• Purée ¾ of soaked fruit in food processor with a little cooking liquid to make a fairly stiff paste. Add lemon juice and let cool.

• Beat egg whites with salt in food processor until foamy. Gradually blend in sugar until mixture is stiff.

• Gradually add in fruit purée. Process at high speed 2 minutes.

• Chop reserved fruit and fold gently into puréed mixture. With a wooden spoon or rubber spatula, fold whipped cream into mixture. Pour into bowls. Refrigerate.

• Serve garnished with fresh mint.

Prunes are rich in calcium, iron, Vitamins A and B, and fiber.

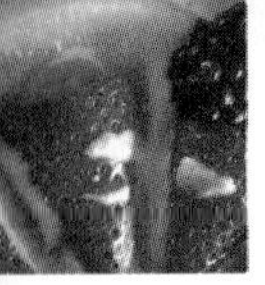

CINNAMON PECAN ROLL

8 SERVINGS

CAKE

3½ cups	**all-purpose flour**	**875 mL**
¼ cup	**sugar**	**50 mL**
¼ cup	**butter *or* margarine**	**50 mL**
1 tsp	**salt**	**5 mL**
1	**envelope fast-rising yeast**	**1**
¾ cup	**milk**	**175 mL**
2	**eggs, lightly beaten**	**2**
1	**egg yolk**	**1**
1 tbsp	**milk**	**15 mL**
	icing sugar	

FILLING

½ cup	**packed brown sugar**	**125 mL**
½ cup	**chopped pecans**	**125 mL**
¼ cup	**raisins**	**50 mL**
1 tbsp	**cinnamon**	**15 mL**
¼ cup	**milk**	**50 mL**

• Preheat oven to 375°F (190°C).

• To make the cake: In a food processor, combine flour, sugar, butter, salt and yeast 30 seconds. Heat ¾ cup (175 mL) milk until warm and add gradually to flour mixture, alternating with beaten eggs. Process until mixture forms a ball. Knead dough 1 minute. Place dough in an oiled bowl and roll to coat all sides. Cover and let rest 10 minutes.

• Meanwhile, prepare the filling. In a bowl, combine brown sugar, pecans, raisins, and cinnamon. Set aside.

• Roll out dough into a 9 x 12 inch (23 x 30 cm) rectangle. Brush top with milk except a border about ½-inch (1.5 cm) wide. Cover with cinnamon filling. Roll rectangle up, starting at long side. Press to seal ends.

• Slide onto a greased cookie sheet. Cover and let stand 1 hour or until doubled in volume.

• In a bowl, mix egg yolk and 1 tbsp (15 mL) milk. Brush roll with yolk mixture. Bake 30 to 35 minutes. After first 15 minutes of baking, cover loosely with foil so top does not brown too much. Let cool. Sprinkle with icing sugar before serving.

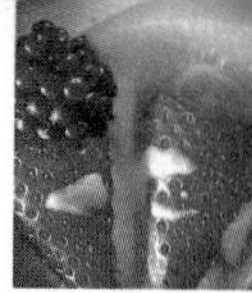

RASPBERRY BAVARIAN

4 TO 5 SERVINGS

14 oz	**frozen unsweetened raspberries, thawed and drained**	**400 g**
3	**envelopes unflavored gelatin**	**3**
½ cup	**cold water**	**125 mL**
4 tbsp	**water**	**60 mL**
⅓ cup	**sugar**	**75 mL**
1 tbsp	**lemon juice**	**15 mL**
1⅔ cups	**whipping cream**	**400 mL**
3	**egg whites, beaten stiff**	**3**
	fresh raspberries	
	fresh mint leaves	

- In food processor, purée thawed raspberries. Set aside.
- Sprinkle gelatin over cold water and let soak 5 minutes.
- In a saucepan, bring to a boil 4 tbsp (60 mL) water. Remove from heat and stir in softened gelatin until dissolved.
- Add sugar and stir to dissolve.
- Stir gelatin mixture and lemon juice into purée. Refrigerate until mixture is nearly set.
- Whip cream stiff.
- Fold whipped cream, then egg whites into purée. Pour into large mold or individual ramekins. Refrigerate at least 3 hours to set.
- Unmold onto a serving dish and garnish with fresh berries and mint.

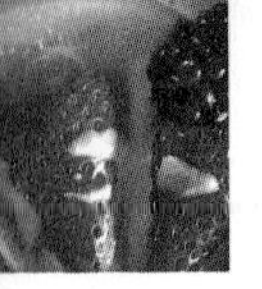

APPLE CIDER CRÊPES

4 SERVINGS

CRÊPES

1 cup	all-purpose flour	250 mL
1 tsp	salt	5 mL
1	egg	1
1	egg yolk	1
1¼ cups	milk	300 mL
1 tbsp	melted butter *or* margarine	15 mL
	corn oil	

FILLING

¼ cup	butter *or* margarine	50 mL
2 lbs	cooking apples, peeled, cored and sliced	900 g
2 tbsp	maple syrup	30 mL
1 tbsp	ground cinnamon	15 mL
¼ cup	dry cider *or* unsweetened apple juice	50 mL
	icing sugar	

- In food processor, combine flour, salt, egg and egg yolk.
- Add milk gradually and mix.
- Add butter. Mix well. Cover and let stand 30 minutes.
- Into a lightly oiled non-stick skillet, pour just enough batter to cover bottom. Cook crêpes on both sides. Set aside.
- To prepare filling, melt butter over medium heat in another non-stick skillet.
- Cook apples with syrup and cinnamon until soft, stirring from time to time.
- Add cider and let reduce until syrupy.
- Fill crêpes with apple mixture and roll up. Sprinkle with icing sugar to serve.

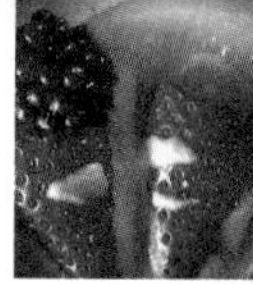

BLUEBERRY MARBLE CHEESECAKE

10 SERVINGS

CRUST

1 cup	cookie crumbs	250 mL
½ cup	ground pecans	125 mL
¼ cup	sugar	50 mL
½ tsp	cinnamon	2 mL
⅓ cup	melted butter *or* margarine	75 mL

BLUEBERRY FILLING

3	8 oz (240 g) packages cream cheese	3
1¼ cups	sugar	300 mL
6	egg yolks	6
3 tbsp	all-purpose flour	45 mL
2 tsp	vanilla	10 mL
2 cups	sour cream	500 mL
1 tbsp	lemon juice	15 mL
1 tbsp	grated lemon zest	15 mL
6	egg whites	6
1	pinch salt	1
1½ cups	blueberry jam	375 mL

• To make the crust, combine all ingredients.

• Grease a 9-inch (23 cm) springform pan. Press mixture over bottom and partway up sides. Refrigerate 20 minutes.

• Preheat oven to 350°F (180°C).

• To make the filling, beat cream cheese until fluffy. Gradually beat in sugar. Still beating, add egg yolks one by one until mixture is smooth. Beat in flour, vanilla, sour cream, lemon juice and lemon zest. Set aside.

• Beat egg whites until stiff with pinch of salt. Fold delicately into cheese mixture with a rubber spatula.

• Partially stir in ½ cup (125 mL) jam to give marbled appearance. Pour into crust.

• Bake about 1 hour. Turn off oven, open oven door and let cake rest in oven 15 minutes. Remove from oven and let cool at room temperature. Cover with remaining jam just before serving.

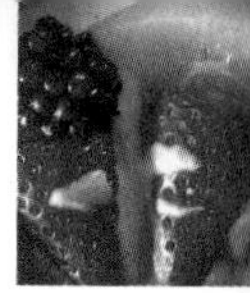

PEAR AND ALMOND TART

8 TO 10 SERVINGS

8 oz	shortcrust pastry	225 g
9 oz	can pear halves, drained	240 mL
	liquid honey, warmed	
	plain yogurt	
	ALMOND CREAM	
4 tbsp	sweet butter	60 mL
3 tbsp	sugar	45 mL
1	egg	1
1	egg yolk	1
4 oz	ground almonds	120 g
2 tbsp	all-purpose flour	30 mL

- Preheat oven to 425°F (220°C).
- Line a 10-inch (25 cm) pie plate (preferably with removable base) with pastry.
- To make the almond cream, beat butter in food processor at medium speed. Gradually add sugar, egg, egg yolk, ground almonds and flour.
- Spread almond cream in pastry shell. Top with pear halves, scored or sliced and evenly spaced.
- Bake 15 to 20 minutes, lower heat to 375°F (190°C) and bake about 10 minutes more.
- Brush top of tart with warmed honey. Return to oven under hot broiler for a few seconds to brown slightly.
- Serve with a dab of plain yogurt.

PEACH ALMOND CUSTARD

8 SERVINGS

1 cup	milk	250 mL
⅓ cup	sugar	75 mL
3	egg yolks	3
4 tsp	unflavored gelatin	20 mL
¼ cup	cold water	50 mL
2 cups	plain yogurt	500 mL
2 tsp	almond extract	10 mL
4	canned peach halves, drained and diced	4

• In a saucepan, heat milk with 2 tbsp (30 mL) sugar over low heat until steaming, but not boiling. Set aside.

• In a bowl, beat egg yolks with remaining sugar until pale and smooth. Still beating, gradually add hot milk.

• Cook in top of a double boiler over low heat about 10 minutes, until thickened enough to coat the back of a spoon.

• Soak gelatin in cold water 5 minutes. Stir into milk mixture gradually. Let cool. Stir in yogurt and almond extract. Stir in peaches.

• Pour mixture into a lightly oiled large mold or 8 small ramekins. Refrigerate 2 hours or until set. Unmold and serve with fresh fruit sauce of your choice.

RASPBERRY ORANGE MOUSSE

4 SERVINGS

1 tbsp	grated orange zest	15 mL
1 cup	unsweetened orange juice	250 mL
¼ cup	sugar	50 mL
2	envelopes unflavored gelatin	2
2 cups	plain yogurt	500 mL
10 oz	frozen raspberries, thawed and drained	300 g

• In a saucepan, combine orange zest, juice, sugar and gelatin. Heat until gelatin is dissolved. Remove from heat. Let set in refrigerator 30 minutes.

• Process mixture in food processor until creamy.

• Add yogurt and raspberries. Process again.

• Pour into individual bowls or a mold. Refrigerate 1 hour. Serve well chilled.

TROPICAL FRUIT WITH MANGO CREAM

6 SERVINGS

2	**mangos, peeled, pitted and sliced**	2
2	**nectarines *or* peaches, pitted and sliced**	2
3	**kiwis, peeled and thinly sliced**	3
½	**pineapple, peeled and sliced**	½
1	**honeydew *or* other melon, peeled, seeded and sliced**	1
	juice of 2 oranges	

MANGO CREAM

1	**mango, peeled and pitted**	1
1 cup	**plain yogurt**	250 mL
	juice of ½ orange	
	juice of 1 lemon	

• Arrange cut up fruit in a bowl. Sprinkle with orange juice. Cover with plastic wrap and refrigerate.

• To make the mango cream, purée mango flesh in food processor with lemon and orange juices.

• Add yogurt and mix well.

• Arrange fruit on plates and serve with mango cream.

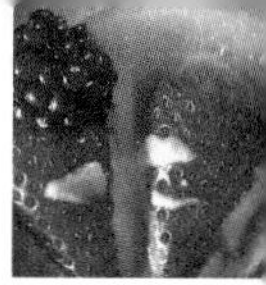

PEACH TART

8 SERVINGS

CRUST

1 cup	**all-purpose flour**	**250 mL**
1	**pinch salt**	**1**
¼ cup	**cold butter**	**50 mL**
¼ cup	**sugar**	**50 mL**
1	**egg yolk**	**1**
2 tbsp	**cold water**	**30 mL**

TOPPING

¼ cup	**soft butter**	**50 mL**
2 tbsp	**sugar**	**30 mL**
2	**egg yolks**	**2**
½ cup	**ground almonds**	**125 mL**
1 tbsp	**cornstarch**	**15 mL**
2 cups	**fresh *or* canned peach slices**	**500 mL**

• To make the crust, sift flour and salt into a bowl. Combine flour mixture in food processor with cold butter just until grainy.

• Add ¼ cup (50 mL) sugar and egg yolk. Process to mix well. Work in cold water bit by bit. Refrigerate 30 minutes.

• Roll out pastry and line a 9-inch (23 cm) greased pie plate. Prick bottom in a few places with a fork.

• Preheat oven to 425°F (220°C).

• Beat soft butter until light. Beat in sugar and egg yolks. Mix well. Beat in ground almonds and cornstarch.

• Spread mixture over pastry. Garnish with peaches, pressing them lightly into batter.

• Bake about 30 minutes.

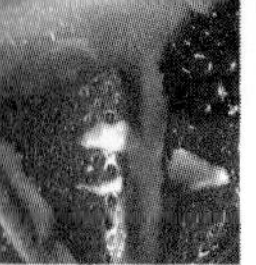

VACHERIN

4 SERVINGS

2 cups	**ice milk**	**500 mL**
1 cup	**whipping cream**	**250 mL**
2 tbsp	**icing sugar**	**30 mL**
1 tsp	**vanilla extract**	**5 mL**
	MERINGUE	
2⅔ cups	**packed icing sugar**	**650 mL**
2	**egg whites**	**2**
3	**drops white vinegar**	**3**
1	**pinch salt**	**1**
4	**egg whites, beaten stiff**	**4**

Meringues must be cooked at a very low temperature in order to stay white; when done, they should be crisp but still tender.

• Preheat oven to 200°F (100°C).

• To make the meringue, put icing sugar, 2 egg whites, vinegar and salt in food processor and process until smooth and white. Pour into a bowl. Fold in 4 stiffly beaten egg whites.

• Grease and flour 2 cookie sheets. On each, make an 8-inch (20 cm) diameter circle of the meringue. Bake in oven 1 hour, then turn off heat and let dry in oven.

(Continued on next page)

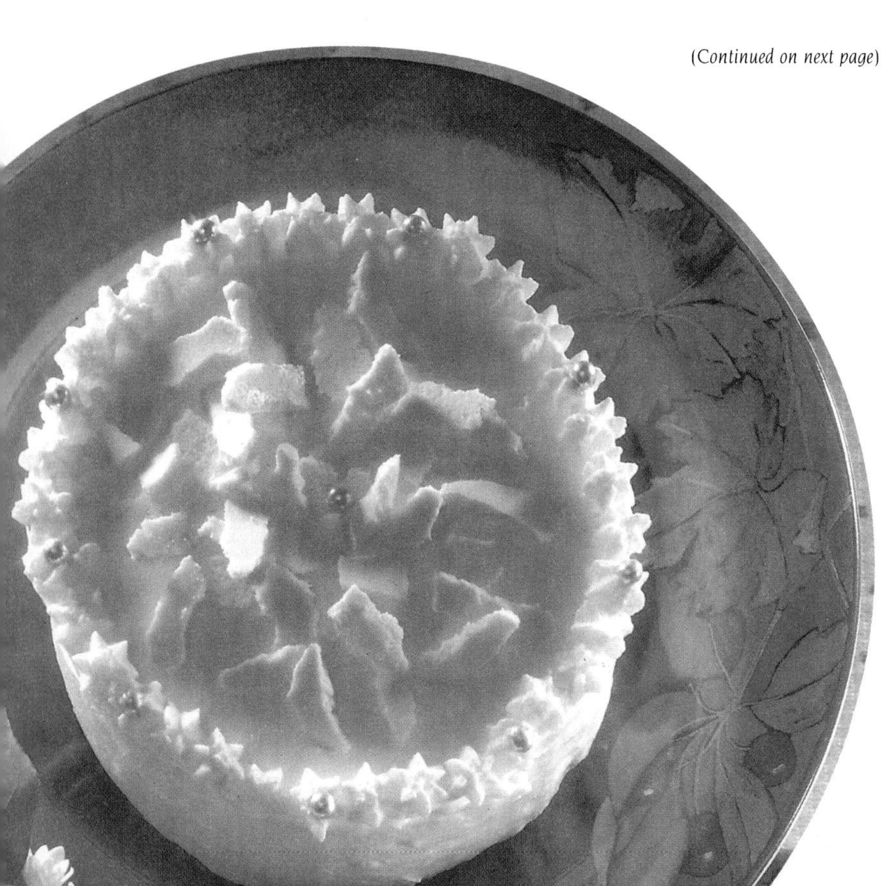

1

Process the icing sugar, 2 egg whites, salt and vinegar until smooth. Fold in stiffly beaten egg whites.

2

Spread meringe in 2 circles on cookie sheets. Bake.

3

Spread ice milk between meringues and place in freezer.

4

Prepare whipped cream topping to cover meringues.

• Arrange 1 meringue on a serving plate. Spread with ½ iced milk and place in freezer 15 minutes. Spread remaining ice milk over first layer, then top with 2nd meringue. Press lightly to seal layers. Return to freezer.

• Meanwhile, beat cream with 2 tbsp (30 mL) icing sugar and vanilla in food processor to form stiff peaks. Spread over meringue layers and keep in freezer until ready to serve.

HOW TO PREPARE MERINGUES

Beat egg whites together with a little vinegar and a pinch of salt to form soft peaks.

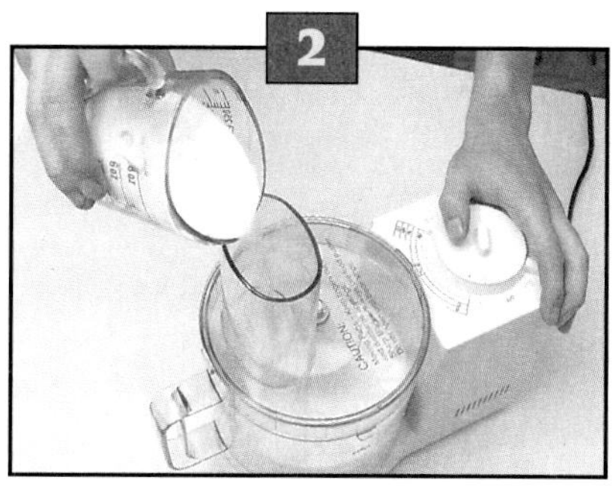

Gradually beat in sugar. Beat until thick and glossy, and mixture forms stiff peaks.

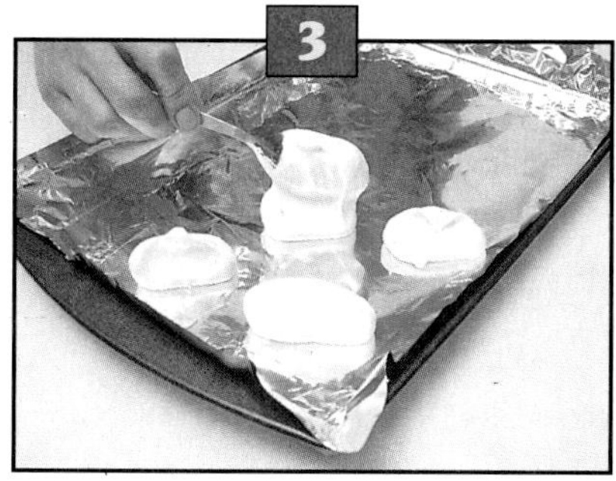

Spoon meringue mixture onto a greased, lightly floured cookie sheet. Bake in preheated 200°F (100°C) oven 1 hour.

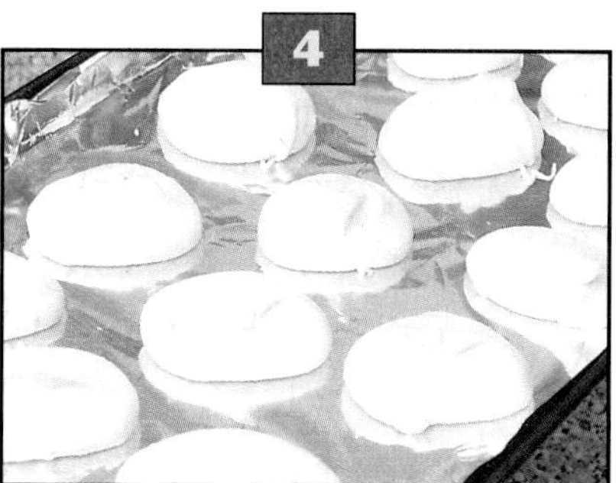

Turn off oven and leave meringues in oven 1 hour. Garnish with fruit sauce or chocolate sauce just before serving.

CHILLED TROPICAL FRUIT SMOOTHIE

6 SERVINGS

2	**mangos**	**2**
½	**fresh pineapple**	**½**
2 tbsp	**fresh lime juice**	**30 mL**
2 cups	**pineapple juice**	**500 mL**
1	**can coconut milk**	**1**
2	**kiwis, peeled and diced**	**2**
½	**mango, peeled and diced**	**½**
	sugar	

Mangos are rich in beta-carotene and Vitamin C.

• In food processor, purée mango and pineapple flesh.

• Add lime juice, pineapple juice and coconut milk. Pour into a pitcher, add diced fruit and refrigerate.

• Chill dessert bowls 1 hour in refrigerator.

• To serve, pour sugar in a dish. Turn dessert bowls upside-down in sugar to coat rim. Pour chilled fruit mixture into bowls.

MELON GRANITA

4 SERVINGS

½ cup	water	125 mL
¼ cup	sugar	50 mL
1 cup	diced, peeled honeydew melon	250 mL
1 tbsp	lime juice	15 mL
	fresh mint leaves	

• Heat water and sugar in a medium skillet to boiling. Let boil 3 minutes, then remove from heat and chill.

• Purée melon in a food processor until smooth. Blend in chilled syrup and lime juice. Pour into a shallow metal mold and freeze at least 3 hours.

• Process mixture again in food processor, return to mold, and freeze until firm (4 to 6 hours). Stir from time to time.

• Remove granita from freezer and let stand at room temperature until soft enough to serve with a spoon. Garnish each serving with mint leaves.

BASIC COOKING TERMS

al dente
In Italian, this means "to the tooth", and describes the perfect condition of cooked pasta — still a little chewy, and **never** mushy.

bake
Baking refers to the cooking of anything in the oven. Delicate foods such as custards should be baked standing in a larger container of hot water to prevent drying and overcooking.

boil
To cook in water in which the bubbles are rapidly breaking the surface. Only green vegetables, rice and a few other foods benefit from boiling. Meats and fish, for instance, should be poached or simmered instead.

broil
To cook with the intense heat of a heating element or flame. If using an electric broiler, always preheat it.

deep fry
A fast process in which food is totally submerged in hot oil.

fry
To cook in a thin layer of fat in a skillet.

julienne
Thin sticks of vegetables or other foods cut about ¼ inch (.5 cm) thick.

parboil
To cook partially until barely tender to a sharp knife.

poach
A slow, gentle cooking in liquid which is barely moving.

roast
To cook in the oven without any liquid other than fat.

sauté
To cook by rapid frying in very little fat.

simmer
To cook immersed in liquid in which the bubbles are just barely breaking the surface.

springform pan
A cake pan with a removable base and hinged sides.

steam
The cooking of food in hot vapor instead of liquid.

INGREDIENTS

brown sauce
Also called Espagnole sauce, this is a rich sauce made of thickened and seasoned beef or veal drippings and beef stock. If you do not have time to make your own, you may purchase it ready-made, or substitute a good brown gravy, homemade or canned.

bulgur
A quick-cooking form of wheat made from wheat berries that have been precooked, dried and cracked. Available in health food stores, gourmet sections and Middle Eastern groceries.

celery root (celeriac)
A variety of celery grown for its fleshy white root, sold without leaves.

chili oil
A fiery oil flavored with hot peppers. Available in Oriental groceries, or use cooking oil flavored with hot pepper sauce.

commercial Chinese fondue flavoring
Several manufacturers make liquid or powdered flavoring mixtures for Chinese fondue that are simply stirred into water. If you cannot find one, substitute canned beef consommé.

commercial gravy thickener
A thickener that is specially designed to dissolve in hot liquids without lumping. You can thicken liquids with flour or cornstarch instead, but both these ingredients must be thoroughly dissolved in cold liquid before adding to a hot liquid.

daikon
A long, crisp white Chinese radish. Turnip will provide a similar texture.

dry French shallots
Not to be confused with green shallots, scallions or green onions, French shallots resemble a tiny onion with a reddish-brown papery skin. They have a unique flavor, but you can use a small plain onion instead if necessary.

fillet
A thick, boneless strip of meat. Beef fillet is usually cut from the tenderloin. Pork fillet is also from the tenderloin. Chicken and turkey fillet is white meat cut from the breast.

filo pastry
These very thin sheets of dough are purchased ready-made, usually frozen or refrigerated. It keeps well frozen.

fines herbes
A mixture of chopped aromatic herbs, usually containing parsley, chives, tarragon and chervil.

hijaki seaweed
A dried seaweed used for flavoring, available in Chinese and Oriental stores.

hoisin sauce
A thick brownish-red sauce made from soybeans, spices, garlic and chili peppers. Available in Oriental stores.

imitation crabmeat (surimi)
A crab-flavored product made with fish, and sometimes containing real crabmeat. It is already cooked.

Italian seasoning
A mixture of rosemary, sage, oregano, marjoram and thyme.

konbu seaweed
A dried seaweed available in Oriental stores.

medallions
Thick crosswise cuts of meat from a fillet or tenderloin.

miso
A salty, high-protein paste made from fermented soybeans, popular in Japanese cuisine. Keeps refrigerated indefinitely.

nuoc mam sauce
A highly flavored sauce made from fermented fish. Substitute mashed anchovies.

Sbrinz cheese
Sbrinz is a hard, strongly-flavored Swiss cheese that can easily replace Parmesan.

scallopini
Also known as scallops and escalopes, these are very thin slices of boneless meat. Traditionally, the term applied exclusively to veal. However, it is now possible to buy pork, turkey and chicken scallopini (the last two cut from the breast). All of these are convenient cuts that cook quickly.

smoked sausages
Smoked sausages include frankfurters, weiners, bologna and Mettwurst. Some smoked sausages are now made from chicken, and are a little lower in fat. They are already cooked, but may be simmered, baked or broiled.

soba
Popular style of Japanese noodle made from buckwheat.

sumac
A distinctively flavored seasoning much used in Lebanese cooking. If you cannot find it, use lemon juice, although the flavor will be different.

sun-dried tomatoes
Sun-dried tomatoes pack a lot of tomato flavor. They are available packed in oil, or simply dried. If you purchase dried ones, soak them in warm water for 15 to 30 minutes before using.

tamari soy sauce
Tamari soy sauce is a soy sauce, made with fermented soy beans, but not chemically processed and less salty and sweet.

tofu
Also known as fresh soybean curd, tofu is high in protein.

tournedos
Traditionally, a small fillet of beef cut crosswise from the tenderloin, often bound in bacon or suet for cooking. Many butchers now prepare tournedos from pork, chicken and turkey. Poultry tournedos are cut from the thick boned and skinned breast.

udon noodles
Very narrow Japanese noodles made from wheat.

vol-au-vent
Round cases made of puff pastry. Available ready-baked or frozen, unbaked.

INDEX

APPETIZERS

SOUPS

SALADS

POULTRY

MEATS

FISH AND SEAFOOD

VEGETABLES

PASTA

DESSERTS